efore

ow.

Capability and Quality
in Higher Education

Teaching and Learning in Higher Education Series
Series Editor: John Stephenson

Assess Your Own Teaching Quality Sally Brown and Phil Race
Assessing Learners in Higher Education Sally Brown and Peter Knight
Case Studies on Teaching in Higher Education Peter Schwartz and Graham Webb
Developing Student Capability Through Modular Courses Edited by Alan Jenkins and Lawrie Walker
Flexible Learning in Higher Education Edited by Winnie Wade, Keith Hodgkinson, Alison Smith and John Arfield
Making the Most of Your Appraisal Graham Webb
Transferable Skills in Higher Education Edited by Alison Assiter
Using Group-based Learning in Higher Education Edited by Lin Thorley and Roy Gregory
Using Learning Contracts in Higher Education Edited by John Stephenson and Mike Laycock

Capability and Quality in Higher Education

Edited by

John Stephenson
and
Mantz Yorke

KOGAN
PAGE

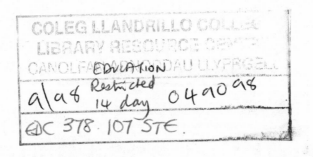
YOURS TO HAVE AND TO HOLD

BUT NOT TO COPY

First published in 1998

Kogan Page Limited
120 Pentonville Road
London N1 9JN

British Library Cataloguing in Publication Data

A CIP record for this book is available from the British Library.

ISBN 0 7494 2570 9

Typeset by JS Typesetting, Wellingborough, Northants.
Printed and bound in Great Britain by
Biddles Ltd, Guildford and King's Lynn

Contents

Foreword

It is likely that, when we look back at changes in higher education, we will identify the 1990s as a revolutionary period. It is a time when it is finally being acknowledged that higher education is an extremely diverse and mass activity that cannot be supported by the elitist arguments of the past. It is a time when, after many years of institutional neglect and in the light of new roles of higher education, teaching is being taken more seriously than ever before. Most importantly, the apparently obvious, but relatively neglected, connection between teaching and learning is being made.

For those of us living through these times it is troubling, as a lot of our assumptions about what it means to be a teacher or a student are being challenged. There are new demands: from governments, from employers, from students. As the enterprise of higher education has grown so large and has developed such an important role in society, there are demands of accountability which previously could not be imagined.

In all this it is easy to lose sight of the essence of higher education. It is above all about learning and about how higher levels of learning in partic- ular can be fostered. Increasingly, it is about learning which will influence what occurs in the future, not just for its immediate value. Whatever else higher education should be judged on, it must be judged on this.

A brief view of the new language of higher education might suggest that it is about matters related to learning. There is a focus on learning outcomes, key skills, competence, employability, standards and so on. A closer analysis, however, indicates that much of what is considered under these headings is about documentation and about appearing to make a difference. There has been resistance to some of these new ideas, but few attempts to articu- late an alternative conception.

The best example of a new way of looking at the challenges of teaching and learning is reflected in this book. It is the view expressed by the Capa- bility movement. Advocates of the notion of capability have focused on education for the benefit of individuals, industry and society as a whole and on the effectiveness of learners in their personal, social and working lives. Not content with simply adopting a vision, the initiators through the Royal Society of Arts and other bodies have translated these ideas into practice through the programme Higher Education for Capability, led by John Stephenson.

While higher education institutions have been battered by external forces with demands for change, Higher Education for Capability has been quietly and systematically focusing the fundamentals of teaching and learning, and working from within to find ways of embedding capability ideas into the curriculum and into institutional practice.

The present book represents an important record of these developments. A significant feature of capability is its holistic and educational focus. This provides a remedy for the crude instrumentalism which has begun to gnaw at the edges of higher education and which for a time dominated dis-cussions of competence in teaching and learning. In the book there are accounts of educational practices which translate principles of capability into specific courses, and of particular interest are reflective chapters by the editors mapping issues and raising intriguing questions about future directions.

The book links capability with the current major theme of quality. It rejects the temptations of the procedure-based, functional approach to quality and points to quality-improving initiatives which do not fit pre-determined categories. It shows how it is important to bring a capability perspective to discussions of quality, in order to avoid the tendency for the quality agenda to be captured by academic disciplines and other groups in ways which reproduce existing boundaries of knowledge rather than challenge them.

The chapters present exciting ideas which trigger creative responses to the challenges of higher education. Capability shifts consideration to the most important question of all: what kind of learning do we need to promote in higher education to equip us for the future?

David Boud,
University of Sydney

Preface

The Dearing Report on the future of higher education in the UK (NCIHE, 1997)[1] raises fundamental issues about the aims of higher education and how those aims might be achieved. The Fryer Report (1997)[2] urges a new national commitment to lifelong learning, with higher education playing a major part. Both Reports see Higher Education Institutions (HEIs) playing a key role in securing the economic well-being of the country into the twenty-first century. Both also see higher education continuing to help students fulfil their personal, academic, vocational and professional potential. When launching the Government's consultation paper on lifelong learning, *The Learning Age* (DfEE, 1998), The Secretary of State for Education and Employment reinforced this duality of purpose of learning by stating:

Learning is the key to economic prosperity – for each of us as individuals, as well as for the nation as a whole.[3]

The Royal Society for the Encouragement of Arts, Manufactures and Commerce (RSA) realised early on, in 1980, the importance of a holistic concept which subsumed both education and training under the notion of 'Capability'[4]. The capable graduate/diplomate would be an effective operator both in employment and in life generally. Since 1980, the rate of change in life and work has accelerated. The globalization of economic

---

1. National Committee of Inquiry into Higher Education, 1997, *Report* London: Department for Education and Employment.
2. Fryer, R.H. (1997): *Learning for the Twenty-First Century:* First Report of the National Advisory Group for Continuing and Lifelong Learning; Sheffield, DfEE.
3. Speech by the Rt. Hon. David Blunkett on 25 February 1998 at the launch of the Green Paper, *The Learning Age*.
4. RSA, 1980, Education for Capability Manifesto, London, RSA. The Manifesto argued that an imbalance between education and training was *'harmful to individuals, industry and society'*. The Manifesto advocated an approach which combined the best features of education and training in the one process, an approach which they called 'education for capability'.

activity coupled with the vast increase in the availability of information have impacted sharply on people's lives, both inside and outside the work environment. Knowledge-based economies require people to be self-starting, self-reliant and good at communications – in other words to exhibit capability (in the broad sense that we use the term). The educational implications of this shift in emphasis are considerable.

Developments in telematics and multi-media technology are transforming how learners engage with specialist knowledge and sustain dialogue with other learners. The volume of 'essential' knowledge in any one specialist field now greatly exceeds the capacity of traditional classroom-based teaching. In response to these changes there is an emerging consensus that the most appropriate priority for HEIs is to help their students to take more responsibility for the management of their own specialist learning and personal development, thereby equipping them for survival and success in the world we do not yet know and which the students themselves will help to shape.

There is, of course, much good practice regarding the preparation of students for the twenty-first century. In some cases this good practice is isolated and untypical of the university in which it is located. Creating a high quality system which encourages and celebrates the development of student capability is a major task, involving changes not only in the way students are taught but also changes in the structure of the curriculum and the culture of the institution itself. Much traditional practice is still based on teachers knowing, teachers teaching, students absorbing and students showing they have learnt what has been taught. Internal and external processes reinforce this top-down control model of university education. Switching to a student-led, teacher-supported system – in which credit is given for what students can do as a result of their learning – has major implications for the quality assurance, assessment and resource allocation systems provided by the HEI, and for the culture of the institution as a whole. It also has immense implications for employers. The danger is that many worthy innovations promoted by enthusiastic academic staff may be frustrated by a failure to make commensurate changes to the infra-structure in which they work.

This book addresses the challenges of developing capable graduates for the twenty-first century, drawing on current experience and practice. Since 1988, Higher Education for Capability (HEC) has worked with HEIs in the UK, Australia and New Zealand on staff and course development projects aimed at the introduction of capability-oriented programmes, ranging in scale from individual modules to multi-partner regional development schemes. Two hundred and fifty-six examples of educating for capability were included in an earlier book *Quality in Learning: a capability approach in higher education* (Stephenson and Weil, 1992), since when over 400 presentations have been made to HEC conferences on different aspects of developing student capability through the higher education curriculum. Other bodies, such as the HE funding councils and the Department for Education and Employment have sponsored numerous initiatives on specific aspects of the curriculum related to student capability, including Guidance and Learner Autonomy, Work-based Learning and the Learning Society. More recently, seventeen universities, accrediting bodies and other organizations have become partners in HEC with the RSA Examinations Board, the University of Leeds and Leeds Metropolitan University, sharing their experience and formulating proposals for further development.

This book presents a synthesis of the accumulating (and often disparate) experience of educating for capability in higher education which is consistent with current resource constraints and quality assurance requirements and which is relevant to the changing circumstances in which we live. The book has four parts. In Part One, Stephenson sets out the capability agenda, exploring its meaning and scope in the context of current trends in higher education and life generally, and focusing on the case for a learner-managed approach. In Part Two, we present examples of how HEC partner institutions are addressing different aspects of educating for capability. Some are making their first tentative moves, others are building half-way houses, and others are experimenting with whole schemes as part of their overall provision. Collectively, these examples show how wide-ranging the changes need to be and they will help anyone thinking of following them to learn from their experience. In Part Three we present a more thematic review of major issues, including the need to provide support for autonomous learners (Stephenson), how students can help each other (Boyle and Evatt), integrating career management into the curriculum (Butcher), using learning contracts to involve relevant stakeholders (Anderson *et al.*) and assessment and quality assurance (Yorke). In Part Four, we present a model for educating for capability based on the practical experience presented in the book and give some suggestions regarding a culture of higher education in which the model can flourish.

Acknowledgements

We wish to acknowledge: the University of Leeds, Leeds Metropolitan University; the Royal Society for the Encouragement of Arts, Manufactures and Commerce, HEC partner institutions and individual members for their continuing support for the Higher Education for Capability project; authors of the chapters in Parts Two and Three; colleagues who presented ideas and examples at 46 HEC events since 1991 and whose collective experience has given us the inspiration and confidence to formulate and present the proposals set out in Part Four; and Liane Pearce, who helped to put the final text together. Responsibility for the content of particular chapters rests with the named authors; responsibility for the overall themes, the compilation of specialist chapters and the structure of the book lies with ourselves as editors.

John Stephenson
Mantz Yorke
March 1998

Glossary

A(P)EL	Accreditation of (Prior) Experience and Learning
AGR	Association of Graduate Recruiters
APWBL	Accreditation of Prior and Work-based Learning
ASSET	Accreditation for Social Services Experience and Training
ASSH	Applied Social Sciences and Humanities
CATS	Credit Accumulation and Transfer Scheme
CBI	Confederation of British Industry
CCTE	Chamber of Commerce Training and Enterprise
CDPLP	The Career and Personal Development Learning Programme
CMI	Career Management Initiative
CV	Curriculum Vitae
DfEE	Department for Education and Employment
DPPD	Diploma in Personal and Professional Development
EHE	Enterprise in Higher Education
FDTL	Fund for The Development of Teaching and Learning
FE	Further Education
GNVQ	General National Vocational Qualification
GPA	Grade Point Average
HE	Higher Education
HEC	Higher Education for Capability
HEFCE	Higher Education Funding Council for England
HEI	Higher Education Institution
HEQC	Higher Education Quality Council
HMSO	Her Majesty's Stationery Office
HNC	Higher National Certificate
HND	Higher National Diploma
ILE	Independent Learning
JMU	Liverpool John Moores University
LCGI	Licentiateship of the City and Guilds of London Institute
LEC	Local Enterprise Companies
LMU	Leeds Metropolitan University
NACETT	National Training and Education Targets

NCIHE	National Committee of Inquiry into Higher Education
NCVQ	National Council for Vocational Qualifications
NELP	North East London Polytechnic (University of East London)
NTET	National Targets for Education and Training
NTU	Nottingham Trent University
NVQ	National Vocational Qualification
QCA	Qualifications and Curriculum Authority
RSA	Royal Society for the Encouragement of Arts, Manufactures and Commerce
SCAA	The Schools Curriculum and Assessment Authority
SEDA	Staff and Educational Development Association
SME	Small and Medium-sized Enterprise
TEC	Training and Enterprise Council
TVE	Thames Valley Enterprise
UNL	University of North London
UTS	University of Technology, Sydney
WBL	Work-based Learning

About the authors

Geoff Anderson is a lecturer in the School of Adult Education, University of Technology, Sydney specializing in human resource development and work-place learning.

David Boud is Professor of Adult Education at the University of Technology, Sydney. He has written extensively on teaching and learning in higher education.

Maggie Boyle is Senior Student Development Officer at the University of Leeds. She has been involved in many initiatives focusing on empowering students initially as part of Enterprise in Higher Education and subsequently within the Teaching and Learning Support Unit at Leeds. She is currently managing the 'Context' project, a national network promoting the use of simulations and case materials in higher education and employment, funded by the Partnership Trust and run in collaboration with CRAC (Careers Research and Advisory Centre).

Val Butcher joined the University of Leeds Careers Service in 1989 after many years of working at the interface between higher education and the world of work, in schools, further education and career guidance. She was seconded to direct the University's Enterprise in Higher Education project from 1991 to 1996, and is now directing the 'Career Management in the Academic Curriculum' project in the University's Careers Service while working half-time in the Teaching and Learning Support Unit as Principal Adviser for Higher Education and Employment. She is a Fellow of the National Institute of Careers Education and Counselling, and researches, publishes and trains regularly in the field of guidance and skills development.

Andrew Castley is Director of the office for Educational and Staff Development at Nene University College Northampton. He was formerly Head of the BA and BSc Combined Honours Programme on which he introduced programme-wide capability approaches. He is Chair of the Staff and Educational Development Association (SEDA) Fellowship Committee and himself a SEDA Fellowship holder.

Jacqueline Davies was until recently a Learning Development Tutor with the National Centre for Work-based Learning Partnerships at Middlesex University. She now works for the Industrial Society.

John Doidge was until recently Head of Staff Development at Nottingham Trent University, and is now Head of Staff Development at Aston University. He has worked extensively in staff development, with an emphasis on quality management and support for allied staff, and as a consultant both in the UK and abroad.

Christine Doubleday is the Higher Education Manager at Heart of England TEC. She has responsibility for encouraging the employability dimension within higher education and Heart of England now have the lead role on higher education on behalf of TEC National Council.

Jean Evatt is a regional officer with the Further Education Funding Council. From 1994–96 she managed the 'Guidance and Learner Autonomy' project at Nene College of Higher Education. Jean began her career as a history teacher and from the early 1980s worked in the further education sector focusing on tutorial support and learner guidance.

Elizabeth Foster has lectured at Leeds University School of Education since 1979. She has managed several educational–business links and research projects, and from 1994–96 was Director of the University's cross-faculty work-based learning project.

Heather Frier is a Qualifications Manager, at RSA Examinations Board, with responsibility for the development of the new National Key Skills Qualification.

Jonathan Garnett is Accreditation Manager and Senior Lecturer in Work-based Learning Studies at Middlesex University.

Jenny Gilbert, after a career in computing, has taught in secondary, further and higher education and is now Teaching and Learning Coordinator at the University of Wolverhampton.

Howard Green is Head of Research Development at Leeds Metropolitan University with responsibilities across the university that include coordinating research assessment and quality assurance of research awards.

Stewart Hase is a psychologist and lecturer at Southern Cross University in Lismore, New South Wales, Australia. His particular interest is in individual and organizational adaptation of which capability appears to be a vital attribute.

Stephen Hunt is the Vocational Qualifications Development Manager for the RSA Examinations Board, with responsibility for the development of NVQs.

Steve Jackson is Assistant Provost (Learning) at Liverpool John Moores University with a brief for the development of teaching and learning initiatives and responsibilities for academic quality and standards. He is also Chair of the City and Guilds Programme Committee.

Trish Lunt is the Work-based Learning Project Officer and the City and Guilds Facilitator at Liverpool John Moores University. She has been responsible for overseeing the operational arrangements for the Licentiate of the City and Guilds, including staff development and training, the preparation of students and the briefing of employers.

Phil Margham is Head of the Academic Development Unit and one of the chief architects of Liverpool John Moores University's modular degree programme. He acts in the capacity of University City and Guilds Coordinator and is currently involved in a major initiative for promoting learning at work.

Pauline McLeman is Associate Dean in the Faculty of Applied Social Sciences and Humanities at Buckinghamshire Chilterns University College. She has responsibility for curriculum development within the Faculty but also has a College-wide role in relation to the enhancement of quality in teaching and learning.

Chris Osborne is *inter alia*, Subject Leader of Independent Learning at Middlesex University.

Barbara Page is Academic Leader, Employability/Capability Development at the University of North London, having previously served as the Director of the Enterprise in Higher Education programme from 1995–96. Throughout her career she has worked with employers in order to increase the awareness within the education system of industrial and commercial practices.

Steve Reynolds is a principal lecturer and academic manager in the School of Applied Sciences, and currently spearheads the University of Wolverhampton's career education initiatives.

Karen Roberts is Education Manager at Leeds TEC. She has a background in secondary education and has previously worked at Calderdale and Kirklees TEC, Leeds TEC and held the role of lead TEC nationally for TEC higher education issues for two years prior to the role being handed over to Heart of England TEC.

Jane Sampson is a lecturer in the School of Adult Education, University of Technology, Sydney in the area of community-based adult education.

Malcolm Shaw is Teaching and Learning Development Manager at Leeds Metropolitan University, with a central role in developing and implementing agreed policy and strategies in relation to teaching, learning and assessment.

Brenda Smith is Teaching and Learning Quality Manager at Nottingham Trent University. She has written widely on teaching and learning, and has facilitated many workshops both in the UK and overseas.

Patrick Smith runs the Staff Development Unit at the Buckinghamshire Chilterns University College. He has a teaching background, working in schools and higher education institutions in the UK and abroad. Much of the work of the Staff Development Unit is concerned with developing learning and teaching activities.

John Stephenson has been Director of the Royal Society of Art's Higher Education for Capability (HEC) project since September 1988 and is currently Head of the International Centre for Learner Managed Learning at Middlesex University. He has spoken and published extensively on the topic of capability – its nature, relevance to the work-place and development in higher education, including *Quality in Learning: A Capability Approach to HE* (with Susan Weil), 1992, Kogan Page, and *Using Learning Contracts in HE* (with Mike Laycock), 1993, Kogan Page.

Since 1994 he has been advising the Australian Capability Network on work-based initiatives involving major employers, universities and training organizations and more recently the New Zealand Education and Training Support Agency on the relevance of a capability approach.

He was Head of the School for Independent Study at North East London Polytechnic (now University of East London) from 1978 to 1988 which pioneered opportunities for full-time and work-based students to plan individual programmes of study to Diploma, Honours Degree and Masters Degree levels based on their own experiences, work interests and longer term intentions.

His doctorate research, at Sussex University, was on students' experiences of learner negotiated programmes and their significance in terms of their work and career development.

He has lead many R&D projects, most recently the joint University of Leeds, Leeds Metropolitan University and Leeds Training and Enterprise Council's work-based learning initiative.

Clare Stoney was a principal lecturer in professional education and development at Leeds Metropolitan University until she took up her present position as the University's Quality Assurance Manager. Clare has also been involved with partnership colleges and universities giving emphasis in recent years to staff development, quality standards and teaching/learning.

Marie Stowell is currently Programme Director for the Combined Honours Degree Programme at Nene University College Northampton. She has been responsible for developing the profiling process across the programme, and is now working on the implementation of a common academic framework. With a background in the sociology of education she has a particular interest in equal opportunities and the management of change in higher education.

Malcolm Taylor is the Partnership Manager at the University of Glamorgan, and is responsible for the implementation of the University's work-based learning strategy.

Mantz Yorke is Director of the Centre for Higher Education Development at Liverpool John Moores University. Previously he served the then Liverpool Polytechnic as Executive Director with responsibility for quality and standards before being seconded to the Higher Education Quality Council as Director of Quality Enhancement. He has collaborated with John Stephenson (HEC) in recent years, running conferences and workshops on the assessment of capability, and contributing actively to HEC's Assessment Network.

He is a member of the Governing Council of the Society for Research into Higher Education and is editor of the Society's journal *Studies in Higher Education*. He has published widely on matters relating to quality assurance and quality enhancement in higher education.

Part 1: The Context

Chapter 1

The Concept of Capability and its Importance in Higher Education

John Stephenson

The quality of purpose

It has been fashionable to judge quality according to fitness *for* purpose, an approach which equates quality with efficiency and takes the purpose as unquestioned, given or imposed. The discussion of quality in this chapter focuses on the question 'What is higher education for?', looking at quality in terms of fitness *of* purpose. The capability movement began debating this issue in 1980 when it published its *Education For Capability* manifesto through the Royal Society of Arts (RSA) in London. This manifesto focused on the limited value of education when it is seen solely as the pursuit of knowledge and intellectual skills for their own sake. '*Individuals, industry and society as a whole benefit*', the manifesto asserted, '*when all of us have the capacity to be effective in our personal, social and working lives.*' When couched in the context of rapid change, the manifesto implies that higher education should be judged by the extent to which it:

- gives students the confidence and ability to take responsibility for their own continuing personal and professional development;
- prepares students to be personally effective within the circumstances of their lives and work;

- promotes the pursuit of excellence in the development, acquisition and application of knowledge and skills.

Higher Education for Capability (HEC) was established by the RSA in 1988 to take these issues into the senior common rooms of the UK and, via its members overseas, to higher education in Australia and New Zealand. Through extensive discussions of the manifesto and its relevance in over 100 higher education institutions, HEC found considerable agreement for the development of student capability as an appropriate aim of higher education. The aim of this chapter is to explore the concept of capability more fully, to set capability in its wider context and to set out some of the issues facing higher education in its delivery.

The concept of capability

Capability is an all round human quality observable in what Sir Toby Weaver describes as 'purposive and sensible' action (Weaver, 1994). Capability is an *integration* of knowledge, skills, personal qualities and understanding *used appropriately and effectively* – not just in familiar and highly focused specialist contexts but in response to *new and changing* circumstances. Capability can be observed when we see people with justified confidence in their ability to:

- take effective and appropriate action;
- explain what they are about;
- live and work effectively with others; and
- continue to learn from their experiences as individuals and in association with others, in a diverse and changing society. (Stephenson, 1992)

Each of these four 'abilities' is an integration of many component skills and qualities, and each ability relates to the others. For instance, people's ability to take *appropriate action* is related to specialist expertise which in turn is enhanced by learning derived from experiences of earlier actions. *Explaining what one is about* involves much more than the possession of superficial oral and written communication skills; it requires self-awareness and confidence in ones specialist knowledge and skills and how they relate to the circumstances in hand. The emphasis on 'confidence' draws attention to the distinction between the *possession* and the *use* of skills and qualities. To be 'justified', such confidence needs to be based on real experience of their successful use. *In association with others* in *unfamiliar* situations has clear implications for the kinds of students' experience of higher education most likely to engender that justified confidence.

Capability is a necessary part of specialist expertise, not separate from it. Capable people not only know about their specialisms; they also have the confidence to apply their knowledge and skills within varied and changing situations and to continue to develop their specialist knowledge and skills long after they have left formal education.

Finally, capability is not just about skills and knowledge. Taking effective and appropriate action within unfamiliar and changing circumstances involves ethics, judgements, the self-confidence to take risks and a commitment to learn from the experience. A capable person has culture, in the sense of being able to 'decide between goodness and wickedness or between beauty and ugliness' (Weaver, 1994).

Capability and competence?

During the 1990s we have seen the development of competence-based national frameworks of vocational qualifications (NVQs) in the UK, Australia and New Zealand which are based on the needs of employers and the national drive to raise the qualification level and effectiveness of the work-force as a whole. These qualifications use industry standard competencies and performance indicators drawn from experienced practitioners. The UK Confederation of British Industry (CBI) has welcomed these developments and has found the use of NVQs beneficial in establishing industry standards and checklists for ensuring those standards are met (CBI, 1997). This competency approach is essentially a top-down control model which aims to secure the effective delivery of current services based on standards determined by past performance. Competence is about fitness for specified purposes.

Capability is a broader concept than that of competence. Competence is primarily about the ability to perform effectively, concerned largely with the here and now. Capability embraces competence but is also forward-looking, concerned with the realization of potential. A capability approach focuses on the capacity of individuals to participate in the formulation of their own developmental needs and those of the context in which they work and live. A capability approach is developmental and is driven essentially by all the participants based on their capacity to manage their own learning, and their proven ability to bring about change in both. Capability includes but goes beyond the achievement of competence in present day situations to imagining the future and contributing to making it happen. Capability is about both fitness of and for purpose. A changing world needs people who can look ahead and act accordingly.

Distinctions between disaggregated competencies and holistic capability have dominated more recent discussions on the concept and relevance of a capability approach. Compared with the late 1980s when the notion of capability was first formulated, there has been increasing emphasis on greater personal autonomy in education, employment and life, suggesting that it may be more useful to pursue this debate in terms of distinctions between dependent and independent capability.

Dependent or independent capability

The cartoonist Gary Larson depicts a group of sheep in a cocktail party, uncertain about where to stand and when to eat. 'Thank God', one says, 'here comes a Border collie'. Sheep, of course, have all the skills for being a sheep – they are expert at both eating and standing. They do both, at the same time, all day. Put them in a cocktail party and they are totally lost, dependent upon the arrival of a controller to tell them what to do. They have the skills but not the confidence to use them when circumstances are totally different. If these sheep were capable (in the sense in which we use the term) they would have three extra attributes: an *ability to learn for themselves*, and to quickly fathom the new environment; a *belief in their personal power to perform* in new situations (they would have the confidence, having spotted the pasture discretely left by the host, to do something about it) and *powers of judgement* (they might even question whether it was appropriate for sheep to be at the party and simply leave).

The Larson cartoon draws attention to the obvious limitations of a dependent mode of behaviour within a changing environment. For the purposes of the present argument, we can identify different situations in which varying degrees of independence are necessary (Figure 1.1). In our daily lives we can find ourselves moving from one type of situation to another, occasionally occupying more than one at the same time when different aspects of our work and lives come together.

Most of us operate, for much of our time, in position Y. In position Y, we are dealing with familiar problems for which we have learned familiar solutions. The context in which we are operating is also familiar. Position Y can apply to the work-place, the home, community activities or artistic pursuits. Good performance in position Y may require technical skills and knowledge of the highest order, or at the simplest level. We give students information about the context; the more complex the context, the more information we give them. We give them information about the kinds of problems they will meet, and details of the solutions which have been found to be effective. We might even give them practice in the implementation of the solutions and evaluation of their effectiveness. We seek to develop student capability in position Y by passing on other people's experience, knowledge and solutions. Though no doubt effective in the context of position Y, the resultant capability is essentially a dependent capability.

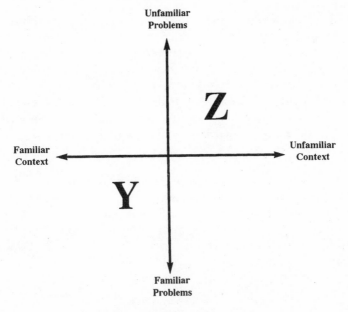

A way of looking at the world of actions

Figure 1.1 *Dependent and independent capability*

But position Y is not the whole of our experience. As indicated above, change is the order of the day. Many more of us will be spending more of our time having to operate in position Z. In position Z, we have less familiarity with the context and we have not previously experienced the problems with which we are faced. The slavish application of solutions perfected for familiar problems may have disastrous effects in position Z. To a large extent we are on our own, either individually or collectively. Very often, what distinguishes effective pilots, effective surgeons, effective social workers, effective teachers, effective builders and effective accountants is that they perform as well in position Z as in position Y.

In position Z we have to take much more responsibility for our own learning. By definition, we must inform ourselves about the unfamiliar context and not simply remind ourselves of what we were taught or trained to do. By definition, we must formulate the problems we have to deal with, not remind ourselves of problems previously learned. We must devise solutions and ways of applying them without the certainty of knowing the outcome, as a way of learning more about both the context and the problem. We need confidence in our ability to learn about the new context and to test possible ways forward from which we can learn. We need confidence in ourselves, and in our judgements, if we are to take actions in uncertainty and to see initial failure as a basis of learning how to do better.

When taking action in position Z, intuition, judgement and courage become important; there is no certainty of consequences based on previous experience. Specialist knowledge and skills are still relevant, but they are insufficient by themselves. It is necessary to appreciate their potential inadequacy, and to have the skills and confidence to enhance them. The solutions devised for the problems which are formulated will be essentially propositional in nature, developments from existing understanding. Evaluation of the consequences of actions taken in position Z will enhance our understanding of, and perhaps even improve, our performance in position Y.

Effective performance in position Z is likely to draw on all components of capability – specialist knowledge and skills, values and personal qualities. Key skills as defined by the Dearing Report (NCIHE, 1997) (the use of IT, communication, numeracy and learning how to learn) are clearly relevant to the above notion of capability, but only so far. They imply a fragmented, restricted, or simplistic view of capability. The Dearing Report comes nearer to describing independent capability when in paragraph 5.18 the Report gives primacy to

> the development of higher level intellectual skills, knowledge and understanding' because it 'empowers the individual – giving satisfaction and self-esteem as personal potential is realized' and 'underpins the development of many of the other generic skills so valued by employers and of importance throughout working life.

Intellectual skills are an important part of the capacity to formulate problems in unfamiliar circumstances. The missing capability feature in the Dearing vision is the packaging of all of the above within a coherent strategy for ensuring students develop the capacity for 'purposive and sensible' action through the formulation of problems in unfamiliar situations.

Preparing people to be effective in position Z is important at all levels of education. It is, however, of particular importance for higher education because it is from our graduates that many of our key people, in work as well as in the community, are likely to be drawn. As the intake to higher education expands and becomes more diversified, the more this will be true. The nation needs its future engineers, business executives, architects, social workers, administrators and citizens to be as confident in position Z as they are in position Y.

Implications for delivering capability in higher education

Student capability is developed as much by learning experiences as by the specific content of courses. If students are to develop 'justified confidence' in their ability to take purposive and sensible action, and to develop the unsheeply characteristics of confidence in their ability to learn, belief in their power to perform and proven powers of judgement in unfamiliar situations, they need real experience of *being responsible and accountable for their own learning, within the rigorous, interactive, supportive and, for them, unfamiliar environment of higher education.* If, as a consequence of being responsible for their own learning they bring about significant changes in their personal, academic, vocational or professional circumstances they will also have justified confidence in their ability to take effective and appropriate action, to explain what they are about, to live and work effectively with other people, and to continue to learn from their own experiences.

Where students are helped to assess their own educational needs, plan a suitable programme, negotiate approvals, secure and use appropriate resources and advice, achieve difficult targets, demonstrate their achievements and plan the next stage of their development, they have in effect successfully formulated and reformulated in the light of experience the problem of their own development. They have flourished in position Z, and dealt with the cocktail party with advice and guidance from, not control by, the Border collie.

This view of the higher education curriculum is at odds with a content delivery model in which staff specify what is to be learnt and how it is to be learnt. The separate development of skills – bolt-on capability – sustains a fragmented model, divorcing personal skills development from the acquisition of specialist knowledge. The Dearing Report (paragraph 9.24) comes to the same conclusion and advocates the development of skills through main-stream curriculum activities. A capability approach is also difficult to develop within modular schemes in which the accumulation of credits is more important to the award of the degree than the internal coherence and integrity of programmes in terms of individual student developmental needs. There are, however, some interesting initiatives exploring ways in which student capability can be developed within modular programmes, some of which are described later in this book (see Chapters 2, 3, 4, 20).

The wider context

Capability and employment

One of the most significant developments in the 1990s has been the extent to which the conventional wisdom among employers has moved in favour of some of capability's most distinctive features, particularly the importance of helping students and employees to be responsible for managing their own learning and development. This trend has been encouraged by dramatic changes in the working environment and greater understanding of the nature of good performance at work. Against the now well understood background of continual and discontinuous technical change, information growth and flatter structures with fewer points of supervision, employment prospects for graduates are significantly different from those that were the norm when university managers with responsibility for designing educational programmes for current students were students themselves. New recruits to the labour market can expect to change jobs every two years and careers every ten and a greater proportion of people are working part time or are becoming self-employed 'portfolio' workers.

In response to these trends there is abundant evidence that employers are looking for autonomous learners as recruits, or are developing the capacity for autonomous learning in their current work force. Every three years, for instance, IBM (UK) requires the members of its professional groups (eg systems analysts, human resource specialists) to demonstrate how they have kept their expertise up to date. Staff negotiate personal learning plans as part of their cycle of personal review (Ashton, interviewed by Stephenson, 1994). Another company, Rover Group, expects all of its workers from the boardroom to the shop floor to maintain personal profiles of their own learning at work (Rover Group, 1994), while the Association of Graduate Recruiters (AGR) anticipates that by the twenty-first century, 'the most significant challenge for graduates will be to manage their relationship with work and with learning' and that higher education needs to 'move from a model of teaching knowledge to one of enabling learning' (Goodman, 1994). Mayo (formerly of ICL Ltd) and Lank argue that '. . . survival in a rapidly changing world is dependent on . . . the capability to learn; and that capability is dependent on the motivation for continuous learning of everybody in an organization within a supportive learning environment.' (Mayo and Lank, 1994, p.vii)

More substantial evidence of the essential requirements of graduates entering employment in today's conditions comes from the recent study of 258 cases by Harvey *et al.* (1997) which concluded that employers are looking for 'knowledge, skills, abilities and personal attributes' including 'intellect, willingness to learn, self-motivation, ie motivation to do the job, develop ideas, take initiative and responsibility', concluding that 'for most employers, intellect and willingness to learn are more important than subject knowledge (pp.63–79). Yorke noted broadly similar needs and interests (within a greater diversity) among 104 small- and medium-sized enterprises (SMEs) (1997).

In America, Peter Senge (1992) writing about the learning organization identified five key disciplines: systems thinking, personal mastery, mental models, building shared vision and team learning and concluded that 'Organizations learn only through individuals who learn. Individual learning does not guarantee organizational learning. But without it, no organizational learning occurs.' (p.139). Most significantly, after 25 years of systematic research into effective performance in more than 600 work environments, Spencer and Spencer (1993) found that underlying personal characteristics such as achievement, motivation, initiative, information-seeking and self-confidence are crucial to good performance and survival.

Growing use of capability approaches in higher education

In *Quality in Learning* (1992), Stephenson and Weil based their model of a capability approach to higher education on 256 examples drawn from UK higher education institutions. Since then over 400 cases have been presented at HEC conferences, many of which have been published in conference reports and the journal *Capability* (see References). Two recent examples of the efficacy of a learner managed learning approach from the 400 conference presentations are of particular interest because they have been subjected to rigorous scrutiny, (a) in the case of Sainsbury plc through cost-benefit analysis, and (b) in the case of Case Western Reserve University's systematic monitoring of student progress by established academic researchers.

(a) Judith Evans, Director of Personnel Policy for Sainsbury's Supermarkets Ltd, a company of 115,000 members of staff in 383 stores which spends £38m per annum on staff training, described the processes and value of self-managed learning within a fiercely competitive industry, concluding 'self-managed learning has given us much more than a traditional training course. As well as people with more skills, it has given us more confident and able individuals who have the courage to tackle the many tough issues brought about by a changing organization.' (Evans, 1997)

(b) Richard Boyatzis and David Kolb *et al.* (1995) have spent the past seven years closely monitoring a capability approach to the development of competence for MBA students at Weatherhead School of Management, Case Western Reserve University, USA, including pre- and post-testing of student performance in key areas. 'The students graduating from the new MBA programmes,' they report, 'have significantly greater capability than they did when they entered,' especially on 'efficiency orientation, planning, self-control, empathy, networking, self-confidence, systems thinking – ie cognitive abilities, personal confidence and effectiveness, initiative, flexibility.' (pp.194–5). Their explanation for this improvement? 'Students' learning goals and learning plans appear to be significantly related to [these] changes. Developing a learning goal reflecting a specific intention to change appears related to significant change demonstrated over the one to two years of the programme.' (pp.194–5)

What these examples have in common is a belief in the power of individuals to manage their own development, whether at work, on higher education courses or in life generally. Learners are directly involved in discussions about what they will learn and/or how they will learn it. Each example is concerned with helping people to be effective in a changing world, with specialist knowledge, personal skills and personal qualities operating in unison. Each is concerned as much about the future as the present. Each is concerned with learning, development and achieving impact.

In the face of such evidence it is difficult not to be disappointed at the Higher Education Quality Council's (HEQC) report of its *Graduate Standards Programme* (HEQC, 1997). Much of the Report is concerned with issues of control of standards rather than the quality of the purpose of higher education. Though showing some awareness of the realities of survival in the outside world, there is an overall lack of grip when it comes to clarity of what is required and how it might be achieved. There is, they discover, 'no shared language or agreed set of measures' though they posit within Annexe C a range of 'best practice' outcomes dealing mainly with traditional academic skills and 'the possession', not proven effective usage of 'interpersonal skills and awareness – communication and presentation; *IT*' and again, 'possession' – not effective use of – 'general employment-related skills'. Self-motivation is confined to independent study skills; specific vocational skills are expected only from courses which are explicitly vocational. The Dearing Report gives a clearer endorsement of the overall capability agenda for higher education, in the name of economic prosperity for the nation and the capacity for lifelong learning for everyone and, as reported earlier, endorses a learner managed learning approach. The Report, however, is less ambitious when dealing with key skills. The skills expected of all graduates (paragraph 5.20) do not include some of the essential skills and qualities which the same Report says are essential in the world of work, including the ability to 'be flexible and adaptable, to work in teams, and to manage their own development and careers' (paragraph 9.17).

Learner responsibility and quality

The Dearing Report proposes greater responsibility to be given to students because it raises the quality of student learning but does not spell out the basis of this assertion. From the evidence of the cases presented at capability conferences (see References), giving students more involvement in the management of key elements of their programmes takes students into deeper approaches to learning through *pro-actively*:

- exploring their own learning needs;
- justifying to others the relevance of what they propose to study in terms of their personal, vocational and academic needs;

- monitoring their own progress against agreed milestones and adjusting their programmes in response to reflections on progress made;
- demonstrating their achievement through the application of their learning;
- reviewing the effectiveness of the programme they planned and completed; and
- planning the next stage of their continuing learning and development.

The drive, willingness and capacity to manage one's own learning, and the propensity to look for learning opportunities when dealing with problems or planning ahead have a different flavour from more bland references to 'learning how to learn'. Teaching study skills, raising awareness of different learning styles and preferences and the provision of a variety of learning materials are, of course, welcome developments but they do not in themselves represent the full richness of a capability approach. Taking responsibility and accepting accountability for the purpose, activity and assessment of learning is of crucial importance. Unless the learner is directly involved in these activities, learning how to learn can easily translate into students being helped to get on with teacher-determined assignments.

Learner responsibility and accountability promote *deep learning* by taking students into a search for meaning, relevance and underlying principles. Their reference point when deciding their learning priorities is relevance to their overall learning goals. Where students have a clearly articulated direction for themselves their eventual programme has an explicit coherence. In teacher determined courses, meaning, underlying principles, relevance and component integration are the preserves of the teacher – if teacher teaches A then A must be relevant to the course. On capability programmes, students to a large extent own their programmes of study and internalize their learning experiences.

Conclusion

In summary, giving students opportunities to be responsible and accountable for their own learning prepares them for effective performance in their personal and working lives, enhances their commitment to their studies, promotes deeper understanding, builds confidence in their ability to learn and helps the development of high level personal qualities and skills. In short, capability education can promote quality education.

There is growing interest among academics in capability-oriented initiatives judging by the high numbers of applicants for development funding for topics such as the learning society, work-based learning, guidance and learner autonomy and more recently, key skills, creativity and high level skills for lifelong learning. The RSA's Campaign for Learning is timely, as is the support for greater autonomy in learning from bodies such as the Council for Industry and Higher Education (Coldstream, 1997) and the CBI (Clark, 1996). Most significantly, the Dearing Report has formally endorsed an emerging consensus in favour of more direct involvement of students in the management of their own learning. What remains is for more universities to tackle the practical problems of bringing it about.

References

Note: the full texts of articles in *Capability* can be seen on the Internet on http://www.lmu.ac.uk/hec/.
* denotes published compendia of cases from HEC conferences.

Assiter, A and Shaw, E (eds) 1993 *Using Records of Achievement*, London: Kogan Page.
Boyatzis, RE, Cowen, SS, Kolb, DA *et al.* (1995) *Innovation in Professional Education*, San Francisco: Jossey-Bass.
Clark, P (1996) 'Funding for capability', *Capability*, **2**(2), 2–4.
Coldstream, P (1997) 'Training minds for the future of work', *Capability*, **3**(2), 2–5.
CBI (1997) 'Reasons to be cheerful', *Human Resource Brief*, August.
*Cunningham, L (ed) (1993) *Student Skills for the New Europe*, Leeds: Higher Education for Capability.
Evans, J (1997) 'Key skills for tomorrow's world', *Capability*, **3**(2), 10–15.
Goodman, C (1994) *Roles for Graduates in the 21st Century*, Cambridge: Association of Graduate Recruiters.
*Graves, N. (ed) (1993) *Learner Managed Learning: Practice, Theory and Policy*, Leeds: World Education Fellowship and Higher Education for Capability.
*Gregory, R and Thorley, L (eds) (1994) *Using Group-based Learning in Higher Education*, London: Kogan Page.
Harvey, L, Moon, S and Geall, V (1997) *Graduates' Work: Organisational Change and Students' Attributes*, Birmingham: Centre for Research into Quality, University of Central England.
HEQC (1997) *Graduate Standards Programme: Final Report*, London: Higher Education Quality Council.
*Jenkins, A and Walker, L (eds) (1994) *Developing Capability through Modular Courses*, London: Kogan Page.
*Laycock, M and Stephenson, J (eds) (1993) *Using Learning Contracts in Higher Education*, London: Kogan Page.
Mayo, A and Lank, E (1994) *The Power of Learning: A Guide to Competitive Advantage*, London: Institute of Personnel and Development (IPD).
NCIHE (1997) Higher Education in the Learning Society, report of the National Committee of Inquiry into Higher Education, London: HMSO.

*O'Reilly, D and Cunningham, L (1998, in press) *Developing the Professional Practitioner*, London: Kogan Page.

*Pauling, B (ed) (1989, in press) *The Virtual University*, London: Kogan Page.

Senge, PM (1992) *The Fifth Discipline*, London: Century Business Rover Group; (1994) 'Employers for capability', *Capability*, 1(1), 13–14.

Spencer, L and Spencer, S (1993) *Competence at Work: Models for Superior Performance*, New York: John Wiley and Sons.

Stephenson, J (1992) 'Capability and quality in higher education', in Stephenson, J and Weil, S (1992) *Quality in Learning: A Capability Approach to Higher Education*, London: Kogan Page.

Stephenson, J and Weil, S (eds) (1992) *Quality in Learning: A Capability Approach to Higher Education*, London: Kogan Page.

Stephenson, J (1994) 'Autonomous self-development in IBM', *Capability*, 1(2), 11–16.

*Stephenson, J and Challis, T (1998, in preparation) *Key Skills in Higher Education*, London: Kogan Page.

Weaver, T (1994) 'Knowledge alone gets you nowhere', *Capability*, 1(1), 6–12.

Yorke, M (1994) 'The external examiner system – in crisis?', in M Yorke (ed) *External Examining for Capability* (pp.2–4), London: Higher Education Quality Council.

*Yorke, M (1995) 'The assessment of higher order transferable skills: a challenge to higher education', in M Yorke (ed) *Assessing Capability in Degree and Diploma Programmes* (pp.5–12), proceedings of a conference held in Liverpool on 8 February 1995, Liverpool: Centre for Higher Education Development, Liverpool John Moores University.

Yorke, M (1997) 'The skills of graduates: a small enterprise perspective', *Capability*, 3(1), 27–33.

Part 2: Building the Capability Curriculum: Some Reports from the Field

Introduction

Building the capability curriculum is a challenge to all involved. Many institutions have now taken up the challenge and have included the development of student capability (or something very similar) in their mission statements: some have gone as far as to establish strategic frameworks within which the development can systematically be pursued. The task of transforming the curriculum in terms of the development of capability is, however, often left to the initiative and enthusiasm of individuals.

Bearing in mind the significant constraints of tightening resources – such as increasing numbers of students and a diversity of competing priorities including research and related activities – there has been an impressive array of initiatives ranging from small-scale localized projects to major institutional programmes. In Part 2 we present a small selection of examples as 'reports from the field' which collectively help us to understand something of what has been done, what is possible and the obstacles that have to be overcome for the possible to be made reality.

Pressure on space has required us as editors to ask contributors to write to very tight limits, and hence some detail has inevitably had to be excluded. The authors of the reports should be contacted in respect of any elaboration that might be sought. The reports cover, explicitly or implicitly, a wide range of issues that impinge on capability and its implementation, though only a sample of these issues is picked up in each.

A concern for quality in learning

A common feature of the chapters in Part 2 is a concern on the part of institutions to raise the quality and relevance of their students' experiences of higher education. None of the writers has been primarily concerned with cost reduction (despite the pressures) although some have mentioned that the need to reduce costs or to increase income has provided the leverage for innovations that would possibly have been undertaken anyway.

The ways in which the institutional concern for quality and relevance are diverse: a reading of the chapters reveals, *inter alia*, the following (a number of contributions could have been listed under more than a single heading, and other headings could have been added).

- Writing of curricula in terms of learning outcomes (Castley and Stowell; Gilbert and Reynolds; Page).
- Working on assessment methodology (Hunt and Frier; Shaw, Stoney and Green).
- Development of partnerships (Foster; Hase; Jackson, Lunt and Margham; Osborne, Davies and Garnett; Taylor).
- Supporting student development in various ways (McLeman and Smith. See also in Part 3: Anderson, Boud and Sampson; Butcher; Evatt and Boyle.)
- Supporting teaching (Doidge and Smith).
- Support for institutions (Doubleday and Roberts).

Institutional approaches

How is capability promoted in institutions? In some (the University of North London, the University of Wolverhampton, Leeds Metropolitan University, and Nene University College Northampton) the approach is strategic at the level of the institution. A policy steer is established (the method may differ between institutions), and the various parts of the institution are expected to follow suit. The tightness of the institutional framing seems to vary across the institutions: in three the expectation is that the various identified skills (which, for individual students, may or may not add up to capability in the sense outlined in Part 1) should appear at appropriate points in the curriculum and be assessed, whereas in the fourth it appears that the framing is more akin to guidance, though it seems likely that, over time, this will be tightened up in order to respond to expectations of comparability and equity.

A theme to come through these reports is the importance of personal and career development (for example, and on a smaller scale than the whole institution developments noted in the preceding paragraph, Buckingham-shire Chilterns University College has specifically addressed the needs of students for career planning). It is possible to see that something of a shift has taken place in the focus of a number of the institutions represented in this collection, from the gaining of a qualification towards the student's preparation for lifelong learning.

Free-standing initiatives

In other institutions capability appears, not in whole-institution commit-ment but in particular institutional offerings. Work-based learning has an obvious connection with capability and lifelong learning, and it is unsurprising that a number of reports dwell on the introduction of work-based learning into particular curricula. Here, too, there is a spectrum of engagement which ranges from the work-place-led programmes supported and accredited at Southern Cross University to the use of the City and Guilds Licentiateship to recognize learning for some sandwich students at Liverpool John Moores University. In between there are examples of work-place/institutional collaboration in which students undertake independent study on a personally-relevant subject while usually taking a selection of 'standard' modules from the institutional prospectus.

Other relevant experience

Not all those with an interest in capability are higher education institutions. National Vocational Qualifications (NVQs) extend to levels comparable to undergraduate and postgraduate work, with a focus on learning outcomes, performance indicators and portfolio development. Training and Enterprise Councils (TECs) and Regional Government Offices are charged with raising the skills level of the population as a whole and are increasingly using their channelling of funds as a lever for change in higher education. We therefore include two contributions from bodies whose work impacts on higher education: from a pair of TECs on their brokerage role, and from the RSA Examinations Board (an awarding body for NVQs) on how the methods used for assessing skills in NVQs can affect the development of capability.

Staff development

Innovations of the kind described in the reports imply, for many staff, changes in the way that they construe teaching and learning and in their actual practices. In a quasi-Newtonian way, change engenders resistance: the report from Nene University College Northampton provides an example of the resistance that had to be overcome. The report from Nottingham Trent University shows how steps may be taken at institutional level to pave the way for developments in curriculum and its implementation. There are those who would argue – as is reported in the area of humanities in one university (Utley, 1997) – that some aspects of capability should have no place in curricula. Given the diversity of views that are held regarding the purposes of higher education, institutions can expect that there will be elements of their staff that will be sceptical about, if not actually hostile to, the neo-vocational turn that government and employers are urging on higher education.

Curriculum development implies staff development. Staff development is a recurring theme in the reports, ranging from relatively local approaches to dealing with the implications of change (such as the switch to learning outcomes and its consequences) to the institution-wide approach taken at Nottingham Trent University. The more that students are involved in determining their programmes of study, the more pressure is exerted on the academic's dual role as both supporter of learning and assessor: the point can be demonstrated by imagining a scaling-up of the independent learning scheme at Middlesex University and comparing this with the typical institutional modular scheme.

Integration, modularity and the assessment of skills

Learning outcomes figure strongly in many of the reports, yet, from the point of view of capability, there is an often unacknowledged tension between the attainment of learning outcomes that might be specified for individual modules and the integration that is a feature of capability. Capability is likely to be rather more than the sum of the individual parts: Hunt and Frier point out, from the perspective of an examination board, that the separate assessment of key skills favours standardization but disfavours a number of aspects of capability (such as transfer and integration). The problem of integration may, in part, be solved if the student contributes to determining the programme of study. Capability requires the student to be able to justify the actions that he or she has taken, and hence brings to the fore the issue of self-assessment. Is reflective commentary, such as that expected at Middlesex University, sufficient, or should further steps be taken towards the development of student responsibility in respect of self-assessment, along the general lines suggested by Boud (1995)?

Partnerships

Many of the developments that have been reported have relied on partnerships of one sort or another, and some are at early stages of their implementation. The University of Wolverhampton has built substantially on what was achieved under the Enterprise in Higher Education initiative, and there are a number of points at which the involvement of TECs has been crucial to the implementation of capability-related ideas (reference was made to the chapter dealing with the role of the TECs with respect to higher education).

Last but not least, resourcing

One issue for consideration, and which is generally not given much attention, is the resourcing of the innovation. While some developments may be of value in educational terms, their unit costs may prove to be too high to be sustained by the institution when the 'pump-priming' money runs out. Worthwhile initiatives sometimes die at the end of pilot work, to the disadvantage of the institution and the dispiriting of protagonists, simply because ways have not been found to carry them forward on an appropriate scale. Major innovations intended to inculcate a new culture of learning cannot easily be sustained by a support culture constructed for the system that the innovations are designed to replace, without appearing to require different (usually interpreted as additional) resources. This is the kind of conceptual and managerial challenge that institutions often find difficult, but nevertheless have to meet if they are fully to achieve the goals that they set for themselves.

References

Boud, D (1995) *Enhancing Learning Through Self-assessment*, London: Kogan Page.

Utley, A (1997) 'Humanities say no to careers in curriculum', *The Times Higher Education Supplement*, no 1296 (5 September), p.40.

Chapter 2

Embedding Capability in the Curriculum: Case Study from the BA and BSc Combined Honours Course at Nene University College Northampton

Andrew Castley and Marie Stowell

Editors' introduction

Castley and Stowell describe the strategy adopted by Nene College to embed capability across a substantial part of the College's curricular offerings. This required a lengthy consultative process designed to achieve a high level of staff support, particularly since the institutional commitment to the personal tutor system at a time of constrained resources implied changes in approach to teaching and learning. The innovation entailed the identification of the skills to be included and their incorporation in learning outcomes. An issue that had to be resolved was whether transferable skills should be developed in a 'bolt-on' module or within subject-based modules.

Castley and Stowell's account shows that the embedding of capability was not plain sailing, a number of staff being sceptical of the proposed changes. The adoption of a method of profiling student performances, seen as an important component of capability, was particularly problematic since it had resource implications which could only be satisfied by adjustments to the way in which staff time was being used, and because a way needed to be found of incorporating it into the assessment regulations.

Introduction

Recent curriculum developments within higher education have emphasized the significance of 'transferable skills' both in terms of relevance to future employment and importance for academic success. In a number of institutions this emphasis has been accompanied by the development of student profiling processes, which provide opportunities for students to reflect upon learning strengths and limitations, set goals for progress and record significant achievements. Such developments are vital ingredients of 'capability'. This chapter describes how a transferable skills framework linked to a personal and academic learning profile provided the structure around which a 'capability curriculum' was developed within an existing Combined Studies programme in a large college of higher education.

Nene College offers programmes ranging from research degrees through taught master's and first degree programmes to diploma and professional courses. The College has 9,500 undergraduate and 950 postgraduate students studying in the areas of healthcare; environmental science; design and technology; social and behavioural sciences; management and business; and the arts and humanities.

Defining capability through structured curriculum development

In 1992 Nene College embarked on a major curriculum development project, which set out to review the aims, objectives and learning processes of the diverse range of subject units making up the College's free-standing BA/BSc (Hons) Combined Studies degree programme. The initiative was driven by the recognition that unstructured and uncoordinated development was increasingly inappropriate within an organizational structure built upon subject autonomy.

The September 1995 intake of around 1,000 students (approximately 40 per cent of the College intake) across 39 subjects was the first to experience the revised programme, but the changes initiated then are, and are likely to remain, ongoing. The project involved a large number of academic staff from across the four faculties, and required the support and approval of institutional managers at senior level.

In reviewing the aims of the Combined Studies degree programme, an attempt was made to realize the commitments of the College mission statement, particularly to 'provide defined academic programmes with clear learning outcomes' and to 'develop students' capabilities and to empower them to achieve their 'fullest potential as individuals and as members of society'. One of the main purposes of the development project was to articulate and give effect to these commitments, and in so doing to provide a commonality of experience among all students enrolled across the programme. Commonality and comparability across subject units were promoted through a number of linked developments which sought to define 'capability':

- a specification for the curriculum design of subject units in terms of learning outcomes;
- the establishment of a framework of transferable skills to be developed and assessed within subject units;
- a generic set of criteria for degree classification, in which a major characteristic of the highest levels is 'the ability to deal with uncertainty'; and
- the development of a student profiling system operating through personal academic tutors.

Learning outcomes

The development project began by seeking to persuade course teams to think in terms of learning outcomes consistent with graduateness: the knowledge, understanding and skills which students should have acquired and developed on completion of their programme of study. This was intended to shift course teams away from defining courses or units of study in terms of aims, content and teaching methods: instead they were asked to specify what students would have achieved on successful completion of a programme of learning, to design learning activities which would support students in achieving those outcomes, and to formulate an assessment strategy which would enable students to demonstrate achievement of the outcomes. In this way learning and assessment were placed at the centre of planned curriculum design. Learning outcomes were established first at programme level and, since they were of necessity generic to a wide range of subject disciplines, they focused very clearly on transferable skills.

Transferable skills

The generic learning outcomes for the programme as a whole provided reference points for subjects in formulating their own outcomes. In defining the generic outcomes, particular emphasis was given to establishing a framework of 'transferable' skills: learning skills, communication skills, group-work skills, problem-solving skills and personal management skills. These were regarded as essential underpinnings to academic achievement across disciplines. It was not being implied that transferable skills were identical across subject disciplines (indeed they are often difficult to disentangle from subject specific skills), or that generic skills could be developed effectively in contexts independent of subject content.

Transferability in this framework related to capability: the ability to integrate and apply specialist knowledge and skills within varied and changing situations, to reflect critically on experience, and to continue to learn and develop. While many subject areas claimed to be already delivering these skills, the demonstration by students of capability and competence was regarded as problematic. It was recognized that, if students were to demonstrate achievement of the Combined Honours learning outcomes, it followed that they required opportunities to develop skills in a variety of contexts and also to generate a considerable awareness of what they were doing. It was for these reasons that subjects were required to be explicit about transferable skills in learning outcome terms.

Generic criteria for degree classification

Having defined the intended learning outcomes for the degree programme and established a framework for the development of transferable skills, it was necessary to make explicit what this meant in terms of degree classifications and assessment criteria, drawing upon a separate initiative within the College which had established a set of generic criteria for degree classifications as a tool for setting standards and maintaining comparability within the College's degree programmes. The capacity to deal with 'uncertainty', which became a defining characteristic of the qualities to be demonstrated for the award of higher classes of degree, was arrived at without explicit reference to 'capability'.

Student profiling

The impact of large numbers, as at other institutions, threatened to make the personal tutor system unworkable and to render academic support for students increasingly remote. However, the values of the institution and a reaffirmation of the personal tutor system by the senior management served to set a context in which the personal tutor system was prioritized as an entitlement for students. Within Combined Honours, the presence of a strong academic student support structure integrated into the curriculum was regarded as vital in ensuring both the coherence of a student's programme of studies and the guidance necessary for individual development. The academic and personal profiling system was to be the mechanism for realizing this commitment.

The Combined Honours profiling system began life in 1992 as a learning action plan, and was developed over the following three years for first year students. All new students are provided with a learning profile document which incorporates self-assessment and action planning proformas, and structured agenda for scheduled meetings with personal tutors. It culminates in a requirement to compile a reflective review of learning. The system is operated by personal tutors. This profile became the 'capability envelope' of the course.

Securing agreement and effecting change

No reader familiar with higher education will harbour the illusion that the changes proposed were received with uniform support and enthusiasm among the 150 or so staff then teaching on the programme. Indeed, many staff questioned the need for change. A two-year development and consultation process was necessary to raise the issues, debate and discuss ways forward, build consensus, negotiate internal politics, develop the curriculum and revalidate first-year units before the first cohort of students entered the new programme in September 1995. Work to embed the 'capability curriculum' continues.

Following an initial series of meetings of subject leaders, in which the programme directors put the case for review of the programme, a consultative document was issued which set out the rationale for change around the themes of 'capability', 'skills', 'profiling' and 'assessment'. A videorecording of a presentation by John Stephenson in 1993 of capability approaches was also distributed. These were essentially staff development resources, and a series of small working groups met to address the various topics.

The intention was made clear at the outset that all subject units would be revalidated under a common process and within a specified framework. A design specification for subject units was drawn up. This included stipulations regarding student learning hours and assessment as well as a standard format, which focused on key aspects of the 'capability' curriculum, for unit descriptions.

Transferable skills: the development process

While the case for development of students' 'transferable skills' was readily agreed, the incorporation of these skills into curricula was a far more contentious issue. Argument took place regarding the relative merits of a separate module of transferable/study skills and the integration of skills within the curriculum of subject units. There was first resistance on ideological, pedagogical and pragmatic grounds. It was acknowledged that skills could only be developed within specific contexts and that the particular perspectives of subject disciplines were important in this respect – and the question of who would actually teach a separate module was clearly contentious. Furthermore, the structure of a first-year programme in which students studied three equally-weighted subject units made the credit value of a free-standing skills module problematic. The development of transferable skills within subject studies became the adopted position. Even so, it was recognized that this would not be without its problems.

From the perspective of the programme directors the problem was one of ensuring that the desired skills *would* be developed through subject studies. Two strategies were adopted in order to ensure this: first, subject staff were required to specify, as learning outcomes, the transferable skills to be developed in subject units and, second, they were required to demonstrate, as part of the revalidation exercise, how the identified skills would be reflected in the teaching, in the opportunities for practice, and in the assessment process.

These strategies were intended not only to support subjects in developing capability within the curriculum, but also to encourage subject teams to make the teaching and learning of 'capability' explicit. In convincing subject teams of the centrality of transferable skills to student success across all disciplines, the programme directors drafted an assignment cover sheet setting out criteria for assessment. This was developed from existing models already in use for a number of subjects, and the currency of generic transferable skills was clearly demonstrable. The adoption of assignment cover sheets for the purposes of student feedback is now established practice across all subject units.

In order to support subjects in reviewing the curriculum a guidance document on writing learning outcomes was produced, and staff development relating to transferable skills was given a high profile through the development period. However, staff have not found the task of writing effective learning outcomes easy. It was recognized in the validation process that few subjects had considered systematically the relationship of assessment to learning outcomes. While all subjects were successful in arguing that the range of transferable skills in the Combined Honours programme would be developed through the subject curriculum, it was clear that this was much more of a reality in some subjects than others. This eventually led to a requirement for subjects to map the assessment strategy to the learning outcomes for a given unit.

Profiling: the development process

Acceptance of the case for profiling was more difficult to achieve. Much debate revolved around the purpose of profiling, the relative value of the profiling process itself and its outcomes, and the extent to which participation in the process should be mandatory or voluntary. These were difficult issues to resolve: those who believed in the validity of the process generally took a voluntarist position, while the sceptics were split between, on one hand, those who argued that students would not take the process seriously unless it was mandatory and, on the other, those who argued that making the profile a requirement of progression to the next stage of the programme would result in instrumental and superficial commitment to the process. The structure of the Combined Honours programme precluded the identification of specific credit for the profile.

This debate was sharpened because of earlier experience with pilot work on voluntary non-credited action planning. This had been implemented within a personal tutor system which had been, as in most institutions, patchy. Staff were concerned that resources did not permit a formally structured profiling process dependent upon regular personal tutor meetings. It became clear to the Programme Directors that the embedding of student profiling not only required acceptance and understanding of its value, but could only be achieved if there were clear resource commitments to personal tutoring.

Since profiling and records of achievement were entirely new to most staff teaching on the programme, opportunities were taken to disseminate successful profiling models used within other courses in the College, and a rationale was developed in terms of the fostering of student independence and autonomy. At the same time, agreement was secured from resource managers that personal tutors should be credited with 1.5 timetabled hours per personal tutee per year. Subjects would have maximum flexibility in delivering the personal tutor entitlement, but this would be prioritized within the teaching hours available. Many subjects chose to introduce 'office hour' systems. In order to assure students' entitlement to academic guidance as part of the profiling process, a standard 'personal and academic learning review' document was provided centrally for all students and staff. This was intended to support and guide students in developing a learning action plan towards the end of the first term, and to evaluate their learning at the end of the year.

The action planning and review processes currently take place with the guidance of the personal academic tutor, with students being referred to various sources of support where there is an identified need for skills development. Students are asked to claim, and provide evidence of, their self-evaluation in the form of assignment feedback from their various subjects. Where assignment cover-sheets have been used, this evidence is readily accessible by the tutor.

The debate over the mandatory or voluntary nature of the profiling process was eventually resolved by making the formal submission of a satisfactory review of learning a condition for compensated progression in the event of a marginal fail in one subject unit. In this way, students were not specifically required to participate in the process, but there could be clear rewards for doing so. The submission rate for first-year profiles now stands at 80 per cent, and student evaluation evidence suggests that the effectiveness of the process depends in large part on the commitment to the process by personal tutors.

The principles and practices involved in profiling in year one are now being extended to years two and three of the degree programme.

Conclusion

Three years on from the validation of the new programme it is clear that 'capability' principles – as incorporated in the emphasis given to 'transferable' skills and student profiling – are now widely, if not universally, accepted. Institutional change within the context of existing course structures was fostered through a centrally defined and managed revalidation process. In part this has been achieved by making explicit a framework for design and delivery of subject units within a large multidisciplinary programme. Thus staff are expected to ensure that courses develop and assess a range of key skills, and that they also provide structured opportunities for students to review and plan their personal and academic development with reference to such skills. This must be demonstrated at validation and made explicit to students in the form of statements of learning outcomes, skills maps, and assignment feedback sheets. Central coordination of the review and validation process, with associated staff development, has been vital to the effectiveness of this aspect of the development project.

Establishing assessment criteria and student entitlements has also proved an effective strategy for defining 'capability'. The integration of assessment, outcomes and learning at both programme and subject level has been an important lever for change in the revalidation process. Commonality and comparability have been important considerations within this context; while subject autonomy is supported, there is a clear definition of minimum entitlements for students.

Chapter 3

An Institutional Strategy for Transferable Skills and Employability

Jenny Gilbert and Steve Reynolds

Editors' introduction

In this description of the University of Wolverhampton's strategy for the development of transferable skills a key feature is the shift of emphasis from the undergraduate degree to the career lying beyond the degree. A number of transferable skills have been identified which respond to the needs expressed by employers, and these have been embedded in statements of expected learning outcomes. Curricular analyses have indicated where there were 'gaps' and over-concentration in learning outcomes (enabling rectification), and the University is well on the way to having all its undergraduate modules written in learning outcome format.

The switch of emphasis towards career development has led to the inclusion of relevant activities at each level of the undergraduate's experience, and Gilbert and Reynolds exemplify this with reference to the field of science. However, when drawing attention to the possibility that information technology might be able to contribute to students' career development they hint at pressures that the approach may be having on staff.

Institutional context and steer

According to key policy-makers at the University of Wolverhampton, the original aim of introducing a 'capability curriculum' was to draw together the academic and vocational aspects of the curriculum and transfer the emphasis from the degree itself to the career at the end of the degree and beyond. The strategic plan of the University has set graduate employability as a top priority with the principal objective of 'the enhancement of academic and pedagogic provision in order to address graduate employment needs.' This is now being translated into better facilitation of students' learning in order to enable them to manage their progress effectively through the 'education-to-work' continuum, and into improved 'destination figures'. Few degree courses are designed principally as preparation for a specific career, but the best-prepared students are those with clear and focused aims and the University believes that this message should be emphasized early on in their courses.

As one of the largest new multi-campus universities in Britain, with 11 constituent schools, the institution recruits a significant proportion of mature and part-time students and, in some disciplines, a large contingent of ethnic minorities. Students at the University are less likely to possess 'middle-class cultural capital' on entry and, with increasing student/staff ratios and the loss of the tutorial model, students in mass higher education will not automatically gain transferable skills through social interaction with other students or staff. Many students develop their transferable skills through activities outside their courses, through membership of clubs and voluntary work. However, the increasing financial pressures and family commitments of local and mature students often reduce such opportunities. The University is responding to this situation by integrating transferable skills, the recording of achievement and career management learning into its fully modular curriculum. The process started in 1988 with the first tranche of Enterprise in Higher Education (EHE) monies. The EHE Initiative was extremely successful in embedding transferable skills into students' activities and fostering their ability to be autonomous learners.

Forming the model: problems, solutions and benefits

Although many modules had assimilated transferable skills, there was no consistent articulation of these skills and students were not always made aware, in advance, of the skills that would be addressed. Although virtually all subject areas were developing skills there was rarely any analysis of the collection of skills that an individual student might be expected to develop through a modular programme. The overriding problems appeared to be how the University might incorporate skills more formally into the curriculum and how it might support students in reflecting upon their development. These had to be resolved within the existing resource envelope, in a situation in which many students would pursue individualized programmes. The solution was the introduction of a new format for describing modules, followed by the validation requirement that each school should demonstrate how it would provide for the recording of achievement and careers education. The new model comprises a curriculum described by the learning outcomes which students are expected to demonstrate:

- the matching of 'bundles' of learning outcomes to assessment components;
- the identification of the transferable skills which are developed and assessed;
- the description of the learning outcomes for an entire student pro-gramme, these outcomes being mainly cognitive outcomes such as the demonstration of analysis and synthesis.

After referring to publications from organizations such as the Confederation of British Industry (CBI), seven transferable skills that employers were seeking from graduates, were chosen, namely those of:

- demonstrating numeracy;
- gathering information;
- using information technology (IT);
- organizing;
- communicating effectively;
- acting independently; and
- working in teams.

Initially the demonstration of numeracy was excluded because of the difficulty of incorporating it into some subjects. This raised concerns which resulted in the decision to add numeracy, but to allow subjects to choose which of the seven skills would be assessed, conditional on approval at validation. In the light of the belief expressed in the Dearing Report that all students should develop the four key skills of communication, numeracy, using IT and learning to learn (NCIHE, 1997, paragraph 9.17), this decision will have to be reviewed.

The introduction of the new model has had a number of effects. It is now much clearer to students what is expected of them in terms of assess-ment, since the matching of outcomes, including transferable skills, against assessment makes this more explicit. Previously, students did not always recognize that they were developing a range of skills. One of the main benefits of the process to date is the mapping of skills across programmes using a matrix. This has brought to light the issues of missing skills and of the over-assessment of others. For example, biology was using poster presentations in most level 1 modules, and computing was burdening students with group work in many modules. It is too early to judge the impact of the introduction of skills in subjects which were previously driven by the need to 'get through' the syllabus but it can be seen that, in disciplines where skills were already being developed, the new model is having the effect of ensuring a more coherent distribution of skills across modular programmes. Having devised the model for the integration of transferable skills into modules, where normally each module assesses only one or two of the University set, there are at the time of writing (September 1997) about 60 per cent of undergraduate modules written in this format. The remainder should be completed over the next academic year. The final phase in the overall framework is the establishment of a careers development programme which will incorporate the students' reflective reviews and action plans.

Career and personal development

As part of the University's reinforcement of mainstream curriculum it is transparently making explicit what hitherto has been implicit and raising consciousness regarding career and personal development. The latter is now being linked to profiling developments. Throughout the emphasis is upon learner ownership of the totality of the learning experience and provision of a tutor-supported, fully integrated approach to career planning activity. As a consequence an overall enrichment of the curriculum has resulted. With the interlocking between higher education and people's working lives becoming a lot closer and more complex, the systematic approach adopted here develops lasting career planning skills which can regularly be re-used at later stages in respect of transitions and lifelong learning.

In many higher education institutions careers education is often a freestanding 'bolt-on' module, usually elective in year two, which is taught on an optional group workshop basis by a central careers service. The University firmly believes that the best way to provide student support is through an embedded subject-specific programme, or module, delivered jointly by academic and careers advisory staff, and complementary to compulsory core materials. The major issue to be faced was how to integrate this into an already crowded mainstream academic curriculum. The pilot school (Applied Sciences) opted for a 'timetabled provision' of careers education and related activities by infusing a career focus throughout the entire undergraduate curriculum. Given the University's culture, however, it has aimed for a flexible approach which can be adapted or customized by schools.

From the outset the University identified and followed three basic premises.

1. It is necessary to enrich student learning early on (focusing upon transition into higher education) by providing a career and personal development focus on job and transferable skills, thereby enhancing motivation.
2. It is necessary to empower students to recognize their own skill repertoires, to evidence and transfer them to new situations, and most importantly, to articulate their capability to potential employers in interviews.
3. For maximum effectiveness skills should be formally embedded, or framed, within a subject disciplinary context, resulting in joint ownership and delivery by academic schools and the University's Employment Services.

Learning a living: a model for integrating careers education

The Career and Personal Development Learning Programme in Science (CDPLP)

CPDLP uses an active learning, student-centred approach, transcending level boundaries and employing core modules to deliver careers education alongside laboratory practicals and activities designed to foster personal effectiveness and basic skills. The programme embodies the Law and Watts model framework of self-assessment (taking stock), opportunity awareness and transition management (coping with change) (see Watts and Hawthorn, 1992). Transition management focuses upon entry to and exit from higher education, and is underpinned by an understanding of the 'world of work'.

A three-pronged plan of attack has been adopted. First, there is an introductory phase (six hours) of career management and personal development as a sort of 'mass inoculation' designed to kick-start students' career planning activities. It comes at the end of semester one in order that students will have settled into the higher education environment. Second, there is a 'booster jab' in year two. This intermediate phase, of nine hours, is delivered intensively at times of low designated activity, and is located principally in the induction and counselling weeks and/or inter-semester periods. Third, the final phase, of nine hours duration, front-loads the double credit rated project module (in year three, or year four in the case of sandwich placement students). The University firmly believes that the final year project has the potential to be an important 'skills demonstrator vehicle' or instrument through which its students can evidence the acquisition and transfer of their skills repertoire, as part of their capability envelope.

The initial phase is delivered via a common central strategy utilizing a 'delivery partnership' approach, whereas later phases are more amenable to customizing by departments. Although the science CPDLP is integrated into the mainstream programme, additional variations on the theme allow 'chunks' to be used appropriately alongside basic study skills and IT units in freestanding modular formats.

Teaching and learning methods now adopted concentrate, not on traditional career guidance mechanisms, but on student career and personal development through the use of active tutorial materials. Students gain first-hand experience in preparing for, and maintaining, employability through using the following:

- self-audits;
- computer-aided guidance packages;
- personal profiling;
- business simulation exercises;
- learning logs;
- role play; and
- case studies.

Key deliverers include academic 'champions of the cause', careers advisers, recent alumni as employer proxies, visiting employers and personnel department staff. Assessment is largely through a combination of learning logs, occupational analysis and group presentations, whose collective outcomes are presented in a portfolio leading to a personal portrayal profile which can be used in conjunction with a curriculum vitae.

Heightening of awareness and dissemination across the institution has been achieved through a series of campus 'internal cascade model' workshops and a one-day annual skills conference on capability and employability. A rigorous evaluation is being carried out on all three phases, which is regarded as an essential part of the development process. Early indications are encouraging the University to believe that the programme is educationally effective and user-friendly. A feasibility study is being undertaken in order to assess whether the use of IT in curriculum-embedded careers' development could ease pressures on staff and CDPLP's dependence upon paper.

The key advantages of embedding CPDLP in the main-stream disciplinary framework are that skills are practised in the context of the subject, and a suitable vehicle is thereby created for the evidencing of student achievement: these increase the credibility of CPDLP in students' eyes. Additionally, issues of validation and accreditation, resource provision, academic support, assessment and quality control are automatically managed through the integration of CPDLP into taught modules.

Students see an appropriate mix of career-related and personal effectiveness skills as leading to increased self-confidence, experience of occupations, and an early start to identification of their career planning needs. Staff benefit from team teaching with careers advisers, and the cost-effective pooling of expertise, ideas and resources. Collaborative working offers the advantage of careers advisory staff acting as surrogate voices for employers and therefore providing a measure of external credibility. On the other hand, academics can provide subject perspectives via the modules incorporating skills development and the internal legitimacy of formalizing assessment, accreditation, resource and validation issues.

Summary

Building upon the solid framework of the specific initiatives of the EHE exercise (1988–93), the policy of accelerated curriculum development now being adopted involves refinements to National Record of Achievement/portfolio-building leading to a progress file:

- integrated careers education provision;
- the assessment of transferable skills;
- the redesign of modules in terms of learning outcomes;
- the development of the IT resources base; and
- a direct emphasis on relevant work experience linked to small- and medium-sized enterprises.

The implementation of this policy will undoubtedly increase the preparedness of the University's graduates for the transition out of higher education and the challenges to be faced later along their career paths.

References

NCIHE (1997) *Higher Education in the Learning Society*, Report of the National Committee of Inquiry into Higher Education, London: HMSO.

Watts, AG and Hawthorn, R (1992) *Careers Education and the Curriculum in Higher Education*, Cambridge: Hobsons.

Chapter 4

The New Capability Curriculum at the University of North London

Barbara Page

Editors' introduction

Page gives an account of how the University of North London (UNL) identified a set of six generic capabilities and is introducing them into curricula in a manner similar to that which the (very different) Alverno College in the United States has pioneered. Modules are being written in terms of learning outcomes, and a mapping exercise is being undertaken in order to ensure that there is an appropriate coverage of the capabilities across programmes of study.

This is an example of how an institution as a whole has chosen to give a particular steer to its curricular offerings, and provides evidence of a careful strategy for implementation which seeks to involve staff in a variety of ways.

Introduction

In 1896 the former Northern Polytechnic (now the University of North London) opened the doors to its first thousand students and, shortly after, began offering degree courses from the University of London. At that time, the institution's mission was to 'promote the industrial skills, general knowledge, health and well-being of young men and women . . . (and) . . . the means of acquiring a sound General, Scientific, Technical and Commercial Education at small cost'. The institution sought to provide access to high quality educational opportunities and to contribute to the social and economic life of the local community. Since that time the

35

University, which has retained its vocational and professional commitment, has grown to provide more than 13,000 full-time students with a choice of around 160 different degree subjects that can be studied as single degree programmes or in major/minor and joint combinations. These programmes have been delivered, since 1992, through a semester-based, fully modularized system, with full-time students taking eight modules each year throughout a three- or four-year degree course. Modules may be 'core' (ie compulsory for a specified subject), 'designated' (complementary to the specialist topic) or 'free' (unrelated to subject specialism). Students can take up to two free modules each year.

The academic work of the University is organized into four faculties or academic areas: the Business School, Environmental and Social Studies, Humanities and Teacher Education, and Science, Computing and Engineering. Each faculty contains several schools or subject areas. Students studying cross-faculty subject combinations are the responsibility of the rapidly expanding Interfaculty Office.

The reasons for change

In recent years UNL has been extremely successful in promoting access to higher education for non-traditional groups such as mature students (70 per cent of its student population), ethnic minorities (44 per cent), and women (55 per cent), and in developing new teaching and learning methods to meet these students' needs. It is now seeking to ensure that its students graduate not only with specialist subject knowledge but also with the skills and capabilities sought by employers. In its Strategic Plan 1996–97 to 2000–1, the University emphasizes access and the need to 'produce graduates who are self-reliant, professional, and are able to use understanding and knowledge to make judgements and take meaningful action' – students who are able to 'fulfil personal, social and employment goals . . . and make a difference'.

The capable graduate

In order to achieve this, the University has identified six core, generic capabilities (key skills) which it considers essential to the concept of graduateness and to graduate employability. These capabilities are fully integrated, developed and assessed within each subject context in the new curriculum, guaranteeing that students possess necessary employment-related skills and abilities. The new curriculum reflects many of the conclusions reached by the Higher Education Quality Council (HEQC) in its consideration of the definition of 'graduateness' (HEQC, 1997) and other recent research into the requirements of employers (eg AGR, 1995; Harvey et al., 1997). It has pre-empted many of the recommendations contained in the report of the National Committee of Inquiry into Higher Education (NCIHE, 1997) concerning the content, delivery and purpose of programmes in higher education.

The capabilities

The University has identified the following capabilities. Students are expected to develop their ability:

- *to act appropriately in the context of social and cultural diversity and the modern day environment*, ie to recognize a range of perspectives on social, cultural and environmental issues relating to subject disciplines and professional activities; to act appropriately in context;
- *to make ethical evaluations*, ie to recognize ethical issues in subject disciplines, professional behaviour and public action; to distinguish between different ethical viewpoints; to establish a personal viewpoint by evaluating alternatives;
- *to think critically, and produce solutions*, ie to identify, describe, classify, analyse, evaluate, synthesize, create, hypothesize, experiment; to think linearly and laterally; to construct the criteria for choice and for alternative solutions;
- *to manage themselves and relate to others*, ie to clarify personal goals; to plan effectively and implement plans within realistic time frames; to identify and address personal strengths and weaknesses; to seek feedback; to take responsibility; to work in a team;
- *to communicate effectively in context*, ie to select appropriate communicative media, including listening, speaking, reading, writing, drawing, symbolising, tabulating, mapping; to use a variety of communication technologies;
- *to seek, handle and interpret information*, ie to identify appropriate information sources; to extract, analyse and interpret information; to select, structure and present information; to recognize and apply the criteria for reliability, validity and sufficiency of information.

The capability curriculum

How it started

The beginnings of the new curriculum go back to mid-1994 when the University and five others (all former polytechnics) invited senior representatives from a small, liberal arts, women's college – Alverno College Institute in Milwaukee, Wisconsin – to present their highly innovative outcomes-based methods of teaching and assessment. Alverno's work has concentrated on enabling students to acquire and demonstrate attainment of specified abilities, which are developed within the context of an academic subject. Alverno's methods produce highly effective student learning and are attracting increasing international interest. Immediately after this event UNL set up a small, cross-institutional working group to identify and elaborate the core capabilities it wanted its graduates to possess. In 1995 Alverno staff were invited to the University to lead two days of staff development, information dissemination, and discussion on the Alverno experience, their methods and processes. Following these sessions, the capabilities identified at UNL were discussed extensively and refined within the University's Boards and Committees, at both institutional and faculty level. Guidance documentation, produced by the Academic Registry, was also considered widely throughout the institution, amended and recirculated. Staff reaction varied from disbelief to disinterest, and from derision to enthusiasm. Many believed it would never happen, and that it was a passing phase. They were wrong.

Structuring change

The institutional framework for change had been established early in the process and is being overseen by a very small, central Curriculum Steering group (chaired by the Deputy Vice-Chancellor, Academic Affairs), whereas coordination across the University is provided by the Curriculum Action Group – a network containing representatives from the faculties, Student Services (including the Careers Service), and the academic support services. Each faculty appointed a member of academic staff to lead and coordinate the work and Faculty Curriculum Action Groups oversaw the development of threshold descriptors specific to discipline areas.

Capability integration

Threshold levels for the capabilities are defined at two levels – preliminary and advanced – corresponding to the distinctions within the degree pro-grammes. A maximum of two core capabilities can be fully integrated, developed and assessed in each module; further core capabilities may be developed in any module, but are not assessed in that module.

At preliminary (year one) level all six capabilities are developed and assessed to a similar level across all subject programmes. Comparability and consistency of threshold levels and their assessment are being achieved through the establishment of cross-institutional, inter-disciplinary groups for each capability. These groups review threshold descriptors throughout the University, define and redefine levels and work towards the articulation of common assessment criteria for each capability. An archive of assess-ments is being established to allow comparison, year on year, between subjects and student cohorts.

At advanced level, certain capabilities can be developed to a greater extent than others, depending on the subject context. Other subject-specific capabilities are also identified and developed. At this level each subject/ discipline area works with groups of employers, practitioners and professional bodies in order to define the levels and assessment criteria for each capability.

Preparing for change

Implementation of the new curriculum is occurring over the next few years. The first stage in the process involved five pilot studies (1996–97) which investigated:

- the integration and development of capabilities in chemistry, history, philosophy, social work, and action, impact, and longitudinal methodologies for curriculum evaluation;
- producing threshold descriptors at preliminary level for each discipline/ subject area;
- locating capabilities appropriately within preliminary level modules;
- rewriting all year one modules in terms of learning outcomes and the associated teaching, learning and assessment methods;
- mapping all single subject and major/minor combinations of subjects in year one degree programmes to ensure that there was an even coverage of all the capabilities, and that students would experience a variety of teaching, learning and assessment processes.

All modules in all undergraduate programmes are being revalidated during the period 1996–98. An extensive programme of staff development, offered both centrally and at faculty level, is under way and the resource and infrastructure requirements for the implementation of the new curriculum have been determined and will be kept under review.

The student experience

Student opportunities and support

The new curriculum is not only shifting the emphasis from teaching students to enabling students to learn but is also giving students more control over the organization and management of their study programme. The introduction of new teaching methods and these, with other concurrent innovations such as IT-based learning and increased module and programme information provision, are giving increased flexibility to programme delivery. Additionally, the academic guidance and support service provides systemised advice and guidance at identified intervention points along students' study programmes, further helping them to plan their learning.

Other educational developments are also increasing capability and employability development opportunities for students. The University offers a year one module in personal and careers development which starts the process of self-reflection and action planning. An advanced level work placement module provides students with a valuable opportunity to gain useful, assessed and accredited work experience.

Changing subject delivery

New teaching methods in history demonstrate the capability-based approach (Castle, 1995). The new history curriculum emphasizes, in year one, the development of oral and written competence, the extraction and analysis of quantitative data, the use of IT, and the critical evaluation of written and visual sources, all within the subject context. Oral communication skills are developed through seminar work, and the oral history assignment has replaced some formal lectures. In the project the students select an interviewee whose experience might illuminate predetermined areas of interest. Students are encouraged to identify the requirements for such a person, to reflect on and to develop the necessary skills required for successful interviewing, and to determine issues which might usefully be addressed. The project is assessed as a 1,500–2,000 word report which summarises the interview and highlights the main areas covered. The oral project has also been adopted in Irish studies.

In social work courses staff are working in partnership with the Central Council for Education and Training in Social Work and employers, focusing on the need for students to understand and cope with the process of change. Teaching involves a small group, problem-based approach facilitated by academic staff and professional practitioners. Coupled with these changes has been the extensive development of resource materials such as module guides, resource boxes (containing additional materials and information on technology-based sources such as CD-ROM, the World Wide Web, and audio-visual materials), and reading packs, all of which enable students to organize and plan their study more effectively.

Another example of the changes in delivery that have taken place under the new curriculum is found in chemistry. Lectures have been abandoned in most year one modules and replaced by a mixture of student-led, small group seminars and tutorials, group project work, and IT-based learning. Regular paper- and computer-based tests are used to ascertain students' underpinning knowledge and understanding of the subject. Module assessment is based on the tests and the production and oral presentation of a poster.

Into the future

This report has touched only lightly on the rapid and intensive pace of change taking place in the University and the extensive work being undertaken in developing and implementing the capability curriculum. Despite the initial reluctance and hesitation among some academic staff, determined and persistent management at all levels in the University, and also time, have worn away much of the staff resistance to the major changes needed. The introduction of the new curriculum took place as planned, in September 1997. However, this first step only marks the initiation of a process which will, over the next few years, see every aspect of the institution's academic programme provision undergo further substantial change – in teaching, learning, assessment, resources development, the role of the external examiner, learning environment, and, of course, changes in study modes. The University is committed fully to these changes and believes they are essential if it is to achieve its mission of guaranteeing the production of capable and employable graduates for the next millennium.

References

AGR (1995) *Skills for Graduates in the 21st Century*, Cambridge: Association of Graduate Recruiters.

Castle, K (1995) 'Oral history for undergraduates: a skills perspective', in A Assiter (ed) *Transferable Skills in Higher Education*, (pp.142–7), London: Kogan Page.

Harvey, L, Moon, S and Geall, V (1997) *Graduates' Work: Organisational Change and Students' Attributes*, Birmingham: Centre for Research into Quality and The Association of Graduate Recruiters.

HEQC (1997) *Graduate Standards Programme: Final Report*, London: Higher Education Quality Council.

NCIHE (1997) *Higher Education in the Learning Society*, Report of the National Committee of Inquiry into Higher Education, London: HMSO.

Chapter 5

Promoting Capability Through the Assessment of Key Skills: Some Lessons from the World of Vocational Qualifications

Stephen Hunt and Heather Frier

Editors' introduction

Key skills are an important component of capability. The RSA Examinations Board has been assessing skills for many years and are currently involved in assessing candidates for General and National Vocational Qualifications (GNVQs and NVQs). Their experience is substantial and, in the case of high level personal key skills, relevant to the development of capability in higher education.

Hunt and Frier describe how the current system of assessment for GNVQs and NVQs encourages the development of capability through its focus on the integration of skills, learner responsibility, transferability and the effective application of skills in real-time situations. However, this capability approach is in danger of being undermined by political and other pressures for standardization through common external assessments. The authors' concerns help us to understand the difference between common standards and individual achievement, and between assessment as a control mechanism and assessment as an educational and developmental tool. Those in higher education who are committed to the development of student capability will find this cautionary tale particularly helpful when planning their own approaches to student assessment.

Introduction

The term 'key skills' is used to describe a range of essential skills which everyone uses in carrying out all kinds of tasks and activities in education, training, employment and in general life. These skills are deemed to be transferable from one context to another, and form the basis of an individual's ability to perform effectively in all aspects of life. It is also believed that these skills will contribute to an individual's ability to respond more appropriately to the future needs of industry and commerce. They are not basic skills, but are about the ability to deal with real-life problems, and ever-changing demands in the world of work and life generally.

There is a fair amount of agreement that the particular skills which are useful in meeting this need are:

- communication
- information technology
- application of number
- working with others
- improving own learning and performance
- problem-solving

While specifications for achievement in these skills have been formulated by a number of organizations, this article refers, exclusively, to those specifications and the assessment methodology developed by the National Council for Vocational Qualifications (NCVQ)[1]. The article looks at the present assessment methodology in the light of the philosophy underpinning the delivery of key skills, and then explores the possible effects of the revised assessment regimes which are presently being introduced.

Current features of key skills assessment

The key skills initiative has been developed and strongly promoted in conjunction with GNVQs and NVQs. It is not surprising, therefore, that the assessment methodology is based on the same principles of competence based and criterion referenced assessment which apply to these qualifications. Some of the main features of this methodology are:

1. Achievement is assessed on the basis of whether the candidate's work, submitted in a portfolio of evidence, matches the published criteria.

---

[1] In October 1997, NCVQ and the Schools Curriculum and Assessment (SCAA) merged to form the Qualifications and Curriculum Authority (QCA).

2. Evidence for achievement in key skills should be gathered from a variety of sources. This indicates the transfer of those skills to new contexts and also improves the reliability of the assessment.
3. In order to establish the validity of competence-based assessments, candidates have to achieve all the specified criteria. Achievement against a sample of the criteria is not regarded as sufficient to show mastery of the skill, and the principles of compensation in assessment are disallowed.
4. To assist with the transfer of key skills to other contexts, the delivery and assessment of key skills should be fully-integrated and contextualized within a student's main vocational or academic programme of study.

The assessment of the key skills at present operates on the basis that a candidate has the responsibility to provide evidence of his or her skills. It is expected that most of the evidence for achievement of the key skills will come from work done as part of the candidate's academic or vocational training programme, but this need not be the only source. Some examples of evidence are:

- a video or tape recording of a discussion or debate in which the candidate took part (for communication);
- a piece of course work which has been produced on a word-processor (for information technology, communication and possibly application of number);
- an assessor's notes of interviews with the candidate's fellow students or work placement colleagues (for working with others);
- action plans and records of discussions carried out with the student's tutor (for improve own learning and performance);
- records of how the candidate manages his or her personal budget (for application of number).

The candidate plays the major role in the generation and collection of evidence, which is usually stored and presented in a ring-binder or lever-arch file, referred to as a portfolio. The candidate is also expected to cross-reference the evidence to the assessment criteria, showing where the evidence matches the specifications. The role of the assessor, who will be a member of the staff of the institution, is to:

- identify opportunities for evidence generation;
- observe the candidate undertaking assessment tasks;
- judge the evidence presented against the criteria;
- question the candidate directly to confirm his or her understanding of principles;
- give constructive feedback.

It is important to note how this assessment process meets the principles of assessment set out above, while, at the same time, it promotes student capability.

1. The candidate is in control of the assessment process to the extent that he or she can decide what material should be submitted for assessment, and when this should happen. This empowerment also promotes self-reliance and personal initiative.
2. The criteria for assessment are made available to the candidate so that he or she can cross-reference the evidence to the criteria. This engagement of the candidate with the criteria proves to be a very valuable development process in itself, promoting reflection on the candidate's achievement.
3. Because evidence can come from across the whole range of a student's studies, and beyond to his or her personal life, the transferability of these skills is enhanced, and the reliability of the assessments is improved.

The student and the assessor are advised to collaborate closely in planning for assessment, and in using assessment as an opportunity to identify development needs. Through this activity students can take an increased responsibility for their own development, and the foundations for lifelong learning are laid.

The key skills assessment process has been criticized for being exceedingly burdensome, bureaucratic, and paper-driven. Nevertheless, it is our contention that the integrated delivery and assessment processes, as described above, do have the potential 'to facilitate reflective and collaborative learning, and to enable people to act in and upon the social world'. (Halsall and Cockett, 1996.)

New features of assessment of key skills

The above assessment model for key skills is set to change. Among the many recommendations made by Sir Ron Dearing in his 'Review of Qualifications for 16–19 Year Olds' are two which have a significant bearing on key skills and the way they are assessed (Dearing, 1996).

First, he recommended that the majority of students be encouraged to take key skills, especially those of communication, application of number and information technology; not only GNVQ students for whom it is compulsory, but also students on A level and NVQ programmes. Some universities have already introduced key skills into their degree programmes. The key skill specifications should be to a 'common standard' irrespective of the route a student is on, and thus they can help to bridge the academic and vocational divide.

Second, in order to improve rigour and make assessment 'more manageable and cost-effective', Dearing recommended that 'The NCVQ should consider the use of appropriately designed, simple-to-use tests for components of the units in communication, the application of number and information technology. These tests should be varied enough to meet a wide range of interests.'

As a result of this report, NCVQ has revised the key skills specifications for communication, application of number and information technology and has issued a revised assessment specification. These new arrangements will be piloted for two years from September 1997, with a range of students presently undertaking A level, GNVQ and NVQ programmes.

The revised model stipulates that at least 40 per cent of the assessment of each skill should be assessed internally, by means of coursework, or portfolios of evidence, and at least 40 per cent should be assessed independently. One form of independent assessment involves externally set tasks which may be either externally or internally marked. The internal and independent components must, when taken together, cover all elements and performance criteria of the key skill. Candidates must pass both components in order to achieve the key skill.

Awarding bodies have agreed that independent assessment will take two forms. For Application of number, there will be an 'end test', an examination lasting one hour which will be offered twice a year. For communication and information technology, there will be a series of assignments which are set by the awarding bodies, marked by the centre assessors, and moderated externally by the awarding bodies. There will be one assignment per unit, and each one will require about three hours to complete, excluding preparation time. The relationship between the externally set test and assignment, and the internally assessed component is not entirely clear at this stage, but it is expected that candidates will continue to collect naturally-occurring evidence which covers the whole specification.

Alternative models of independent assessment for key skills are also being developed by awarding bodies for trial, subject to approval by QCA.

Implications of changes for the development of capability

Whichever models of assessment survive in the future, it is unlikely that the portfolio evidence (the internal component) will be lost entirely, or its weighting reduced much more. Attempts earlier this year to produce a 100 per cent external assessment model had to be abandoned because of its unmanageability. Nevertheless, the introduction of any amount of external assessment will make a considerable impact on the potential of key skills to fulfil their broader aims. In respect of these broader aims there are two questions which need to be asked:

- what effect will an external test or assignment have on the *integration* of key skills into the main area of study, and the *transferability* of those skills?
- how will the *development* of capability be affected?

There is serious concern that the introduction of an external test or assignment will reduce the degree of integration between the key skills and the main area of study. Despite Sir Ron Dearing's wish that these tests should be 'varied enough to meet a wide range of interests', and NCVQ's assessment specification stating that the assessment scheme must emphasize the contextualization and application of candidates' knowledge and understanding, it is clearly impossible for an awarding body to set tests and assignments which integrate fully into a wide range of different areas of study. It is well known that assessment approaches influence the teaching styles and content, as teachers aim to improve their results by teaching to the test, so we can expect that as the assessment of key skills is separated from the assessment of the main study, the delivery of the key skills will also become disintegrated. This will have an unfortunate effect on the transfer of these skills to vocational and real-life contexts.

Nigel Blagg and Associates point out (Employment Department, 1993), that transfer of skills from one context to another does not happen by chance, but can be facilitated through appropriate teaching techniques such as 'hugging tactics', and the use of 'challenging whole complex tasks' and 'guided, co-operative learning'. If teachers are teaching to an assessment which contains a large and important portion of external testing, it is our belief that less use will be made of these techniques to enhance transfer, thus undermining a major rationale for the key skills.

This can also have the unfortunate consequence of reducing the student's motivation. Blagg comments (Employment Department, 1993):

Intrinsic motivation is likely to result from meaningful learning which builds from the learner's current understanding and experience. . . . Thus it is important to:

- choose interesting contexts that relate to the learner's interests, needs and experiences;
- embed theory in practice, and practice in theory, so that one informs the other on a continual basis;
- establish the purpose for each learning activity and ensure the objectives are clearly understood by the learner. This is especially important where the importance and relevance of the activities are not immediately transparent to the learner.

Decontextualizing a large part of the assessment process can have the effect of demotivating and ultimately alienating the very students who should benefit from the key skills approach to teaching and learning.

The other area of concern is that of the ownership of the assessment process and what that does for student capability. To quote from Blagg again:

If learners are to become truly autonomous, they must be given genuine opportunities to take responsibility for their work. All too often, learning experiences are selected, directed and assessed by the teacher/trainer with the learner being a passive and sometimes unwilling participant in the process. Placing responsibility on the learner is closely concerned with the idea of ownership. This will be enhanced by (*inter alia*):

- extensive use of active learning projects focused on 'real life' problems which oblige learners to take on a measure of responsibility for their own learning;
- learners assessing and recording their own learning and identifying their own development needs.

With 40 per cent of the assessment of key skills becoming externally managed, and especially if this is seen as the most important part, the responsibility of the candidate towards assessment will be significantly undermined. Students will be the passive recipient, once more, of an assessment process, and they will not have the power to remove the external component from their overall portfolio, if they feel it does not represent their potential. The development of capability is not best served by this process.

From the above, it will be seen that in many ways key skills are at a cross roads in their development. After some initial opposition and practical difficulties surrounding their introduction, a measure of success has been achieved in implementing them in a way which is designed to achieve maximum benefit in terms of skills transfer and student capability. Credit for this is due to the huge efforts and personal commitment of the teachers and trainers involved. The danger now is that because of calls for greater reliability in assessment, the scope for promoting capability through the key skills assessment process may be undermined. Fortunately, the pilot project is only beginning and one can hope that the evaluation of the pilot will take these broader issues into account.

References

Dearing, Sir Ron (1996) *Review of Qualifications for 16–19 year Olds*, Hayes, Middlesex: SCAA Publications.

Employment Department in association with Nigel Blagg Associates (1993) *Development of Transferable Skills in Learners, Research and Development Series*, report no 18, Moorfoot, Sheffield: Employment Department.

Halsall, R and Cockett, M (1996) *Education and Training 14–19: Chaos or Coherence?*, London: David Fulton Publishers.

Chapter 6

Reconciling Quality and Standards with Diversity

Malcolm Shaw, Clare Stoney and Howard Green

Editors' introduction

Leeds Metropolitan University (LMU) have developed what appears to be an effective way of facilitating flexible course provision within a common framework based on generic criteria which describe the level of performance required for different awards.

Shaw, Stoney and Green describe how the creation of a taxonomy of learning outcomes, derived from the University's mission and designed to assure comparability across the wide range of university provision, has supported the initiative of faculty staff to develop programmes which facilitate greater student responsibility for their own learning. The taxonomy not only achieves its primary goal of contributing to the assurance of the quality and standards of the University's programmes in general but also provides autonomous learners at all levels (including postgraduate research) with tools and reference points for articulating their learning needs and describing their achievements.

Introduction

Among a number of paradoxes contained within the Dearing Report (NCIHE, 1997) is to be found the seemingly incompatible notion of benchmarking standards across the whole of the higher education (HE) sector alongside exhortations to continue to value and to preserve the diversity of provision across the sector. Leeds Metropolitan University, in its approach to aspects of curriculum development, has been trying to address such apparent paradoxes for some time now – particularly in relation to attempts to assure the quality and standards of its course provision, while respecting and valuing the diversity within its student body, its academic, vocational and professional disciplines, its course programmes and its academic staff.

The approach that has been developed is much more to do with providing a university guide and steer through frameworks developed collegially and *nothing* to do with leading by the nose *nor* dragging by the scruff of the neck. We illustrate here how a particular initiative – around learning outcomes taxonomies – provides a framework (but not a straitjacket) that can begin to ensure some consistency in certain aspects of quality and standards in curricula. This has allowed a degree of latitude and freedom to academic staff, in respect of their professional skills and integrity, to enable them to respond to the diversity in their course and subject cultures, in their student intake, as well as in their vocational and professional contexts.

Context

A capability mission

One of the significant influences on the general approach to quality and standards at LMU, and the inherent focus on the curriculum within this, has been the parallel development and implementation of a more comprehensive and planned University-wide approach to aspects of the development of teaching, learning and assessment. This has been initiated and coordinated through the Academic Quality and Development section of the Academic Registry.

The strategies and relationships that have guided this work are shown in Figure 6.1, where the origins of our teaching, learning and assessment policy have been clearly rooted in the University's mission. The policy also has been reflected strongly in the strategies and plans developed by faculties and courses and has been supported by a range of guidance documents as well as specific projects identified and selected through general consensus across the University. Complementary to this has been an approach to the processes of dissemination and implementation that has acknowledged and been sensitive to principles currently espoused more particularly in the literature around *the management of change*.

The University mission in particular emphasizes the notion of an applied learning and capability approach through four of its major goals:

- to promote effective application of innovative approaches to learning and teaching;
- to develop the curriculum in support of lifelong learning;

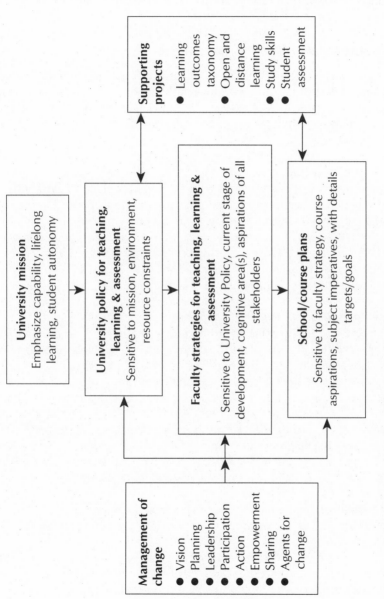

Figure 6.1 *Framework for teaching and learning development*

- to review progress annually in addressing the development of capability in the curriculum;
- to increase opportunities for student involvement in the determination and management of their own learning.

From mission to policy and procedures

The University policy reflects these concerns but extends them to include and promote the wholly inherent and equally important issue of assessment. This policy contains in all eleven guiding principles among which, and of particular relevance here, we find (with extracts from Notes for Guidance shown in italics):

- Teaching, learning and assessment strategies will focus on learner development that is consistent with the broad concept of capability in HE and that indicates significant planned and appropriate increases in responsibility for learning and assessment being placed on the learner. *Such strategies will need to include aspects of a capability approach such as: lifelong learning skills; personal, interpersonal and group skills; self-esteem, empathy and social values; problem formulation, analysis and solution; synthesis and evaluation; creativity, intuition and imagination; the application of the foregoing skills in communicating, doing, designing, making, organizing and creating in situations that are (or approximate to) real-life.*
- Assessment must be valid, appropriately formative and summative, and clearly consistent with stated learning outcomes, levels of study and vocational contexts and, where assessment is for an award, it must demonstrably reflect accepted national standards for such an award. *The formative and summative functions of assessment will need to be clearly identified, distinguished and specifically indicated to students in clear and accurate briefs. The validity of assessment is demonstrable by its congruence with stated learning outcomes. So, module outlines and evaluation, course annual monitoring and review, external examiner comments must specifically address assessment and related issues of validity, reliability (see next point) and standards.*
- Assessment must be reliable, based on clear, open and explicit criteria, and must be kept constantly under review for efficiency as well as effectiveness. *Reliability is a product of clear, explicit and available criteria that can inform the actions of both tutors and students. Efficiency is closely related to the pursuit of assessment loads that are programmed to avoid bunching and are kept to a minimum by the use of carefully selected and varied diets of assessment that may include sampling and joint assessment of modules. Effectiveness is*

also influenced significantly through strategies for ensuring the validity and reliability of assessment. In all cases prompt and well focused feedback to students will be an identified and defined goal.

Faculty diversity of interpretation

Faculties were charged with the task of producing explicit strategies that were congruent with University policy as well as being sensitive to the current stage of their own development within applied learning and capability, the imperatives of their subject areas and the particular aspirations and needs of the range of stakeholders that impinge upon their courses. A small number of short extracts will help to give an indication of the sort of directions proposed in such strategies:

'. . . the faculty recognizes that its current use of paper-based approaches is merely a step towards a largely IT-based future, which must facilitate and deliver learning through remote access.'
'. . . the faculty is aware of the need to develop the telecommunications network infrastructure to allow and facilitate remote access to learning resources.'
'. . . faculty sees emerging themes as being independent learning and open or distance learning associated with part-time provision.'
'. . . independence in learning is seen to be sensitive to a capability approach, but vocational perspectives are also viewed as essential along with a broad approach to skills that encompasses theory as well as interpersonal and group skills.'
'the main thrust . . . is towards the provision of open learning materials, accepting that this needs to be managed in a way that provides real cost benefits.

So faculties have been encouraged to express their own individuality and diversity but within the context of a University steer which is itself consistent with our mission.

Supporting projects

It is probably quite evident, from some of the faculty priorities identified briefly above, how the University came to focus on the need to support a major project on *open and distance learning*. In a similar way common concern for *study skills* and for *student assessment* clearly emerged as major issues across the institution during early stages in the process of developing and implementing the policy. So a major survey across the University into the methods and procedures in student assessment has been completed and a project on the embedding of learning skills into the curriculum is just about to report.

Learning outcomes taxonomies have a more established tradition within the University, having been first developed around 1988 as a means for guiding levels of learning, particularly in Credit Accumulation and Transfer Scheme (CATS) contexts. They have subsequently, in more developed and adapted forms, become a feature of many significant areas of mainstream undergraduate provision at LMU, as well as more recently helping to guide postgraduate provision including research awards. It is this particular taxonomic aspect of the supporting project work on which we shall focus our attention here.

Learning outcomes taxonomies

Undergraduate taxonomies in use within the University identify a set of broad generic skill domains that typically might include: technical skills, organization and planning, communication, group and interpersonal, data collection and interpretation, theory and principles, analysis and reflection, application and reflection, synthesis and evaluation, creativity. Indicative generic learning outcomes that might be expected at each of three under-graduate levels in each of the specified domains are suggested, thus providing a guidance matrix with which it is possible to calibrate courses in order to begin to ascertain the extent of their skills coverage and the levels of their learning outcomes. Originally it was the development within the University of large modular schemes and the wish to assure some comparability of standards across the many and diverse awards within such schemes that led to the more widespread use of such taxonomies. Shaw and Stoney (1995) have provided a more detailed account of the origins, format and content of such taxonomies and describe a particular model that was originally developed to help to guide the rational integration of some 19 different, but associated, undergraduate awards (involving 2,000 full-time students) into a unified modular scheme. It has proved interesting to note the similarities between such taxonomies and the outcomes that have recently emerged around *graduate attributes* from the Higher Education Quality Council's *Graduate Standards Programme* (see HEQC, 1997).

A natural extension of the above work resulted more recently in the development of a prototype generic taxonomy to address postgraduate levels of study. It was felt that diversity of experience (as well as diversity of student background) was potentially much greater at postgraduate levels, where many students were not necessarily part of large cohorts on highly prescribed programmes of study. In fact, in the case of research awards there was a sense that students were quite understandably following highly individualized programmes of study. The prototype postgraduate taxonomy, which is still undergoing trials in a range of contexts, comprises the same set of domains as those reported in the undergraduate taxonomy above. Outcomes within each domain are differentiated at the moment in three levels – labelled as M level, MPhil level, PhD level. A more detailed description of the taxonomy and the outcomes of initial trials is provided by Shaw and Green (1996).

The taxonomies in practice

A variety of uses

As we have indicated, initially the taxonomy's value was intended to be mainly in relation to improving the accuracy and confidence with which modules were calibrated at specific levels by considerable numbers of staff across the whole of a large modular scheme which was up for review. It was about trying to assure, at the curriculum design stage, that broadly comparable standards were *written in* across a diverse portfolio of awards. It was also about trying to ensure the cognitive progression and quality of the experience of a diverse body of students. However, it emerged from evaluation that other perceived values were being identified by curriculum developers engaging with the taxonomies. These were identified in the undergraduate context partly by Shaw and Stoney (1995), where the additional value for such taxonomies was identified by users to include:

- helping to ensure that the outcomes of modules are assessed appropriately;
- assisting with the development of appropriate criteria for module assessment;
- providing a common lexicon and assisting with curriculum debate;
- assisting with the assurance of coherence and progression through levels;

In a follow-up evaluation of a taxonomy, Stoney and Shaw (1996) reported further specific uses of the taxonomy identified by staff that had emerged during two years of application as:

- helping with student briefing for active learning;
- directing students to achieve at appropriate levels;
- negotiation of criteria in self- and peer-assessment settings;
- advising and subsequently assessing students in claims for experiential learning;
- pitching modules with similar content at different levels;
- facilitating staff transfer between the teaching of modules at different levels.

It is perhaps appropriate at this time to point out that versions of the taxonomy are embedded in the course documents and curriculum practice of about half the University's undergraduate provision.

The complementary postgraduate version is growing in use and there is serious and wide-ranging debate surrounding the wholesale adoption and the continuing development of the research awards variant across all research awards within the University. This seems entirely appropriate in view of calls within the Harris review of postgraduate education for standardizing the nomenclature of awards, effective quality assurance and greater clarity regarding the awards offered (HEFCE, 1996). These concerns are largely echoed by the UK Council for Graduate Education (1996) and extended to include concerns around standards. The former HEQC, under the auspices of the new Quality Assurance Agency, is beginning to take on board the urgings of Harris and is extending the undergraduate work of the *Graduate Standards Programme* (HEQC, 1997) into the postgraduate arena.

Some issues

Debate between academic staff around the postgraduate taxonomy has been, in general, quite positive and constructive with concerns emerging such as:

- the extent to which the domains are discrete;
- the extent to which the domains represent a hierarchy of skills;
- the relative importance and weighting of the domains for different subjects;
- the relative importance and weighting of domains for different awards;
- the need to separate product and process outcomes.

The taxonomy has also been welcomed warmly in initial discussions with research students, where it has been seen as one means to demystify the research award and provide a better idea of what is expected of them.

Conclusion

What we have attempted to illustrate here is the way in which managers, with overall institutional or faculty responsibilities for quality and standards in teaching, learning and assessment, have been providing frameworks and guidelines within which course designers and curriculum developers across the University can operate. Such guidelines and frameworks must help to assure a degree of confidence in the quality and standards of what is offered while at the same time allowing course teams to respond appropriately to a rapidly and constantly changing higher education scene, as they perceive it. There is obviously a careful balance to strike between pip-squeaking control and total anarchy. We would not claim to have found the fulcrum, but we are searching for it. Moreover we expect that the position of the fulcrum, like everything else in higher education, will be subject to change over time, whether planned or increasingly in response to events beyond our control.

References

HEFCE (1996) *Review of Postgraduate Education*, (Harris report), Bristol: Higher Education Funding Council for England.

HEQC (1997) *Graduate Standards Programme: Final Report*. London: Higher Education Quality Council.

NCIHE (1997) *Higher Education in the Learning Society*, report of the National Committee of Inquiry into Higher Education, London: HMSO.

Shaw, M and Green, H (1996) 'Standards in research awards', *Innovation and Learning in Education*, **2**(3).

Shaw, M and Stoney, C (1995) 'Assuring quality and standards in a large modular scheme', *Innovation and Learning in Education*, **1**(2).

Stoney, C and Shaw, M (1996) 'Assuring standards in a large modular scheme: two years on, *Innovation and Learning in Education* **2**(1).

UK Council for Graduate Education (1996) *Quality and Standards of Postgraduate Degrees*, Warwick: UK Council.

Chapter 7

Can Higher Education Deliver Capability?

Elizabeth Foster

Editors' introduction

The example described in this chapter is a capability-focused programme designed from scratch and tested as a pilot with 'real' students. Although the Work-based Learning programme of the University of Leeds is a small part of the University's portfolio (but targeted to grow substantially), for the students taking part it represents the whole of their experience leading to full university awards at any level from Certificate of Higher Education (Level 1) to full honours and masters degrees. The programme is the nearest example in the book to a complete work-based capability programme. It is a student led partnership between the University and the student's work-place focused on the development of student capability through problem-based projects related to the field of work. Features include learning contracts, peer support, cross-discipline work, opportunities for advanced standing and assessments based on student defined final products and critical self-review.

Of particular interest is the fact that this programme, which has no conventional syllabus, exams, classes, modules or attendance patterns, is based in one of Britain's mainstream universities. Leeds is a typical civic university recruiting in the main high level school leavers to courses designed by academic staff, delivered through lectures, seminars and workshops and assessed by conventional examinations (with some interesting variations stimulated by the University's excellent Enterprise in Higher Education programme and other initiatives). To be accepted as a substantive scheme by the University (which it has been), the pilot programme needed to demonstrate how intellectual rigour and comparability of standards were to be secured on student managed problem-based programmes. The report which follows focuses on the way comparability of level has been achieved without detriment to the programme's aims and principles.

Introduction

Recent recommendations for higher education to focus upon lifelong learning and skills propose the UK economy as the key beneficiary. (HMSO, 1994, 1995, 1996; DfEE, 1995; NACETT, 1996; Dearing 1996; Armstrong 1996). The wider life and well-being of individuals and society are usually identified as additional benefits rather than pivotal motives.

The Work-based Learning Programme (WBLP) at the University of Leeds (Foster 1996) provides evidence that a programme can be developed which places capability at its core, addressing the expectations, knowledge and skill requirements of higher education and employers and also developing learners' capability in their personal and professional lives.

The background to the Programme

The WBLP was developed by a pilot project at the University sponsored by the Department for Education and Employment (DfEE) and the Leeds Training and Enterprise Council, in partnership with City and Guilds of London Institute (CGLI), Higher Education for Capability (HEC) and four employers: a manufacturer with a well-established training culture; a major regional theatre; a national fine art organization and a two-person video-production enterprise.

The University of Leeds has an international reputation for research excellence and, with over 21,000 students on campus is one of the largest universities in the UK. Its mainstream programmes are three year degree courses for 18–21 year olds. The WBLP is a radical departure from these and challenges existing structures and mores. It is not based on modules or pre-determined course content yet establishes comparability with other qualifications of the University of Leeds. It is work-based, individually negotiated and self-managed. It offers higher level learning opportunities which are *differentiated*, starting from each learner's distinctive experience and knowledge; *progressive*, taking them forwards in their learning; and *work-based*, designed for students in full-time work and focusing their learning on, at, through and for their work to meet their own and their employers' professional, development needs.

The tripartite relationship

An individual's WBLP is centred at the intersection of self, university and work, drawing from and contributing to each area. The deliberate blend of all three in a learner-managed, problem-focused programme gives each student a key role in determining the start and end points of their Programme, its content, modes of study and assessment. The process of the learning is as important as its content. Learning through reflection and experience, self-management of learning and responsibility for determining personal and professional development (Kolb 1984; Boud *et al*. 1985, 1993; Schön 1983, 1987; Candy *et al*. 1994; Bélanger and Gelpi 1995; Longworth and Davies 1996) are key skills developed within the process of the WBLP. A student who does not have, or cannot develop, these skills will not be able to determine and carry out a personal WBLP which truly integrates self, work and higher education.

Programme focus

While some aspects of work-based learning have focused on the accreditation of existing expertise and knowledge (Fulton *et al*. 1996; Brennan and Little 1996), it is fundamental to the Leeds model that *improved capability* at work is an explicit goal and that reflection on the learning process is a required part of the assessed products in the form of a Personal Review of Learning. It is also expected that the work-based learner's accomplishments will have some original or creative features with responses to new problems, or solutions that are innovative for that work context. In some cases, wholly new knowledge (Eraut, 1995) may be generated. In others, ideas or practices familiar to experts in other contexts may be brought to bear. In all cases, simple mastery of existing procedures or texts is not sufficient and students must make reference to contexts external to the problem being investigated.

Each student addresses two inter-related problems: the problem of managing their own educational and professional development and the specific problems, challenges or issues related to their work. The problem of their own development is to audit their strengths and opportunities and clarify their needs and ambitions, personally, educationally and professionally. The solution is the programme of study they put together to help them get there. Such problem-focused work-based learning differs from most university courses which are designed and delivered by academic staff for students who have limited experience of the world of work and are based on fields of knowledge in discipline areas. The WBLP places students at the interface of traditionally different cultures, exploring work-focused and work-related issues in the context of university knowledge, scholarship and values. This leads to programmes which are very different from those of traditional students and may combine aspects drawn from more than one academic discipline.

Some examples

One pilot student, a theatre sound technician, noted a relative lack of understanding about how people hear and the discomfort which some experience from particular sound effects. He constructed a programme combining physics, physiology and music to improve his insight into the hearing process; challenge established and often outmoded ways of sound production; generate more creative and effective sound designs and improve accessibility to the theatre for the aurally impaired. The facility to target learning and academic support towards such specific projects is rarely available within traditional programmes and is one of the key needs of able, diligent, purposeful learners in the work-place.

Integrating university with work is another key feature of the programme. A student with the Textiles Department is investigating the effect of detergents and other chemicals on fabrics. Four days a week of her work in an industrial project team provides a core focus for her programme. Already an acknowledged 'on the job' expert, a degree will make her eligible for management posts. Her programme included support to obtain a Licentiateship of the Textiles Institute and she entered her degree programme at level three.

Building on their particular knowledge and requirements, students construct discrete programmes which sometimes have academic coherence only in their individual circumstances. An occupational nurse supervised in psychology integrated a package of modules 'tailored to suit my abilities' into her study with the objective of investigating stress in the work-place. She will not be assessed on the modules but on products which include an in-company survey, comparison with external data, a stress awareness exhibition, plans for future stress-awareness workshops, supporting essays and a 2,000 word report. A partner in the video company, having found other courses with set modules structured around academics' perceptions of learning needs and priorities unsuitable with 'too much time on irrelevant things', is investigating ethical forms of company governance with a view to building capacity and expanding the business, a process she found personally and professionally rewarding, and directly helpful in moving the business forward and increasing its profits.

Programme structure

The Programme (Figure 7.1) has a common sequence of four learning stages (enquiry, exploration, development and demonstration) and formal

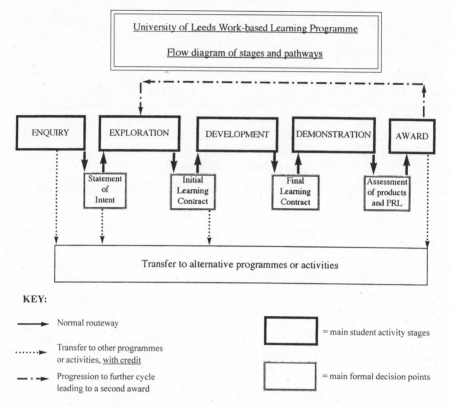

Figure 7.1 *Programme structure showing stages and formal procedures*

procedures (statement of intent, initial learning contract, final learning contract and programme criteria) which guide and support learners through their individualized work-based learning programme. Although programmes are customized to individual students, the processes and support-needs are common and students may work in tutor-led groups and in student-led learning sets as well as in a one-to-one relationship with their university tutor and work-place mentor.

The *enquiry stage* is brief and takes place before formal enrolment in the University. It introduces students to the novel concepts and practices of this unusual Programme, assists them in ascertaining its appropriateness in the light of other opportunities in higher education, training or the work-place and guides them in constructing their *statement of intent*, a matriculation document.

Successful registration of the statement provides entry to the *exploration stage*, a diagnostic phase during which learners audit and clarify their existing knowledge and skills, determine their learning and development needs and relate these to the expectations and opportunities of the University and their work-place. Cross-referencing evidence to the *general criteria* (see below), students may propose an advanced level of entry into the Programme. This has enabled many students without standard minimum entry qualifications to propose undergraduate programmes commencing at levels two or three and also postgraduate programmes. Depending upon their intentions and progress, at the end of this stage students prepare a credit-bearing exit contract or an *initial learning contract*, successful registration of which permits entry into the *development stage* (when the bulk of a student's work takes place).

During the *development stage* subject-specific tutors provide guidance and challenge in specialist areas. The programme is refined and students negotiate a *final learning contract* specifying the precise nature of their full Programme, its modes and products for assessment and enter the last, *demonstration stage* of the Programme when the final end-products are assembled and presented. Learners may re-negotiate contracts at any stage.

Programme criteria

In a programme of this type (particularly in a traditionally academically oriented university), with no traditional entry requirements and no set curriculum, syllabus, teaching or assessment specifications, criteria to guide the Programme and its assessment were essential. An early task for the project was thus to determine the means whereby the WBLP could be *comparable in level to the learning achieved by campus-based students*. A two-fold analysis was undertaken of the characteristics which staff in the University identified as contributing to 'graduateness' at Leeds and the features which distinguished level and minimum threshold standards. The characteristics and attributes were identified through seminars with academic staff from all faculties drawing on their own expertise as well as the work of others within and without higher education. After two days the first seminar group moved from a statement that *I know in my guts what a first is, describing it is something else* to the identification of *the criteria that really matter*; six working proposals identifying the particular requirements of university programmes for work-based learners; and six *key variables* which indicate the *level* at which students are working, namely *complexity* of concepts, variables, influences; *autonomy* and control; *relevance* and impact; *integration* of content, skills; *abstractions*, generalizations and transfer; *creativity and innovation*.

From this the project team generated an embryonic set of criteria which became the central quality assurance mechanism for the Programme. They comprise common standards and expectations which bear a relationship in intellectual level and operation to other programmes of the University at the same level. The generation of these general criteria took the project team many months during which there were many meetings with interested parties and further seminars and consultations with committees. Seventeen versions of the criteria were produced en route to the final version and comment sought from over 100 people on- and off-campus.

The general criteria contain five *problem-focused fields* which help to clarify the essential nature of the Leeds WBLP as problem-centred (Table 7.1).

Table 7.1 *The five fields of the general criteria for work-based learning*

Field	Criteria
1	Formulation of the problem
2	Generation and design of possible solutions or responses
3	Implementation of solutions or responses
4	Evaluation of outcomes
5	Organization and presentation of all activities.

Each field is elaborated through the identification of a number of *aspects*. In all there are 23 aspects, with Field 1 (the largest) containing seven and Field 3 (the smallest) just two. As an example, Field 2 is amplified as follows.

Field 2: The generation and design of possible solutions or responses

(a) is in response to a range and a review of alternatives
(b) shows awareness of knowledge and skills base
(c) is consistent with the scope of the problem
(d) is consistent with the planned time-scale of the problem

By applying the six key *level variables* to each aspect of the general criteria a description of progression through different levels of undergraduate and postgraduate learning was generated, with the six variables imposing a degree of control and coherence (Table 7.2). A level 1 achievement is described as a positive achievement without expressing a negative relationship to higher levels and progression through the levels to the highest (masters) has both consistency and meaningfulness across the 23 aspects of the criteria (Foster, Saunders, Stephenson, 1995a; Foster and Saunders 1996; Foster, Saunders, Stephenson 1996).

In this student-led and learner-managed programme the explicit identification of criteria and level provides rigour, transparency and guidance for assessment and programme construction. They are a framework for determining entry level, content, implementation and assessment of each

Table 7.2 *Level statements for Field 2 aspect a): the generation and design of possible solutions or responses is in response to a range and a review of alternatives*

Level	Indicators
L1	Adopts a solution proposed by others. Recognizes alternative solutions exist.
L2	Recognizes the potential of a range of solutions. Makes some assessment of the relative merits of a number of different solutions. Explores two or more and provides distinctive rationale for choice.
L3	Reviews and assesses a range of alternatives, including original solutions. Identifies strengths and weaknesses of them. Presents rationale for solution chosen.
LM	Recognizes ambiguities and contradictions of alternative solutions. Argues original case for chosen solution, recognises limitations and incongruities.

student's Programme, enabling learners, tutors and employers to engage in the Programme processes and they establish comparability of level within diverse, discrete WBLPs as well as with the University's more traditional programmes of study.

Capability and personal growth

Coffield recently drew attention to a variety of issues surrounding the concept of the UK as a learning society (Coffield 1997). One of these is that for many students higher education has become the transmission of 'unwanted answers to unasked questions' (Popper, 1976). The WBLP at Leeds has sought to address this. First, the Programme belongs to the individual learner *and* their employer *and* the University. So the questions are those which all three parties are asking. By negotiation a consensus among the three parties is developed which draws from the requirements, expectations and culture of each. Experience suggests that the consensus does not exist in the abstract and it grows only by virtue of dialogue, the growth of understanding and learning by each party; it is likely that the consensus will have to be built largely from scratch for each individual programme or each individual learner (Foster 1997).

A further aspect of the WBLP is the nature of the answers achieved. They cannot be assumed to be 'given' (in the sense of taken for granted) nor are they 'delivered' (in the sense of provided to the learner by those with greater authority). They are developed, fought-for and contended. They are informed and guided by the bringing together of expertise from learner, tutor and work-place mentor; they are founded upon theoretical knowledge and understanding; they are discovered, researched and tested in the real contexts of work, the work of the individual and other experts and the 'answers' must be considered in the light of alternative and contradictory explanations or findings and ethical and societal considerations. The process of the learning and the process of structuring the programme are fundamental elements in the learning of the individual student (and their mentors and tutors), in the building of each individual's programme and in the products of the learning. In this respect the Programme seeks to bring together information processing on the Kolb model (Kolb 1984) with the social contexts of the learning (Bruner, 1966) and to engage the learner in a process which develops their personal capability and their autonomy both intellectually and personally.

The Programme is a capability programme. It is about self-knowledge and the integration of personal qualities with knowledge and skills. It continually requires students to hypothesize, plan, research, reflect, evaluate, and re-plan. It's about building skills and knowledge using wide contexts and frames of reference to meet unfamiliar circumstances. It is learner-driven, problem-focused and integrates the student's experience and needs with the values and expectations of higher education in a personal learning programme. The nature of the process; the content and context of the learning; the products for assessment each require from the learner some degree of growth in personal autonomy.

Clashes of culture

At times, learners found the emphasis on processes and reflection frustrating: hoarding information seemed more important. A manufacturer spoke of *right first time*; she wanted learning to be achieved quickly with immediate and productive returns as in good training courses; for academics, knowledge input through mass lectures seemed to offer better prospects than spending time developing students' personal and academic self-sufficiency. For all partners, the shared responsibility for the programme presented difficulties; the cultural norm gives responsibility for learning in higher education to the specialist provider, the university; this programme gave all parties a role, for some learners, employers and academics this was too great a cultural shift.

Challenges and gains

For all the students in the pilot, the process proved extremely challenging. Some found the elements of diagnosis, projection and negotiation too demanding or ill-suited to their current stage in life but most ultimately agreed with the analysis of one who had learned a lot 'both about my subject and also about myself and I do think this is a thoroughly worthwhile thing for me to be doing'. A more recent recruit, reflecting on her progress through the enquiry stage, was sufficiently confident and informed about her personal diagnosis and audit to comment that 'the evidence of my ability to complete the Programme is outlined throughout this initial learning contract'; sufficiently aware of her development, personally, academically and professionally to conclude that 'the Programme has already provided me with a stronger commitment to be focused on my work-based learning problem target. I am more confident in my writing skills ... My profile has dramatically increased (at work) and this is exciting and challenging for me. My knowledge and expertise ... has been exploited ... giving me an increased involvement in the team programme. I am constantly winning support of the colleagues who were not convinced about this way of learning.' So much has this individual gained from her involvement with the Programme that she already anticipates benefits which, although expressed in the work-based context, undoubtedly encompass broader life skills: 'In the future, when I have completed the Work-based Learning Programme I will be able to make independent suggestions for new experimental designs and to take initiatives when the unexpected arises. This will enable me to become a more effective team member by allowing me to make a larger contribution to project work.'

The gains were not limited to the learners. Their employers also found the Programme of great benefit not only in linking organizational learning with the expertise of academics but also in increasing the frequency and depth of collaborative working across entire organizations rather than within small departmental groups, increasing staff skills and formalizing time for strategic thinking. Initial findings suggest that the Programme is indeed a capability programme, benefiting both individuals and organizations in a broader field than economic performance alone.

References

Armstrong G (November 1996) *Speech to DfEE Conference on Work-based Learning*, London.

Bélanger, P and Gelpi, E (1995) *Lifelong Education*, Dordrecht: Kluwer Academic Publishers.

Boud, D, Cohen, R and Walker, D (1993) *Using Experience for Learning*, Buckingham: Open University Press.

Boud, D, Keogh, R and Walker, D (1985) *Reflection: Turning Experience into Learning*, London: Kogan Page.

Brennan, J and Little, B (1996) A Review of Work-based Learning in Higher Education, London: Open University/Quality Support Centre.

Bruner, J (1966) *The Culture of Education,* Cambridge, Massachusetts: Harvard University Press.

Candy, P, Crebert, G and O'Leary, J (1994) *Developing Lifelong Learners Through Undergraduate Education,* Canberra: Australian Government Publishing Service.

Coffield F (1997) 'Can the UK become a learning Society?', Fourth Annual Education Lecture, London, School of Education, King's College.

Dearing, R (1996) *Review of Qualifications for 16–19 Year Olds,* London: DfEE.

DfEE (1995) *Lifetime Learning,* a consultation document, London: DfEE.

Eraut, M (1995) *Developing Professional Knowledge and Competence,* London: Falmer.

Foster, EJ (1996) Comparable but different: work-based learning for a learning society, *The work-based Learning Project Final Report 1994–1996,* DfEE.

Foster, EJ (1997) 'Crossing the Styx: cultural issues in work-based learning, *Higher Education Digest,* Supplement, spring 1997, Issue 27, London: Open University, Quality Support Centre.

Foster, EJ and Saunders, JP (1996) 'Different but comparable: establishing criteria for work-based learning to match the levels of university awards', K Percy (ed) *Towards a Learning Workforce,* Lancaster: Department of Continuing Education.

Foster, EJ, Saunders, JP and Stephenson, J (1995) *Seminar on Criteria for Degrees: Report on Proceedings and Proposals,* Leeds: The University of Leeds and Higher Education for Capability.

—— (1996) *The University of Leeds Work-based Learning Handbook* (3rd edn), Leeds: The University of Leeds Work-based Learning Project.

Fulton, O, McHugh, G and Saunders, M (1996) *Work based learning and its accreditation: Can higher education deliver? The evaluation of the Department for Education and Employment's work-based learning theme, final report,* Lancaster: Lancaster University CSET.

HMSO (1994, 1995, 1996) *Competitiveness,* London: HMSO, Cm 2563, 2867, 3300.

Kolb, DA (1984) (ed) *Experience as a source of Learning and Development,* London: Prentice Hall.

Longworth, N and Davies, WK (1996) *Lifelong Learning,* London: Kogan Page.

NACETT (1996) *Skills for 2000: Report on Progress towards the National Targets for Education and Training,* London: NACETT.

Popper, K (1976) *Unended Quest,* London: Fontana/Collins.

Schön, DA (1983) *The Reflective Practitioner: How Professionals Think in Action,* New York: Basic Books.

Schön, DA (1987) *Educating the Reflective Practitioner: Towards a New Design for Teaching and Learning in the Professions,* San Francisco: Jossey-Bass.

Chapter 8

Work-based Learning for Learning Organizations

Stewart Hase

Editors' introduction

Higher education institutions are not only concerned with developing the capability of students registered on their courses. They also have a role to play in helping organisations develop their own capability through the capability of their employees. In this Chapter, Hase describes how Southern Cross University in Australia uses a learner managed learning approach to work-based learning for this purpose.

The chapter includes a description of the approach devised by Southern Cross University and a summary of some of the lessons they have learnt from the experience of using learner managed learning in a variety of organizations. Some of these lessons transfer to the higher education context, such as the need for effective leadership, flexible provision, learning support, accreditation and responsiveness to different levels of learner readiness. Of particular importance is their observation that learner managed learning, as in higher education, requires a willingness to work towards a paradigm shift in the culture of the organization.

Integrating learning and management structures

Over the past two years we, at Southern Cross University in Australia, have been developing a work-based learning model that attempts to integrate learning activities and human resource management systems. Our interest in doing this is based on a belief that while the development of capability is more effectively facilitated by active learning experiences rather than by traditional passive methods, it may not be enough. There needs to be what amounts to a paradigm shift in the culture of the organization itself towards learner managed learning (Graves, 1993), perhaps moving towards the capable organization.

In its simplest terms work-based learning is learning that takes place at, from, and through an individual learner's actual work environment. Learning opportunities are ever-present at work, irrespective of what trainers may organize and structure. Work-based learning turns what is a 'natural state of affairs' into a powerful tool for learning and development (Gattegno, 1996). This paper describes our experience of implementing a work-based learning model in a number of Australian work-places.

The need for a learner-managed model

As a number of commentators on working life (Emery and Trist, 1965; Field, 1995, for example) have pointed out and as most of us have experienced, our social world is becoming increasingly unpredictable and the rate of change seems to increase exponentially. Globalization and changes in national economies, in particular, have had enormous impact on the work-place. In Australia this has meant, among other things, deregulation and work-place reform as the nation attempts to compete in a rapidly changing environment. Emery and Trist (1965) describe our environment as turbulent, in which there are rapid changes in organizations and in the way in which they interact with each other.

Survival in this environment requires organizations to adapt by acting as open rather than closed systems. An open system is more than just homeostatic or reactive – it is dynamic and recognizes that the environment influences its behaviour, that itself is having an impact on the environment and that the environment itself is dynamic. Adaptation requires careful and continuous monitoring of what is happening outside as well as inside the organization, the capacity to respond quickly, risk-taking, flexibility, creativity, pro-action, and the capacity to learn. For many organizations this requires giving up maladaptive behaviour such as hierarchical and divisional structures, excessive control, old values and methods of operating, being inward looking, being overly cautious, and having strictly defined strategic plans and outcomes, (Crombie, 1995). Most importantly, organizations need to invest in developing capable people who will have the necessary attributes to cope with turbulence. According to de Geus (1988: p.70) the 'only competitive advantage the company of the future will have is its managers' ability to learn faster than their competitors'.

Creating learning experiences is one thing. Developing a learning culture in an organization is another. So, we were interested in not only following

HEC's examples in developing learning situations that would help people to develop capability and to become learners, but also in integrating these into the day-to-day operations of organizations for the purpose of cultural change.

A model for work-based learning

The work-based learning model with which we have been working focuses on the whole system while still recognizing the need to develop capable individuals. We have been primarily interested in developing the 'capable organization' where there is a commitment to the idea of a learning culture by senior management and a recognition that there is a need to implement wider change rather than just a new training initiative. This is an important issue and means that there must be some careful, early planning of exactly what is to be done and how it is to be put in place.

Given that an organization has chosen to implement the work-based learning model we can assume that the commitment has been made at the highest level. This is clearly vital since implementation requires paradigm shifts in the way learning and management are perceived (Davies and Hase, 1994). Organizations will vary immensely in their structure and the sophistication of their human resource management systems. Our experience is that the work-based learning model needs to be designed to have the 'best possible fit' within the current organizational structure rather than attempting to force rapid change in an environment that is not yet ready. It is also possible that while there is a commitment from senior management to work-based learning there may have been little preparatory work at other levels. It may be necessary to build into the model, at a very early stage, additional change management processes involving all stakeholders.

There are four major immediate stakeholders in this model. They are: the individual learner; the person's supervisor or boss; a mentor or learning facilitator; and a coordinator of the work-based programme. If accreditation of the learning is involved then a representative of the accrediting agency is involved.

The process begins with the individual's job description and key performance indicators. At performance appraisal time and using whatever systems the organization might have developed the supervisor works with the employee to identify specific learning needs based on performance deficits, future change in work functions, changes in key performance indicators, and the employee's career goals. A learning plan (or contract) is developed and signed off by both the supervisor and the employee. If an accrediting agency such as a university is involved then an academic or trainer will also help develop the plan with a particular emphasis on assessment.

The learning plan can vary but will contain the key elements of objectives, how the objectives will be met, the resources to be used, a work-based project and how the learning is to be evaluated or assessed. The plan is driven by the needs of the learner and centred around work-place experiences. The supervisor's role in negotiating the plan, providing resources, understanding the needs of the employee, linking the goals of the employee and the organization, and providing support is critical.

Throughout the process of achieving the learning plan's objectives a mentor, chosen by the learner, is used to provide feedback, to 'bounce ideas around', and to guide. Most often mentors will have content expertise in the area but they will always have coaching skills since a key aim of work-based learning is for people to develop learning skills. A coordinator takes responsibility for, organizes, supports and monitors the work-based learning programme.

Following the development of all documentation the stake holders are briefed carefully about their roles and about the work-based learning model. Briefing sessions are usually held in groups to enable maximum opportunity for discussion. Since the model requires two major paradigm shifts – involving management style and learning – careful preparation for implementation is vital. Sometimes it is necessary to utilize a Search Conference or similar technique to encourage active participation by all stakeholders to prepare for change.

Some of our experiences

Leadership

One of the most important factors that contributes to the successful implementation of a work-based learning model is a commitment from senior management for a more effective way of delivering training. Since the ideas associated with the model demand paradigm shifts, organizations that choose to apply have usually, but not always, undergone structural change towards flatter management, teams, greater flexibility and responsiveness, quality processes and other aspects related to enterprise development. These organizations have already moved towards performance appraisal systems and are often well down the track towards an enterprise agreement. Less structurally advanced organizations do become interested in work-based learning but are more likely to want more structured training, at least in the early stages, as a 'just in case' measure. Where the full model has been implemented in large, highly bureaucratic organizations we have found acceptance to be slow. The lesson seems to be to implement the model into small organizational units.

Different situations require different emphases

While the principal components of the model described above are usually kept intact, specific design features make each work-based learning experience different. Some of the variances include: learning plans versus learning contracts; the use of external as well as internal mentors; the degree of emphasis on using structured training materials; accreditation; their scope – most have been gradually introduced following a pilot programme; the extent to which the learning is truly learner driven; and interaction between participants.

Industrial issues

Industrial issues have been an important feature of work-based learning design. As Ford (1995) claims the establishment of an enterprise agreement (or its equivalent) is a significant developmental feature of the learning enterprise as a means of recognizing achievement. While an enterprise agreement is not essential to implement work-based learning, issues that need attention include the binding nature of learning plans (some organizations fear using the term 'learning contract'), the rewards for completion or the implications of non-completion, and the additional responsibility for mentors and coordinators. Some service organizations have well-developed promotional systems into which work-based learning can be integrated, usually along with accredited programmes.

Employer confidence in the process

On the other side of the coin, the employer demands value for money and wants to be assured of worthwhile outcomes. To some extent introducing work-based learning is a risk since it does involve doing something quite different from what is expected in a normal training programme. Clear, measurable learning objectives in the learning plan help develop employer confidence in a method that appears unstructured and *ad hoc* compared with the more familiar structured training programme where employee participation is highly visible though simply turning up.

Time commitment

One of the issues to be addressed is the time commitment required on the part of supervisors and mentors who see their work-based learning role as additional to their normal work activities. The inclusion of these roles in job descriptions and the provision of reward systems is important to institutionalize work-based learning.

Support for learning

Providing access to learning resources other than mentors is a problem for some organizations. One client of ours, a large public sector organization, already had a suite of self-directed 'in-house' programmes, the completion of which was essential for promotion or movement into other areas. It also had a reasonable library. The 'in-house' programmes were redesigned to incorporate the work-based learning model.

In comparison, a rural-based organization spread over a large geographic area has special problems in accessing information and even mentors. That organization's response was to use the telephone more, use e-mail and develop a network of mentors rather than assigning a single mentor to an individual. One advantage, however, was that work units tended to be small cohesive groups of people who provided support to each other, and where everyone knew what was going on. This organization also chose to use externally-accredited programmes and had the provider redesign self-directed programmes to include work-based learning.

Capability and competencies

In Australia there has been considerable national effort expended in the establishment of industry-specific competencies and competency-based curricula. Some care has to be taken with organizations that rely heavily on competency attainment to drive training and employee advancement. It is important that the learning plan should take the learner through and then beyond competency to capability. The plan may consist of two forms of assessment: one might be based on competencies; and the other could be built on a work-based project with much broader outcomes.

Accreditation

Accreditation is an important issue for some organizations concerned that employees obtain the maximum benefit from learning. Sometimes the provision of appropriately accredited training or education is part of the employer's contribution in an enterprise bargaining agreement. One public sector organization with which we worked enabled us to develop a subject we imaginatively called 'work-based learning'. This subject is essentially a learning plan involving an academic along with the supervisor and the learner in the establishment of objectives and outputs. In particular, the academic is interested in helping the learner to access appropriate resources and in the form and depth of the assessment which is still focused on the work-based project. Along with other participants we had to coach the academic carefully in the ways and ideas of work-based learning. Academe still has the rather disturbing habit of believing that it knows what is best for people to learn and how best it should be delivered.

Learner readiness

As might be expected learners vary in their ability to adjust to work-based learning. Some need more structured learning experiences with an emphasis on content and find it difficult to adjust to independent learning. More support needs to be given to these people and early identification of problems by the mentor or supervisor is essential. Others find the challenge and freedom to manage their own learning an opportunity to take themselves forward.

Benefits to individuals and organizations

Some of the reported benefits of work-based learning include:

- an improvement in the range of a person's skills and competencies;
- increase in learning activity; an acceptance of the need for ongoing learning;
- the development of the skill base of trainers;
- improvement in work practices and financial savings as a result of projects;
- less reliance on expensive and sometimes *ad hoc* formal training;
- imaginative work-based projects; and
- team development as work units become involved in projects.

The future

The above learner managed work-based learning model is one attempt to get to the core challenge that confronts organizations in today's shrinking globe – to increase their adaptability to rapidly changing circumstances. The development of individual and organizational capability appear crucial to having this capacity.

Possible obstacles

The acceptance of learner managed work-based learning and other change models, however, is hampered by a number of factors that include:

- a misunderstanding on the part of our education system about the way in which people learn;
- the divide between different components of post-compulsory education;
- the current emphasis on competency and its measurement;

- the need to develop resources rather than programmes so people can manage their own learning; and
- management that emphasizes control rather than leadership.

The challenge for the future, if we are to help people and organizations to become more capable, is to find ways to make what amount to major paradigm shifts take place in the way we view learning and management.

References

Crombie, A (1995) *Maladaptive responses to turbulence*, unpublished paper, Canberra, Australia.

Davies, AT and Hase, S (1994) *Factors Facilitating Co-operative Education*, Canberra: AGPS.

De Geus, A (1988) 'Planning as learning', *Harvard Business Review*, March–April, 70–88.

Emery, F and Trist, E (1965) 'The causal texture of organisational environments', *Human Relations*, **18**(1), 21–31.

Field, L (1995) *Managing Organizational Learning: From Rhetoric to Reality*, Melbourne: Longman.

Ford, W (1995) Integrating people, process and place: the workplace of the future, paper presented at the Australian Quality Council, 8th National Quality Management Conference, Melbourne, Australia.

Gattegno, G (1996) *Work-based Learning*, Lismore: Norsearch.

Graves, N (ed) (1993), *Learner Managed Learning*. Leeds: World Education Fellowship.

Stephenson, J (1992) Capability and quality in higher education, J Stephenson and S Weil, (eds) *Quality in learning*, London: Kogan Page.

Chapter 9

Accrediting Sandwich Training: the City and Guilds Licentiateship

Steve Jackson, Trish Lunt and Phil Margham

Editors' introduction

The year of work placement in an undergraduate sandwich programme (sandwich programmes include at least one period of work placement, typically of a year's duration as the third year of a four-year programme) has been widely acknowledged as being of particular value in the development of capability, since it provides both a context for the testing of what has been learned to date and an enrichment that can be incorporated into final-year studies. An issue for modular schemes has been how to place a publicly-visible value on the learning achieved during the sandwich year.

Jackson, Lunt and Margham describe how Liverpool John Moores University has piloted, in partnership with the City and Guilds of London Institute, the use of the latter's Licentiateship as a vehicle for recognizing the value of the sandwich year. They indicate some of the successes of the venture and the need for staff development, and draw attention to the resource implications of taking the initiative beyond the pilot stage

Background

Liverpool John Moores University (JMU) is a metropolitan university with approximately 20,000 students, of whom about 13,250 are full-time and 6,750 part-time. The University offers a broad portfolio of academic programmes with a particular focus on vocational and professional education.

Currently around 2,100 students are registered on sandwich degree programmes with an increasing number of students undertaking work-based learning opportunities in both vocational and non-vocational programmes.

JMU first introduced the Licentiateship of the City and Guilds of London Institute (LCGI) in September 1994 as a pilot programme for sandwich students in two of its (then) 16 schools. In the first year 18 students registered for the programme. The pilot was managed as a small project in order to assess the progress of students and to evaluate resourcing requirements. During the academic year 1996–7 the number of students participating increased by nearly seven-fold, 136 students being registered from four different schools. The numbers are expected to increase again next year as more schools become involved with the programme. In addition, since 1996 the University has acted under delegated authority from City and Guilds to oversee the development of the Licentiateship for students following Graduate Training Programmes run by the University of Liverpool in conjunction with the Merseyside Innovation Centre.

The University introduced the scheme, in partnership with City and Guilds, for a number of reasons which related to both the structure of its award programmes and corporate objectives. With the development of a University-wide modular credit framework (the Integrated Credit Scheme) in 1990, the decision had been taken to redefine module and programme objectives in terms of learning outcomes. It became increasingly clear that many of the outcomes could be achieved through experience outside the lecture theatre and practical laboratory. In particular, sandwich degree tutors commented on the amount of learning that took place in students' placement year and, for an institution that claimed to award credit for demonstrated learning achievement it seemed appropriate to find a way of recognizing this learning at work.

Following the designation in 1992 of the institution as a university, there was much discussion about the 'mission' of the University and the direction that developments would take in the future. The University wished to retain the reputation it had developed as a polytechnic, particularly in the areas of vocational and professional education. The agreed purpose was to produce graduates who were 'ready for work', having had a sound academic training and having developed the appropriate skills to apply their learning in the world of work. The LCGI was one of a number of routes through which these objectives could be realized.

The key decision was how to accommodate credit for 'off-campus' learning within the new University structure. Simply to have added extra credits for the sandwich year would have introduced disparities in the total credit rating of sandwich and non-sandwich programmes and raised issues about employers' responsibility for assessment which, at the time, the University was not confident could be addressed. An alternative was to offer a dual award – the sandwich degree plus a University certificate for learning completed at work. This would avoid the problem of integrating credit into existing awards and allow for a broader definition of what students might be expected to achieve from their placements. However, many felt that a university certificate lacked recognition and cachet with employers. There was concern in the University about the level of student commitment to an award which would not necessarily help them to gain employment.

The solution was to look for external recognition of high-level work-based learning. The LCGI offered a number of distinct advantages.

- City and Guilds is the largest vocational awarding body in the UK – well-known by employers and with its programmes having a good reputation for the development of practical and applied skills
- City and Guilds already had in place a well-defined structure for recognizing students' learning in the work-place. The senior awards framework provided '. . . a single progressive structure related to industrial and business careers . . . designed to help increase the numbers of qualified people at higher levels within the workforce.' (City and Guilds, 1995, p.2). In addition to the Licentiateship there were other levels of award (Graduateship, Membership and Fellowship), to which students could progress during their careers.
- The focus of the Licentiateship was on the personal development of students and required the practical application of professional skills, knowledge and understanding in employment. It was very much in line with the University's desire to enhance students' employability.
- The scheme could be managed under delegated authority from City and Guilds. It did not require a costly or extensive new support framework.
- City and Guilds had well-established criteria for assessing personal skills in the work-place which not only recognized practical competencies but also the development of maturity, confidence and the ability to work with others.
- As with the University's new commitment to learning outcomes, the requirements for the LCGI were defined in terms of the level of student achievement and not in terms of time-on-task. Students were required to demonstrate their learning and not simply receive credit for having been on placement.

Organization

The two schools that participated in the pilot project (the Business School and the School of Biomolecular Sciences) had long-established procedures for managing sandwich students on placement. In the case of the Business School, the total number registered for the BA Business Studies sandwich programme was large and, as a consequence, the School had established a unit to provide support for students in off-campus learning activity. This unit provided a focus at school level for managing the student experience and coordinating the implementation of the LCGI. Within the School of Biomolecular Sciences the numbers involved were smaller, and much of the support for the scheme came from an individual tutor who had overall responsibility for student placements.

At an institutional level support for the scheme has been provided by the University's Academic Development Unit. This is a team holding responsibility for the introduction of innovations in the University's portfolio of academic activity and for managing project initiatives. The Unit has provided training for staff in the supervision, management and assessment of the LCGI as well as support for much of the initial work of the students. It has also visited employers and assessed portfolios. It would have been very difficult to have established the programme without the resources of this central team to work alongside academic staff who were already, in many cases, considerably stretched in their institutional roles.

The University established two staff in the Academic Development Unit with defined responsibilities for the LCGI: the *University City and Guilds Coordinator*, whose responsibilities were to act as the contact point for the LCGI programmes within the University and to promote and co-ordinate programmes within Schools in order to ensure the integration of the programmes into the administrative procedures of the University, and the *City and Guilds Facilitator*, whose responsibilities were to promote the development of arrangements during the period of the project and subsequently to explore ways of embedding the scheme within the University.

Quality assurance

The standard of the LCGI is defined by City and Guilds in the following terms.

The Licentiateship of the City and Guilds of London Institute denotes the ability to understand and practise the principles of a technical subject or professional activity. This ability is to be demonstrated in the context of advanced education and training and/or employment. The level of competence required is that which could be expected of a holder of a National Vocational Qualification (NVQ) at level 4, with subsequent relevant work experience at the same level, or the equivalent acceptable to the Institute. (City & Guilds, 1995, p.3)

The benchmarking of the award against NVQ level 4 is particularly significant as it provides a widely-recognized standard which complies with the NCVQ awards framework and allows the University to make links with initiatives for the development of key skills which are currently accredited via one or more NVQ key skills units at levels 3, 4 and 5. One of the principal advantages of adopting the LCGI has been the ability to develop and interpret the objectives of the award within the context of the subject disciplines involved. The procedures for assessment are rigorous but, unlike NVQs, they allow some scope for the use of discretion by tutors and supervisors. The award is based on students' achievement and the standards are defined in terms of outcomes.

The criteria for the LCGI are expressed in terms of both the general ability and understanding of students and also their personal skill development. Students must achieve the appropriate standard in both elements to receive the award. In this way the LCGI takes into account both the students' proficiency at work and also their transferable skills. Personal skills are defined in terms of:

- self-management and development
- management of tasks
- communication
- working with others
- applying knowledge
- applying initiative and problem-solving

On the basis of the experience with developments in work-based learning, the University introduced an additional category to the listing of personal skills: students' ability to review and reflect on the learning achieved in the work-place. Each of the elements of personal skill development is assessed using defined performance criteria. The process of assessment is conducted by both the work-based supervisor and the student's academic tutor.

Evaluation

The University has run the scheme successfully for the past three years and is currently conducting an independent evaluation to assess its impact and viability. The exercise involves not only the collation of existing information from students, academic staff and work-based supervisors but also the collection of qualitative material from the key managerial stakeholders; school directors, careers managers and employers. The aim is to establish whether or not the scheme is fulfilling its stated objectives of enhancing personal skill development and graduate employability.

The anecdotal evidence received to date suggests that the scheme has already had some impact. Comments from employers indicate that they appreciate the emphasis in the scheme on transferable skills:

We are giving them experience in kind and by doing the scheme hopefully giving them an edge that will get them certainly an interview, and hopefully jobs, when they graduate . . . To be able to get something additionally as a qualification, which objectively looks at their year, can only be good.

In addition there is an awareness that proficiency in the work-place is not sufficient evidence in itself that students have acquired the ability to be successful in their chosen careers:

The aspects of personality the LCGI programme addresses are ones not normally discussed in our society. Science undergraduates especially are unused to concepts such as awareness or self-confidence and are uncomfortable thinking in this way.

It is also apparent that students have recognized the potential advantages of following the programme and achieving an additional award for their sandwich placement year. When asked to identify the benefits of the experience, two commented:

Being able to critically evaluate my learning process and consequently amend my faults and improve on them. It has also helped to develop my management skills.

My placement was a very good one and it afforded me many opportunities. Perhaps a lot of responsibility was placed on me (for a sandwich student) but I appreciated this as it made me feel like one of the team . . . I now see that I can function well as a team member or an individual in the world of scientific research.

They also identified the point that the additional qualification was a very useful addition to their own individual curriculum vitae and that it was particularly helpful to be able to include a well-informed work-based supervisor as a referee in job applications.

Many of these comments were echoed by the external verifier who was appointed to oversee the programme. However, she also pointed out a number of areas in which there was scope to improve the management and support of the scheme. Two issues of particular importance were identified: the need for further staff development activity in order to ensure that academic tutors were fully aware of the requirements of the scheme and were familiar with the assessment criteria, and the need for better preparation of students before starting their placements.

The staff development issue is being progressed by support from the Academic Development Unit for individual tutors new to the programme, and by the sharing of good practice between the Business School and other schools coming into the scheme. Student preparation has presented more of a challenge. For many students, particularly those from a scientific background, the concept of identifying and recording personal skill development was a completely new departure and one which ran counter to the training they had received. Many found themselves in working environments which positively discouraged the use of individual initiative when dealing with scientific processes. Tasks in which they were involved had to be conducted methodically and in accordance with strict procedures. The skills that were required were those relating to the following of established codes of practice, and not those of coming up with bright ideas or experimenting with new approaches. The whole focus of the LCGI – on individual development – did not fit so well into the employers' culture, and many students faced difficulty in appreciating what was required of them in terms of the performance criteria for the award.

Students from the Business School had far less difficulty than those from Biomolecular Sciences in preparing for the requirements for the LCGI. Not· only did the Business School already have in place a well-established programme of preparation for the sandwich year but also the whole culture of Business Studies is one which encourages self-reliance, team-work and personal reflection. Students viewed the requirements for the award as simply an extension of what they were doing already.

The School of Biomolecular Sciences, on the other hand, had not managed initially to free up curricular space to allow a similar introduction. The response to the problem has been twofold. A more comprehensive induction programme has been introduced for science students, which includes sessions on skills such as team-building, assertiveness and time management. Students have, in addition, been encouraged to keep a log of their personal skill development throughout the programme, which covers skill development in their concurrent lectures and practical classes.

Issues for the future

Considerable progress has been made since the first cohort started on their LCGI in September 1994, and the University is now keen to explore ways of extending the opportunity to other subject disciplines. Interest has spread to other subjects which currently include a sandwich year and a number of schools are now involved. This has occurred partly through staff contacts and dissemination within the University, but in some areas it has been students, aware that their friends are involved with the scheme, who have approached their tutors to ask if they can also register for the Licentiateship.

Having established the principle that students may benefit from a more structured approach to recording their achievements in the work-place, it is logical to consider ways of making the award available to students on non-sandwich programmes – particularly those which include a significant element of work-based learning. At present, students are required to have completed four semesters of higher education before embarking on the

LCGI and it is expected that the period in training or relevant work experience will stretch over a calendar or academic year. Some relaxation of these requirements would allow other categories of students to become involved – for example, part-time students who study while at work, and postgraduate students who spend blocks of time in the work-place as part of their vocational training.

In the longer-term there is potential for integrating the award within a more clearly articulated framework to support the development of key skills at all levels in the University. The personal skills element of the scheme, together with the detailed performance criteria, provide a comprehensive model for managing student development – and many of these criteria apply to other activities in which students engage, such as voluntary work, student tutoring, part-time employment, involvement in the Students' Union, and the management of clubs and societies. Activities such as these provide opportunities for students to develop additional skills and capabilities which could be accommodated within a broadly-based skills agenda for the University.

Progressing these ideas requires some consideration to be given to the issue of resourcing. The LCGI is an award additional to that for which students originally register and hence there is a need for additional resources to support it. The principal costs include a registration fee to City and Guilds and, more significantly, the time of academic staff to support students in preparation for their placements, in overseeing their progress and in assessing their portfolios. To date, the University has dealt with these resource requirements through a mixture of school and project funding as well as a considerable amount of goodwill and commitment from those staff who have been involved. If the scheme is to develop in the future it will be necessary to find a better solution to the funding issue. Ultimately it may be necessary to look for support either from the students, who benefit from receiving an additional award, or from employers who benefit from having better prepared, more self-reliant graduates.

Reference

City and Guilds (1995) *Senior Awards of City and Guilds – Licentiateship* (LCGI), London: City and Guilds.

Chapter 10

Guiding the Student to the Centre of the Stakeholder Curriculum: Independent and Work-based Learning at Middlesex University

Chris Osborne, Jacqueline Davies and Jonathan Garnett

Editors' introduction

In this chapter, the authors report on the experience of Middlesex University in providing opportunities for students to take responsibility for key aspects of their own learning. Two examples are described; one in mainstream campus-based studies for undergraduate students, the other largely off-campus in work-based learning. By comparing the use of learner managed learning in these two contrasting contexts, the writers have identified common features which throw light on the process as a whole.

Of particular interest is the use of Independent Learning (ILE) within traditional academic studies. Though not the whole of the students' undergraduate programme, ILE has been warmly received and has had an impact on other activities in the University through shared modules and supervision. Issues related to student motivation and quality assurance are addressed and guidance is offered to the reader. Learner managed learning in the University's National Centre for Work-based Learning Partnerships is on a larger scale both in terms of student numbers and proportion of the students' overall experience of higher education. Extensive use is made of accreditation for prior learning, skills support, learning contracts and portfolios.

Together, these two examples give confidence that significant innovations can be made within higher education institutions (HEIs), even when resource pressures are high. Anyone looking for ideas on how to introduce a learner managed approach to capability education will find this chapter useful.

With increased recognition, as expressed in Dearing's 'new compact' (Dearing Report 1997), that students are now key stakeholders, well-placed to actively shape the curriculum to their needs, it requires little prescience to anticipate that as stakeholders (shareholders?) they will increasingly seek 'value for money' return on their investment, with the notional value of a degree (a 'commodity') reflecting its exchange value in the global knowledge economy.

Matching the curriculum to the student is most effective when the curriculum adapts to student interests and needs, not vice versa. This entails strategies for teaching and learning which require students to become active learners *and* curriculum managers, able to identify and build on their own interests (and recognize those of employers). Dearing provides a vision of a future society where learning is an ongoing, lifelong process; but many novice students (on-campus school leavers and work-based employees) still engage with higher education on *its* terms rather than their own. In Independent Learning (ILE) and Work-based Learning Studies (WBL), however, involvement is fundamental as students undertake negotiation, reflection, action planning and critical thinking in order to progress; in so doing they discover why travelling toward an award is often more valuable for the student than just getting there.

Independent learning at Middlesex – the basic concept

ILE at Middlesex University arose to cater for students (often mature) wanting more personally meaningful study opportunity than conventional curriculum provision. Within the constraints that the topic of study must:

(a) lend itself to genuine (and respectable) academic study, and
(b) must not duplicate existing taught modules,

students can design up to half their total programme (modules) for years two to three. For a proposal to become a 'learning *agreement*' (renegotiable), the student must identify, and recruit the support of, a tutor to oversee (and grade) the work. A further distinctive feature of ILE working is that, although the student proposes the means (and criteria) of assessment, a minimum 10 per cent of the marks for each module is obligatorily assigned to a '*reflective analysis*' wherein the student presents his/her estimation of what has (or has not) been achieved (and thereby, while not determining a grade, can valuably inform the grading tutor).

ILE also provides other opportunities. Some students lack awareness of the means to do well in their studies and of the demands of higher education (and of a subsequent career). The workshop-based level 1 Language and Communication Skills module addresses 'studentship', while a Career Planning level 1 module, run by the Careers Service, enables students to relate study programmes to possible career openings and requirements. Other modules (level 3) allow for individual (or group) negotiated work placements and (externally commissioned) project-based activities. A feature of such modules is their potential cross-accreditation (transfer of academic credits) into other subject areas thereby enriching the learning opportunities beyond ILE itself. The most significant ILE development, however, was its use as the 'cradle' for establishing work-based learning within the University. Such was the success of this initiative that WBL soon became free-standing as the National Centre for Work Based Learning Partnerships.

Work-based learning studies at Middlesex – the basic concept

WBL at Middlesex University is a means of recognizing and developing the learning which takes place outside the classroom, learning which could be at higher education level but does not conveniently map on to conventional higher education. 'Work' is interpreted widely, and incorporates the learning activity arising out of paid and unpaid employment. The *distinctive* character of WBL at Middlesex is that it does not assume a deficit model of student knowledge and skill but takes as its starting point the learning that the individual has *already* developed. By taking the Accreditation of Prior and Work-Based Learning module (APWBL), available on-campus, at a distance or in the work-place, students create a portfolio capturing their full knowledge and capabilities. They can then build on this, through a planning module, to devise customized programmes of study, entirely work-based or incorporating elements of taught provision, at certificate, diploma, degree and masters levels and beyond. Students negotiate with employer and University in generating a learning agreement showing rationale, coherence and intended outcomes, culminating in at least one major work-based research project. These projects are distinctive as they address a real work issue or problem calling for investigation and for application of current knowledge; the related capability lies in the end product, which has to work.

Initially WBL was used as a return-to-learning option, developing the self-esteem of mature students interested to access conventional university programmes, but growing links with employers and the work of staff has enabled WBL to develop a new provision which concentrates on continuing professional development as a field of study in its own right whereby individuals and their employers develop the process to suit their needs. Increasingly this is giving rise to WBL programmes devised out of organizational capability frameworks and collaborative projects, which is proving highly attractive to students and employers alike. The Centre has now attracted over 700 students from some 50 organizations across industry, the community and the public services, involving diverse occupational areas and levels of seniority. The recent Doctorate in Professional Studies (the DProf) is being used by people at the highest levels of their organizations to develop major change projects in their work places and/or in their professions.

Employers are important stakeholders in the WBL programme. Their specific involvement can range from endorsing the employee-student's learning agreement through to contribution (where institutional partnership is well developed) to the design, delivery and assessment of the WBL programme.

The role of accreditation in work-based learning studies

WBL starts with student learning already achieved, but uses the A(P)EL process to move far beyond delivering specific credit for exemption purposes. It encourages students to reflect on, and use, their learning achievements and interests to plan both the subject content of their eventual programme and their future personal development. Inevitably, students initially see learning as activity, as things done; and they encounter difficulty in expressing underlying knowledge and skills. The student's adviser mediates this process and helps elicit learning in both the process and outcome terms needed for academic accreditation. While there is a tension related to coaching students to familiarize themselves with the learning vocabulary and discourse of higher education, and to define their learning against academic level descriptors, the process has proved to be a powerful transformative one as many student reflective essays plainly reveal.

Common features, and challenges, of ILE and WBL

What then do ILE and WBL have in common – and why differentiate? Taking the latter point first, a distinction relates to the base of the learner. For 'conventional' undergraduate and postgraduate students ILE provides campus-based possibilities of individualized study and patterns of working. For other potential students, however, the possibility of combining study with activity within the work-place itself confers advantage on the WBL approach.

Commonality exists, however. Jaques (1991) lists 11 criteria indicative of active, self-managed and independent student learning, namely who determines: topic selection; pace of learning; learning tasks; learning resources;

outcomes; provision of feedback; changes in direction; the nature and criteria of assessment; grades; and evaluation procedure. ILE and WBL could each respond 'the student through negotiation with tutors' to most of these criteria, although assessment standards remain fundamentally a tutor preserve. Similarly, both ILE and WBL lend themselves to deep learning by their scope for independence in learning, personal development, problem-focused working, reflection, learning by doing, refinement of learning skills, project work, and group work (see Gibbs 1992), to which we might add personal responsibility for learning and a high level of motivation. Both also recognize that achieving desired outcomes requires appropriate groundwork, giving students the 'tools to do the job' (ie learning to learn), appropriate support, and a clear understanding of the nature and significance of their undertaking.

Student preparation and support: both ILE and WBL normally require students to take preparatory (planning) modules to convert raw ideas into a structured proposal. This usually involves identifying and working with the tutor who will support the subsequent work; it also introduces students to others who, although proposing different themes, can provide valuable alternative perspective and support. It is vital that students realize that independence is not isolation – and that isolation is frequently prejudicial to good work. For this reason, ILE students are required to have (and document) at least two meetings per subsequent module with their tutor to discuss work in progress, to negotiate any changes to the learning agreement, and to obtain formative feedback on work already done; WBL operates similarly but also runs a duty tutor scheme to provide more immediate support to off-campus learners.

A distinctive feature of WBL is that, for the initial APWBL module, students receive an open learning pack, and are allocated a personal adviser and complementary workshops (usually up to three one-to-one one-hour guidance sessions and three two-hour workshops over one semester). Stimulus workshops, delivered at the university or at the work-place, promote peer collaboration and deeper understanding; distance learners receive more regular coaching utilizing telephone, fax and e-mail. Also, as the WBL curriculum evolved it became apparent that students needed help in approaching project activity. The research methods module equips students to identify, collect and analyse information for problem-solving. Unlike a conventional research methods course it focuses on the worker as researcher and on the development of an individual research portfolio to support the project component (research proposal) of the programme. The module cultivates research awareness and capability of specific relevance to the work-place.

The *learning agreement*: for both ILE and WBL the learning agreement is fundamental to students accepting responsibility for managing their own learning (a prerequisite for lifelong learning capability) and to recognizing process factors in learning. So, students in the ILE planning module negotiate the parameters of their proposed work to derive the (renegotiable) learning agreement showing the overall ILE programme and the learning outcomes and assessment criteria for individual modules. One common problem is student difficulty in moving outside the received model of higher education and traditional modes of working (particularly assessment): renegotiability not only covers changes of vision and direction but also accommodates growing student confidence in independent learning.

Similarly, the WBL planning module requires the student to actively engage with curriculum, question how the intended programme has both a fitness for and fitness of purpose, and explain the rationale for including any accredited learning (carried over from the APWBL portfolio), together with the anticipated learning outcomes from taking additional taught modules, studying research methods and undertaking their project. Students must also address the impact the programme will have on their work-place and on their own continuing personal and professional development.

Tutor identification: both ILE and WBL have a (small) core group of staff, but both need other tutors, or work-place mentors, to support specific students. In ILE, tutor recruitment is left to the student (with guidance), partly as an early initiative test but partly to recognize personal compatibility. Topic-relevant tutors can be hard to locate, however, and often need some introduction themselves into the nature of ILE. Furthermore, when conventional, long-planned module teaching has long since filled work programmes, tutors are being asked, in effect, to take on the latecomer ILE student as an act of charity! Many do, however, and relish the personalized working with a motivated student on an original study (described by one as 'something like undergraduate research'), as offers of repeat service indicate. In WBL, expansion of student numbers means the core team continues to grow and key tutors from other areas of the University are contracted for project supervision in advance.

An experiential process: although students approach ILE and WBL with an idea (sometimes exotic!) of what they want to study or explore, whether for interest or for a purpose, this is almost invariably articulated in terms of content (syllabus). Recognition of broader learning outcomes (personal development, capability) usually requires some tutor effort to tease out. Yet, as the best students come to realize, the real success lies not in what is studied but in how one goes about it – in short, that it is the process itself that engenders the significant learning. And that the greatest benefit generated is the ability to learn for oneself in a society where received knowledge can become rapidly outmoded. Perry's stages (1978) of student maturation from a 'dualistic' position to acceptance of relativism and uncertainty have parallels in student development in ILE and WBL where an early primary concern with knowledge acquisition tends to evolve into recognition that the real measure of learning is personal growth of self as learner. That ultimately it's not what you know that matters, it's not even what you do with what you know, but what you do when you don't know – and how efficiently and effectively you do it.

Assessment aspects: one major challenge facing ILE and WBL is to ensure academic equivalence to conventional (taught and discipline-based) learning. ILE addresses this in two ways. First, no student can take more than half their level 2–3 modules in ILE (which means that students experience traditional higher education, obtain some measure of normal requirements and standards, can spread the risk of their total endeavours, and in so doing provide a benchmark for comparing ILE grades with those obtained elsewhere). Second, by having tutors from conventional discipline teaching, prevailing standards are applied to ILE negotiated work. It is perhaps not surprising therefore, that, although there is some indication that ILE may have a flatter 'bell curve' in terms of overall grade distribution than more conventional modes of study (some students seize the opportunity offered by ILE, others are exposed for poor organization and self-discipline), there is usually reasonable correlation between ILE and other grades assigned to individual students.

A second challenging aspect is that of self-assessment. As one mature ILE student observed, the student proposes (negotiates) the work and is responsible for completion, only to be assessed by a tutor (albeit one with whom the student has, hopefully, been working closely). This reveals an inherent tension between the 'pure' notion of independent learning (with its goal of self-knowledge and the ability to self-assess) and the University's need to ensure standards.

The reflective analysis goes some way to giving the student influence in assessment (by showing how a setback was turned from potential disaster to positive learning advantage, for example; or by explaining where and why certain lines of exploration were consciously excluded, rather than have them interpreted as blind spots) but can itself be problematical: it can run counter to usual student expectation, while it also assumes students can analyse their own learning. Many students, even with the recommended 'learning log', still have great difficulty in extricating and articulating their achievement and development beyond a narrative of work events, while guidelines can result in point-by-point responses rather than a genuine holistic review of learning and of self-development (process).

In this context, WBL now incorporates peer assessment of presentations of research proposals. This is extremely effective and leads to incisive and perceptive questioning by the peer group (WBL values highly the ability to debate, solve problems and articulate standpoints in a team or group situation – Costley, 1996). The need for the project to be useful to the employer or sponsor organization as well as academically valid highlights fitness-for-purpose criteria which do not always sit comfortably with conventional higher education expectations of assessment. Finding the optimum balance of tutor/self assessment and of guided/intuitive reflection is a matter deserving of further consideration.

A focus on change and responsibility: as Ackoff (1974) observes, 'a curriculum is a solution to a problem which does not exist . . . [so] . . . because what one learns is not nearly as important as learning how to learn, and because questions are at least as important as answers, students should design their own curricula'. Both ILE and WBL allow students to do this, to perceive their study needs as a total picture before concerning themselves with the focused detail of individual modules: students are enabled to operate on as well as in their chosen sphere of work, and so come to operate in a context of flux, accustomed to locate themselves with regard to a mutable and evolving (uncertain) future. It is no longer appropriate in our society to assume or expect that someone else will make sense of information and events and impart their conclusion for others to follow: to be properly adaptable means to be willing to make analyses and decisions, and to take action, oneself. In ILE and WBL this is exactly what students learn to do.

Conclusions: the future

Experience suggests that ILE is not suited to all takers, particularly those fresh from school, without groundwork support. As with WBL, it is a process of growth as much as a methodology for learning, and students need preparation for this, as do teaching staff (teachers certainly are not redundant, but may require some re-orientation). In recompense, ILE and WBL offer student and teacher a rewarding experience, a real meeting ground of student-identified need, tackling real issues, with tutor as enabler (and sometimes 'devil's advocate') in a process of learning development (for both). No more silent seminars or half-hearted tutorials: discussion now necessarily originates with the student, whose needs are real, and where the focus is as much on the learning process itself as on the knowledge, understanding and skills being developed. As Gray (1997) observes, 'the secret of learning, of course, is in the process, not the outcome', pointing out that it is only through negotiation that there can be valid ownership of learning, with 'the job of education [being] not to gain compliance but to help individuals work out matters for themselves . . . [and] to develop autonomous individuals who use rationality, common sense and experience to inform personal values'. And, in a society where 'the rate of turnover of useful knowledge is already very high, and increasing, [the] ability to decide what must be learned, and then to do it fast and effectively, is thus a survival skill, in work and indeed for the rest of life . . . the choice is not between being a dependent and an independent learner, but rather being a more or less effective learner' (Baume 1994).

Independent and work-based learning are not without their challenges but not without their benefits. Both now offer other subject areas (and teachers) and the means, via cross-accreditation of ILE and WBL modules, to expand and enhance learning opportunities for students majoring in fields currently without such openings. In so doing, independent learning becomes available to a greater number of students (without generating problems of tutor availability). Also, while WBL is firmly established at postgraduate level, ILE is yet to fully explore the possibilities at this level for students who are seeking an award for self-directed learning that, even if career-related, is not specifically work-focused.

The evidence is accruing of the potential for students to thrive when given the opportunity of independence. The need now is to extend this to a wider range of students, and to recognize the implications of such extension in terms of preparing students, and (no less importantly) their teachers, for operating appropriately. All parties in higher education can learn from what is essentially a joint endeavour that erodes the traditional power relationships noted by Gray (1997); but, for students, the prime value of ILE and WBL is that the experience of the process of learning, of learning to learn, endures when that which was learnt has long been forgotten or outmoded.

References

Ackoff, R (1974) *Redesigning the Future: A Systems Approach to Societal Problems*, New York, John Wiley.

Baume, D (1994) *Developing Learner Autonomy*. Birmingham, Staff and Educational Development Association (SEDA paper 84).

Costley, C (1996) 'How argument relates to graduates in their work and lives', in M Riddle (ed) *The Quality of Argument: a Colloquium on Issues of Teaching in HE* (pp.31–8), Middlesex University, School of Lifelong Learning and Education.

Gibbs, G (1992) *Improving the Quality of Student Learning Through Course Design*, in R Barnett (ed) *Learning To Effect* (pp.149–65), SRHE/Open University Press.

Gray, H (1997) 'Instruction, teaching and the oppression of learners', *Capability*, 3(1), pp.2–4.

Jaques, D (1991) *Authority and Dependence in Higher Education*, in McDowell, E (ed*) Putting Students First*. Birmingham, Staff and Educational Development Association (SEDA paper 64).

Perry, WG (1978) *Forms of Intellectual and Ethical Development in the College Years: a scheme*. Holt, Rinehart & Winston.

Sneddon, I and Kremer, J (eds) (1994) *An Enterprising Curriculum: Teaching Innovations in Higher Education*, Belfast: HMSO.

Chapter 11

The Partnership Framework at the University of Glamorgan

Malcolm Taylor

Editors' introduction

This is a case study of partnership which involves Training and Enterprise Councils, employers and the University of Glamorgan in the development and implementation of study programmes which are based on the needs of the work-place. Students create, in conjunction with the University, 'bespoke' learning contracts appropriate to their work-related needs.

Within the context of partnership, Taylor describes the practically-oriented 'Meister' Programme which is designed to develop technical personnel skills appropriate to business and management. The commitment to lifelong learning is very clear, and is consistent with recommendations in the Dearing Report (NCIHE, 1997) regarding regional partnerships and lifelong learning.

The University of Glamorgan, located in South Wales, has approximately 17,000 students attending its 200 courses. The University's mission is to provide and promote access to high quality learning opportunities for all those able to benefit, and to foster economic, social and cultural development, particularly in Wales, through the extension and application of knowledge. In accordance with this mission, the University's academic bias is towards vocational and applied education, and cooperation with the Training and Enterprise Councils (TECs), local industries and voluntary organizations in the development of key skills and initiative in employees.

At an early stage the University acknowledged and recognized the impact of the competency movement on education and determined to offer higher level National Vocational Qualifications (NVQs) as a development route complementary to more traditional programmes. The availability of NVQs allowed the University to claim further credit for its vocational bias, but these awards fell short of fully integrating the concepts of capability and competence into its own awards.

As a way of integrating capability and competence, the University's Academic Board has now approved a Strategy for Work-based Learning, thereby acknowledging the value of work-based learning and its relevance to higher education.

The Strategy for Work-based Learning

The Strategy defines work-based learning as that which takes place within the normal work-place of the learner, and as characterized by the testing of theoretical knowledge within a practical work context. It defines the work-place as any formal organisational structure within which work occurs, including voluntary organizations.

The Strategy is based on the following principles:

- accredited work-based learning carries the same status and credibility as learning achieved through more conventionally-delivered means;
- work-based learning programmes are characterized by a mutually interactive interrogation between theoretical principles and practical application;
- the learning undertaken in the work-place is incorporated within structured and accredited programmes of study;
- the learning does not itself have to be gained through formal accredited courses, but can arise through experiential learning.

The core of the Strategy is to develop a regulatory Partnership Framework through which the University's wide range of modules and awards is linked to the work-place needs and learning opportunities of prospective students and employers.

The Partnership Framework

The Partnership Framework, the vehicle to be used to deliver the Strategy for Work-Based Learning, responds to initiatives such as the *Realising our Potential* (Duchy of Lancaster, 1993), the *National Training and Education Targets* (NACETT, 1995), and *People and Prosperity: An Agenda for Action in Wales* (Welsh Office, 1996). The Framework recognizes the need to stimulate the growth of the Welsh economy by developing the skills and initiative of employees, and by targeting the numerous small- and medium-sized enterprises within South Wales through partnership with the TECs. The Partnership Framework offers students the opportunity to gain higher education qualifications through a combination of existing University modules of study, accredited work-based projects and the accreditation of experience. It offers an innovative learning and development opportunity by recognizing not only the value of work-based learning, but also the opportunities available for matching work-based learning outcomes with the learning outcomes of University modules.

The Partnership Framework's key aims are:

- to provide comprehensive, accessible and high quality learning opportunities;
- to provide further opportunities for lifelong learning especially, but not exclusively, of a vocationally-orientated kind;
- to provide a holistic learning experience employing the resources of a candidate's work-place and integrating the academic environment of the University; and
- to promote the capability of a wide range of employees and their associated work organizations.

Among its objectives are the following:

- to respond to local employers' needs and the higher educational needs of the local workforce;
- to ensure partnership between industry and the University, facilitated by TECs; and
- to provide a flexible operational structure for the recruitment of students from the work-place into higher education.

A Partnership Office has been created to act as a focal point for the implementation of the new strategy, whose tasks are to:

- network with external organizations;
- liaise with departments regarding the development of student-centred programmes of study;
- act as a focal point for Partnership students;
- provide advice and support to students seeking accreditation for prior learning; and
- provide advice, support and staff development to departments regarding the implementation and accreditation of work-based learning.

Accreditation of learning

The Partnership Framework encourages employees within the work-place to engage in four kinds of learning experiences:

- compiling portfolios of evidence in order to demonstrate existing competences and skills that have already been developed at the stage of enrolment, and that lead to higher education credits through the assessment by the University of previous learning and experience;
- the use of learning contracts and learning support groups as a means of expressing a student's individually-negotiated study programme;
- completing, as part-time students at the University or its partner institutions, a selection of modules specified in the learning contract (modules being taken from any disciplinary field within participating departments); and
- engaging in project work within the work-place, the projects being linked with learning outcomes for particular modules offered by the University (in this way it becomes possible to translate a traditionally-taught module at the University into a project-based enterprise that attains the same learning outcomes).

Conventional modules of study are assessed using the assessment method agreed within each scheme module. Where prior experience is claimed, or work-based projects are negotiated to replace conventional assessments, students are expected to provide appropriate evidence of actual work activity together with an appropriate narrative which links the work activity to the theoretical framework of the relevant academic module(s), thereby demonstrating both knowledge and its application in practice.

Supported by the Partnership Office, students create a unique learning programme which addresses their particular needs. A learning contract specifies the content of the study programme, and identifies:

- the extent to which the accreditation of prior learning (APL) is to be claimed;
- the modules to be studied;
- whether assessment is to be work-based or via traditional methods;
- the level and credits to be awarded; and
- the named award to be gained on satisfactory completion of the study programme.

The learning contract states the programme of study that the partnership student is proposing, the thinking and justification behind the proposal, the time within which the programme is to be completed, the resources necessary to achieve success and the type of evidence that will be presented to assess the learning outcomes achieved. Within the learning contract, therefore, issues of coherence and continuity of learning across modules and projects will be addressed. The coherence statements are derived from and proposed by learners, but the University department or school has the final decision about the academic standing and value of the agreed learning programme. The contract is agreed following full consultation with departmental staff, work-place mentors, employers and other parties who are to help provide the learning experiences and assess the learning outcomes.

The contract is made-up of three parts:

1. work-based learning (projects, design problems, etc);
2. modules of study chosen from the University's Prospectus (or from appropriate courses on offer at other higher education institutions); and
3. the APEL portfolio, where appropriate.

A learning contract typically covers the equivalent of a year's programme of study. Partnership students can thus expect to propose and work through a series of learning contracts during the course of their studies.

Although the Partnership Framework is a new initiative, there have already been significant responses from schools and departments which demonstrate the institution's commitment to implementing the new strategy. While it is anticipated that the Framework will eventually impact on activities throughout the campus, early inquiries have focused on the subjects of electronics, mechanical engineering, business, management and accounting. The Framework is also being used as a vehicle to promote the University as a whole, rather than the more usual piecemeal approach taken by individual departments.

An example of partnership: the 'Meister Programme'

One example of departmental collaboration which addresses regional, long-term development needs is the 'Meister Programme', which combines modules from the Departments of Electronics and Information Technology, Mechanical Engineering and the Business School. It is the Partnership Framework, with its scope for customized and flexible development programmes, which has enabled the University to create the 'Meister Programme' in association with external partners. This innovative programme seeks to upgrade the technical skills of participants while offering them the opportunity to explore key aspects of business and management. The name reflects the quality and excellence of the original German approach to the development of master craftspersons and emphasizes the technical element of the programme. However, unlike the German approach, the focus of the University's Meister Programme is on initiating and stimulating the development of the all-round skills required by the engineering, science and technology managers of the future. It provides learning opportunities that are based in the work-place and academic environments, and that are linked to the developmental needs of both the organization and the individual. The programme seeks to recognize competence through the identification and accreditation of uncertificated and experiential learning, while developing capability through learning gained via conventional methods which can then be practised in the work-place.

The University of Glamorgan embarked on the Meister Programme in response to a demand from the South Wales business community for more management training. Many companies felt that their technical staff needed to improve their problem-solving, negotiation and leadership skills. They wanted a practical approach rather than the more theoretical approach of local MBAs. The need was highlighted by the three local TECs which all enthusiastically assisted in the development and promotion of the programme, together with support from the Welsh Development Agency.

Programme objectives

The formal objectives of the programme are to enhance the abilities of participants by providing them with the opportunity to:

- update and extend their technical skills and expertise;
- develop a commercial edge and awareness to the business needs of their own organization and of their suppliers;
- gain an appreciation of the purpose and role of management;
- enhance their people and general management skills;
- acquire a reflective, yet progressive approach to their personal development; and
- work towards a recognized higher education qualification.

Programme content and delivery

Participants all study the same managerial and business modules but select technical modules which are appropriate to the needs of both the organizations and themselves. The programme consists of attendance at the university, residential weekend sessions, industrial visits and assignments within their companies. The success of the programme is dependent upon the full and active commitment of participating companies, which can demonstrate their commitment by:

- their close involvement in the initial discussions identifying the specific learning needs of their participants;

- releasing participants from work for one afternoon and evening per week as well as occasional Saturday morning activities; and
- selecting a mentor within the company to offer general support to the participant.

The accreditation of learning provides an opportunity for participants to receive formal recognition of their learning and development. Participants are expected to be qualified to at least HNC, HND or NVQ level 3, and their developmental activities will be geared to studying for credits at the next level.

The first pilot of this initiative is just concluding, and feedback from participants and employers has been very positive. Its success, in the eyes of employers, has been achieved by designing a bespoke programme which allows them to select key areas where development is considered to be vital to the company's and the individual's growth. The University and its TEC partners are now looking forward to commencing another Meister Programme with participants from a diversity of occupational sectors including automotive components, aircraft maintenance, energy utilities and manufacturers of prefabricated garden equipment.

It is the University's belief that the Partnership Framework has the potential to address the recommendations in the Dearing Report (NCIHE, 1997) for regional partnerships and lifelong learning. The Framework's focus on work-based learning provides individuals and employers with an opportunity to accredit lifelong learning within a context of economic development and growth. The opportunity to study and be assessed through work-based projects removes a major obstacle to individuals and employers who are anxious to take up development opportunities but find that the conventional patterns of attendance and study conflict with both work and domestic constraints. While it is anticipated that most students will seek accreditation towards a first or higher degree, the availability of credit for single modules also offers the opportunity to accredit development undertaken as Continuous Professional Development.

References

Duchy of Lancaster (1993) *Realising our Potential: A Strategy for Science, Engineering and Technology* (Cm 2250), London: HMSO.

NCIHE (1997) *Higher Education in the Learning Society*, Report of the National Committee of Inquiry into Higher Education, London: HMSO.

Welsh Office (1996) *People and Prosperity: An Agenda for Action in Wales*, Cardiff: Welsh Office.

NACETT (1995) *National Training and Education Targets*, National Advisory Council for Education and Training Targets.

Chapter 12

The Career Management Initiative at Buckinghamshire Chilterns University College

Pauline McLeman and Patrick Smith

Editors' introduction

McLeman and Smith provide evidence of the effective collaboration between Thames Valley Enterprise and Buckinghamshire Chilterns University College regarding the development of an initiative aimed at developing students' career management capability. A feature of interest is the introduction of pilot schemes that reflected the nature and priorities of the different faculties involved, rather than a central prescription. Work in the Faculty of Applied Social Studies and Humanities is highlighted, and shows inter alia that, although students may, early in their time in higher education, possess skills relevant to career management, it is often necessary to develop their awareness that they actually do possess them and can use them. The experience of a 'mock' application and interview process involving employers (another aspect of partnership) is shown to have had benefit for the students involved. An issue for the future is how to extend the pilot initiative across a broader front when the pump-priming funding ends.

The origins and features of the Career Management Initiative

The Career Management Initiative (CMI) had its origins in extra-curricular provision developed within the Faculty of Technology designed to help students optimize their chances of success in the job application, selection and interview process. The idea of helping students to 'make the most of themselves at interview' received a very positive response from students and stimulated a more systematic approach to developing and trialling a short programme.

A Steering Group consisting of staff from both careers and guidance and faculties, as well as employers, met regularly over a six-month period to develop an outline programme which could be tailored to the needs of faculties. This period allowed a team spirit to develop, which was to prove invaluable in the running of the programme. The support, in a number of ways, of Thames Valley Enterprise (TVE) gave the staff involved the time to organise the programme and to reflect upon its outcomes.

'Working with the grain' of departments and faculties was to be a central feature of the CMI, with the result that the three pilot projects (in the faculties of Applied Social Sciences and Technology, and in the Business School) were quite different from each other despite following the same four stages.

Since the intention was to evaluate the effectiveness of such an initiative, the role of both formative and summative evaluation was emphasized from the beginning and an External Evaluator joined the Steering Group early on. The Steering Group met regularly to monitor progress, as did those staff involved with the implementation of the three pilots. In developing the programme the Steering Group was at pains to reconcile the demands of a programme which addressed the needs of the students while keeping to a minimum the extra workload which would be placed on both staff and students.

From self-audit and review to selection: the four stage model

The Steering Group identified four stages which would structure the students' experience:

1. Skills awareness
2. Opportunity awareness
3. Intelligence gathering, CV and application preparation
4. Handling selection and interview processes

This structure, similar to that outlined by Cross (1996), was designed to allow a progressive focusing of students' awareness, understanding and experience of seeking and securing employment. The faculties face different issues in terms of the expectations and preconceptions of students. For example, students from the Business School are fairly confident of securing employment within the corporate and commercial sector and, within that expectation, are relatively flexible in terms of what they will consider. The position with regard to social science students is more varied. Students taking courses which include psychology and criminology typically anticipate employment as 'psychologists' or 'criminologists', but without any very clear idea about what kind of work this may involve. The reality is that for both subjects it is likely that a postgraduate qualification will be needed as the basis for discipline-related employment. For sociology students the issue is somewhat different, since they often have very little idea of what their future career might be.

For all of the social science students the starting point was to enable them to develop a clear view of the range of skills and knowledge they had acquired through their studies, to facilitate the development of skills relevant to securing employment, and a realistic, open-minded approach to the range of opportunities available to them.

The role of transferable/generic/key skills

The CMI was at pains to focus on the idea that students following undergraduate courses should, in addition to acquiring and developing subject specific knowledge, also develop key skills. While there is debate over what the term comprises, key skills are taken to include, in relation to the CMI:

- communication skills, both oral and written;
- flexibility and the ability to handle change;
- information technology skills;
- learning to learn and adapt;
- numeracy and basic computational skills;
- planning and organization skills;
- problem-solving skills; and
- team work and team roles skills.

As well as seeking to enhance students' abilities to perform to the best of their abilities in the selection market, the CMI is a means of addressing students' lack of awareness of the existence and importance of such skills. Experience from the pilot demonstrates that, once aware, students develop the ability to employ such skills and that their confidence increases rapidly.

Innovation strategy: the experience of the pilot in applied social sciences and humanities (ASSH)

The Faculty had been aware for some time of the difficulties faced by social science students as they embarked on the search for employment in that the students often found it extremely difficult to reach a clear view of what they wanted to do, or of the kind of employment for which their degrees had prepared them. This awareness was heightened by one of the points made in the Teaching Quality Assessment of sociology which indicated that, while there was clear evidence that our students had gained important transferable skills, they were often not aware that they had done so and therefore were unable to make best use of these skills in their subsequent careers. For this reason it seemed clear that the primary focus for the ASSH pilot should be on developing students' awareness of their own strengths and skills, their ability to identify the kind of occupation that would suit them and their ability to present themselves, and what they had to offer, *effectively* to prospective employers. It was also decided that the pilot should, as far as possible, reflect the process of seeking and securing employment realistically, in order to provide students with some experience of the procedures they would face.

During the summer of 1996 all social science students about to enter the final year were informed about the pilot and invited to participate. It was explained that this would be in addition to the requirements for their degree programme and that no credit would be awarded in respect of the degree. The fact that 35 of these students (drawn from all five social science degree programmes) were prepared to undertake what was, in effect, an additional module bearing no credits in their final year is an indication of the importance that they attached to developing skills and abilities in support of their search for employment.

The programme for the pilot consisted of four workshops held on Wednesday afternoons throughout the first semester. The workshops were run by different teams representative of the cross-section of expertise contained in the Steering Group. The dates and topics of the workshops were as shown in Table 12.1.

Outcomes of the ASSH pilot and its evaluation

ASSH pilot students were brought together in late May 1997 for an open discussion which was video-recorded. Evidence from the video-recording, along with observations from students, staff and the external evaluator collected during the course of the innovation indicate the following.

Greater career awareness

One of the principal intentions of the pilot focused on broadening out students' often somewhat narrow conceptions of possible careers. '[A]t first they (the students) didn't want to hear that they might not go directly into psychology or criminology . . . but that changed.' This shift in expectations along with the development of a more flexible attitude towards what might

Table 12.1 *The workshop programme*

Date	Details of the workshop
November 1996	*Workshop 1: What have you got to offer? (two hours)* • Self-analysis of strengths, weaknesses, skills and aptitudes. • Induction to PROSPECT (Careers Software) • Review of skills required by employers and the transferable skills embedded within the social science degree programmes.
December 1996	*Workshop 2: Where are the opportunities? (two hours)* • Careers destinations for social science graduates. • Sources of information about career opportunities. • Introduction to CV preparation.
January 1997	*Workshop 3: Psychometric testing (three hours)* All participants completed a standard psychometric test, individual feedback was provided at the final workshop. Following this workshop, participants were asked to select, from a range of mock advertisements, a job for which they wished to 'apply', and then to prepare and submit a letter of application, application form and CV.
February 1997	*Workshop 4: Selection procedures and interviews (two days)* This workshop took participants through some of the range of selection procedures and activities currently used by employers, including: • selection interviews; • individual presentations; • group problem-solving exercises; and • an in-tray exercise. The students were interviewed for the jobs for which they had applied by professional personnel/human resource managers drawn from the College and from local organizations. Each interview was video-recorded so that the 'applicants' could review their own performance in the light of feedback provided by the interviewers. Feedback was provided on an individual basis, based on the results of the psychometric tests administered in the previous workshop and, on a more general basis, about the interviewers' views of the applications, CV and interview performances.

be both feasible and possible in terms of employment, took time to occur, but would appear to have been achieved. 'I was prepared to go along with it, because I didn't have any real idea about what I might do, in fact, I hadn't even thought about it . . . so this came as something of an eye-opener, suddenly I didn't feel stuck.'

It was clear that those students who completed the programme not only enjoyed it, but found it helpful. This was evident, not only in terms of what they said but, more convincingly, in the nature of their participation, particularly during the final two-day workshop. Over the course of those two days it was impossible not to notice the way in which, as a group and individually, they had grown in confidence.

Given the comments of the quality assessors that social science graduates at the College needed to be helped to identify the skills and qualities they had gained from their courses, it was pleasing to note that a number of participants commented specifically on this, one drawing attention to how much clearer she was now about what she had to offer an employer and that she was now considering a much wider range of possibilities.

Increased levels of confidence

Assessing improvements in states of mind such as general confidence is fraught with difficulties, for the evaluator has to rely on self reports, the observations of others and the general 'feel' or 'climate' of activities observed within the workshop settings – all of which are open to misinterpretation. The consensus, however, in relation to this pilot is that students' confidence had received a huge boost. One student remarked, after one of the early sessions, 'I feel so much more confident about what this degree has to offer.'

Applying for 'real' jobs and being interviewed by human resources managers from local companies made the preparation, selection and interview process appreciably more significant than if the exercise had been undertaken by College staff. Having gone through the experience, students felt much more assured about their ability to perform. 'Interpreting the information from job adverts, what you thought they were asking for, and finally putting it all together . . . the difference was really useful . . . actually doing it.'

Tutors too noticed a difference: one, on seeing students he had previously taught two years before, reported, 'The difference in confidence, in what I would have termed diffident, even withdrawn students, is dramatic.'

Developing key skills

It is not that students are lacking such skills: rather, it is that they are not aware of their existence or of their significance in relation to continued learning and the challenges represented in jobs. During a coffee break in the final workshop the students themselves brought up importance of these skills, one saying, 'You don't realize they're important but, in a way, they're perhaps more important, well as much important, as the stuff you've learned in the subject.'

Specific skills relating to the operation of groups and teams also attracted the students' attention and interest, particularly the recognition of different approaches to problem solving and listening to the views of others: some sample comments were: 'we all arrived knowing different things – just like real life,' and 'It's not *what* you say, but *how* you say it.' 'It's also how what is said is listened to,' and 'Some people leap to conclusions with no evidence, others have got the evidence, but keep quiet . . . you've got to somehow get it out of them.'

An exercise requiring the students to adopt roles in which each was required to argue for a concealed agenda or opinion which they had been given and with which they might not necessarily agree, raised both ethical and tactical issues that were implicit in one student's comment: 'It was difficult, but fun, arguing for something you don't believe in.'

Extending and embedding the CMI: some lessons for the future

In the monitoring and evaluation process staff were eager to explore how best to 'fit' the CMI with the students' needs and their course requirements. Integrating it into an existing module was not an alternative in this case, thus its placement was of particular significance.

Timing and spread of workshops

Placing the pilot in the final year meant that students were asked to make an additional commitment at a time when they were preparing dissertations and working for their final examinations. It is perhaps surprising that so many did so. In fact, attendance held up reasonably well until the third workshop which had been scheduled inadvertently for semester one revision week.

The participants felt that workshops should be scheduled over the second semester of the second year and into the first semester of the third year, and that students should be encouraged to use vacation work to reflect on their development of key skills. At the same time the students made the point that the existence of the CMI should be advertised early in their courses and its relevance spelt out. Evidence from the literature (Cross, 1996) reveals that, the earlier such provision is introduced, the better is the students' attendance and the greater the impact on their career development.

Having noted the extremely high levels of enthusiasm and involvement of the participants, it was suggested that, if such a programme can have such a significant impact on the way students participate, there would be a benefit in scheduling it to start at the very beginning of the degree programme, with perhaps reminder sessions later in the course.

The involvement and commitment of staff and students

One of the dangers of developing new and additional provision is that, once the innovator has moved on, the innovation is not sustained. In order to minimize this happening, those involved with the CMI were at pains to 'spread the word' by means of a three-part strategy:

(a) encouraging colleagues to drop in on sessions during the final two-day workshop;
(b) ensuring that the Dean of Faculty shared lunch with the students and was able to discuss the initiative informally with them; and
(c) inviting the students to a follow-up discussion which was video-recorded, edited and will be used to advertise the CMI to subsequent cohorts using staff and students from this first cohort as advocates.

Embedding and extending

While it has been interesting and rewarding to run the pilot so successfully, this initiative will only be of real value if it can now be extended to all students. The pilots have been, and are being run, on the enthusiasm of the members of the Steering Group supported by the contributions of others both internal and external to the College. The costs of the pilots have been met jointly by TVE and College funding. If the initiative is to be taken forward, its value to faculties will need to be recognized and its resourcing be taken over by them. This will involve managing the transition between the joint funding which continues until summer 1998 and the funding of the initiative by faculties alone after that time.

To credit-rate or not?

A more difficult issue relates to how such provision should be offered. If it is to be offered as a non-credited optional extra, as was the case with the ASSH pilot, two issues are raised. First, students would be expected to increase their workload at a time when many are saying that their courses involve too many modules, and second at a time when financial constraints mean that many have to undertake paid employment. The ASSH experience shows that the students will take on additional work if they are convinced that it will be to their benefit. One option under consideration is to employ graduates from the first CMI to work with staff on subsequent CMI provision in a peer learning/supplemental instruction approach.

One strategy that might help would be to credit rate the CMI as a module and include it in degree programmes. If this were done it could even be made compulsory if that were thought to be appropriate. The introduction of joint honours and major/minor courses makes this very difficult, especially where course teams are trying to reduce the total number of modules taken at any one time, and in some cases course teams feel that they are struggling to work out how to cover the subjects adequately. It is likely that some course teams would perceive its inclusion as weakening their programmes if space had to be made for this initiative.

A Transcript of Personal Development

Discussion at a late Steering Group meeting centred on the search for some means of accommodating the valuable lessons of the CMI, and producing something in the nature of a framework within which other 'personal development' initiatives could be located. Wary of the unwieldiness and lack of definition of both portfolios and records of achievement, the Group came up with the idea of establishing a Transcript of Personal Development.

The Transcript would sit alongside the students' mainstream course and they would be encouraged to reflect on their total experience in terms of personal development and record significant developments in the Transcript. The Transcript would be characterized by its brevity, consisting merely of a listing, or inventory, of experiences and achievements. The Transcript would make it easier for students to demonstrate to employers the steps they had taken to acquire appropriate skills and might encourage them to look beyond the collection of marks for academic work.

This idea is neither unique nor particularly new. Brunel University has explored a similar scheme in its Diploma in Personal and Professional Development (DPPD). In this case the DPPD is specifically related to work placement. Currently a number of other institutions are developing similar programmes, particularly in relation to career planning.

The kinds of item that could be included in a Transcript of Personal Development would vary between faculties and courses, but would be likely to include a range from basic study skills, through more specialist subject-related skills, to career planning and development activities. At the same time, it could also provide the means through which other kinds of extra-curricular activity could be recognized, such as serving as a student representative or Students' Union Officer. Clearly such an approach would need to be framed very carefully in order to ensure that the opportunities provided were relevant, manageable and of an appropriate standard.

Concluding discussion

In its current form the CMI represents a fairly satisfactory first attempt, but much still needs to be done in order to improve it. Phase Two, starting in October 1997, seeks to address some of the issues and dilemmas identified and discussed below. The publication of the Dearing Report (NCIHE, 1997), particularly Recommendation 11, concerning the closer integration into academic affairs of careers education and guidance; Recommendations 17 and 21, with their emphases on key skills; and 20, in relation to the development of Transcripts, was welcomed as a vindication of much of the work that had been invested in the CMI.

The issues and dilemmas which the Steering Group currently face include the following:

- retaining the integrity of the CMI as more faculties wish to be involved and process larger numbers of students;
- whether the CMI should become a free-standing module in its own right;
- developing a workable definition of the Transcript of Personal Development;
- validating the contents of the Transcript; and
- whether there should be a minimum and/or maximum number of entries included within the Transcript.

Given the very different needs of faculties and their students, the creation of a uniform approach to career management across the College appears to be an unlikely prospect, despite the increasing recognition of the importance of the CMI in students' undergraduate experience. The Transcript appears to offer a flexible and credible means of recording achievements, and it too will be monitored and evaluated in order to determine its usefulness.

While the CMI's principal focus has been on student learning and development, implicit in the approach has been a commitment to staff and professional development built around a loose interpretation of the action research cycle in which review and evaluation are significant elements.

References

Cross, I (1996) 'Careers and the graduate', *The New Academic* (summer), 8–9.

NCIHE (1997) *Higher Education in the Learning Society*, Report of the National Committee of Inquiry into Higher Education, London: HMSO.

Chapter 13

Using Staff Development as an Agent of Change

John Doidge and Brenda Smith

Editors' introduction

This case study describes an institutional approach to educational and staff development which can create the conditions in which a commitment to capability can flourish. Based at Nottingham Trent University, a feature worth noting is that staff development is not seen solely in terms of academic staff – other members of the University's staff are openly acknowledged as having an impact on student development.

Doidge and Smith show also how the University is being able to exploit external funding to develop the quality of teaching, to the apparent benefit of both staff and students.

Introduction

Nottingham Trent University (NTU) is one of the largest universities in the UK. It has grown considerably during the 1980s and 1990s and now embraces nine faculties and some 24,000 students. It offers one of the widest ranges of student education, which includes a considerable emphasis on vocational courses by full-time, part-time and distance learning modes of study.

The University has been keen to adopt a strategic approach to developing the capabilities of all staff and in 1993 adopted a Staff Development Plan and a Teaching and Learning Plan which engendered and supported change.

A 14-point Teaching and Learning Statement gave vision and direction to further developments, supported by appropriate staff development networks and programmes.

The University adopted several mechanisms to implement its strategies, and this chapter gives an outline of two particularly important approaches – one supporting the personal and professional development of staff and the other concentrating on developing the professional skills of academic staff that particularly enhance the student learning experience. Both affect student capability – the first incidentally, the second directly and identifiably.

Developing institutional capability

Several approaches to developing capability were discussed at a conference organized in 1997 jointly by Higher Education for Capability (HEC) and NTU. A key theme was the concept of the 'capability envelope' – the cultures, systems, competencies, developmental structures and people that define institutional capability. NTU described its use of staff development as an agent for change and development within this 'envelope'.

The University has utilized both internal and external approaches to staff development, through which it has developed a range of award-bearing programmes for all staff, and has reviewed and revised communications at all levels. Recently the University has reshaped strategic plans at University and local level in order to encompass other institutional mechanisms such as appraisal, service level standards and statements, and objective-setting at every level. Of particular significance are the following:

- the continuing review of its staff development provision for all staff;
- the commitment to Investors in People as a benchmark for institutional staff development and management processes;
- the strengthening of appraisal procedures in order to ensure that training and development needs are focused and related to institutional plans, and are capable of monitoring and evaluating progress;
- the provision of a transparent system for promotion and reward for all staff;
- the development and delivery of National Vocational Qualifications (NVQs) at all levels for its staff (including Assessor development and the support of faculties which are setting up NVQ systems to underpin industrial links and student placement activities);
- the requirement that all new academic staff without a formal teaching qualification become qualified through the NTU Staff and Educational Development Association (SEDA)-accredited scheme;

- the introduction of the concept of reflective, self-managed learning and peer review for teaching staff through its Higher Education Funding Council for England (HEFCE)-funded 'Sharing Excellence in Teaching' project; and
- the provision of management training and development at every level and, in 1997–98, of an extended programme of management training and support for new heads of department and senior managers in order to ensure that they are equipped to carry out this key role (this includes a compulsory introductory module for new heads, and a series of core modules from which heads and other senior managers agree, through appraisal, their continuing professional development for the year, this being supported by distance learning materials, mentor and action learning group processes).

The University was among the first to require teachers without a formal teaching qualification and/or relevant and substantive experience to take a formal induction programme (now Module I of the Postgraduate Certificate in Teaching in Higher Education). This extensive support to new teachers embraces elements of mentoring, portfolio development and reflective learning, and has been tested against the rigorous SEDA accreditation process.

The University has also sought to accredit as much as possible of its internal staff development programme for all staff groups – management, technical, administrative, research and teaching staff. Through the Education Faculty Credit Accumulation and Transfer Scheme (CATS) scheme, accreditation of a portfolio of personal and professional development programmes for support and technical staff has also been available.

NTU was conscious of a gap in its support for teaching and other staff who have responsibilities outside the classroom and in the critical area of learning support. In 1996 a discussion paper to HEC and SEDA led to the development of a course proposal leading to a master's degree in higher education. The course structure mirrors that of the teachers' course. Inelegantly titled 'Postgraduate Certificate in Pastoral, Managerial and Learning Support', the course has as a target group admissions tutors, placement tutors, course leaders and faculty administrative staff, although it is open to others.

This extensive development process has been aimed at bringing together many of the elements of lifelong learning described by Senge (1992), in order that staff and students are embraced by a supportive institutional environment and demonstrable commitment at the most senior level to their development.

The 'Sharing Excellence' project

In this section is described the way in which the University has embraced a project called 'Sharing Excellence' in order to enhance the capability of its teaching staff through reflective practice and the dissemination of good practice. A key feature has been the involvement of students as partners.

In 1995 the HEFCE invited universities to bid for monies from a newly created Fund for The Development of Teaching and Learning (FDTL). The aim of this fund was to disseminate more widely the good practice that had been highlighted in the subject reports following the outcome of a teaching quality visit by HEFCE assessors. The University already had in place its Teaching and Learning Statement and had undertaken pilot projects on both peer observation and student feedback. The FDTL provided an ideal opportunity to develop and enhance this work further. The submission resulted in a successful bid relating to peer review and exchange of teaching excellence. The working title of the project became 'Sharing Excellence', with its aims to:

* share actively the skills and good practice that led to the designation of 'excellence' for teaching and learning;
* encourage the creation of a University-wide culture that recognize[d] the value of excellence in teaching and learning;
* provide a network of support and exchange;
* provide a system for effective use of student feedback by staff;
* disseminate existing and future good practice in teaching and learning more widely and effectively internally and externally.

The project is steered by a group which is chaired by the Deputy Vice-Chancellor. The Project Manager has responsibility for working with departmental subject coordinators. In each subject area there are between 20 and 40 staff divided into small groups. The peer review mechanism works in the following way. One lecturer observes two colleagues in each group and, in turn, is visited twice and given feedback. All the staff involved have received training in observation skills and the giving and receiving of feedback. Staff participating include professors and principal lecturers, part-time staff and research demonstrators. Good practice identified at small group level is passed to subject and faculty level. Subject coordinators organize faculty events to discuss themes resulting from observation and issues that need to be addressed. The holding of a whole-University 'Good Practice Day' on teaching and learning acted as a main focus for staff across the institution to meet together and share experiences.

A key feature is a widespread system of student feedback developed by the Student Coordinator. A staff resource pack on student feedback has already been developed in order to help departments and faculties develop their practice in respect of student feedback. This includes not only different ways of collecting feedback, but when to collect feedback, supporting student representatives, carrying out an audit, and evolving a strategy.

Students' views regarding teaching and learning have been video-recorded. The following comments exemplify some of the student views and highlight the importance of students in the learning process.

The more staff talk to each other about teaching the better it is for us. Peer review seems like a useful way of swapping ideas and encouraging each other.

The staff in our department seem to have been quite heavily involved in the project this year. I think it's made them more self-conscious. Well . . . more conscious of what they're actually trying to achieve in each session.

It's strange how little changes make such a difference to a lecture. The only obvious effect was that the overheads were bigger and clearer – but somehow the way she explained things became more straightforward as though she had thought through everything really thoroughly.

A web site has been developed in order to disseminate the outcomes and share good practice, initially within the University but, eventually, to a wider audience. A special edition of the University's teaching and learning journal *TALK* was devoted entirely to the Sharing Excellence Project and can be accessed electronically via the teaching and learning enhancement web site http://www.talec.ntu.ac.uk.

Under development is a Teaching Portfolio. For most staff this is intended as a vehicle for reflection on, and enhancement of, their teaching and learning practices. It also enables a member of staff to provide evidence in support of a claim of excellence in teaching and learning.

The Project has been running for 12 months, and already some important lessons have been learned.

Planning

A well-planned project, with clear outcomes, milestones and with an evaluation and dissemination strategy enabled the team to start on time and work to clear targets. Many innovations are started by a group of individuals with good ideas, but who do not think through the implications and the resources required, and who give little consideration to the need for staff release time if they are to carry out the activity appropriately.

Project management

It is essential to have good project management with a team of coordinators working at the local subject level who can motivate and cajole, as well as interpret and amend material to suit the local subject area. Additionally, a network of people across the University who work and learn together, and who share their talents and materials, has a synergistic effect as well as making efficiency gains.

Support

Strong and active support from senior management is essential. As noted earlier, the Deputy Vice-Chancellor chairs the Steering Committee which consists of deans and heads of department. Senior management needs explicitly and implicitly to support teaching and learning for, if it takes teaching and learning seriously in public statements and in practice, the chances are that the staff will do likewise.

Strategy

The development of a strategic infrastructure with high levels of awareness throughout the university is important. The Sharing Excellence project has included well-organized dissemination of training and materials, close liaison between coordinating staff from different departments and a network of support from both senior management and colleagues at local level. The network of support is essential if project activities are to be implemented effectively and changes embedded into faculty structures, faculty mission statements, curriculum frameworks and teaching practices. For embedding, a critical mass of senior support is needed – which takes time and energy, but is essential if the 'good work' is not just to fade away.

Evaluation

Evaluation and reflection are essential parts of good professional practice and themselves need to be embedded. As Hawkins and Winter (1997) observe

Reflection is far from instinctive. It needs to be forced in every way possible. It must be built into agendas and required in reports. It also requires trust. Reflection must be developed as a habit, the habit of learning.

The personal habit of critical reflection is essential. It is the basic building block of an institution which is able and willing to respond appropriately to changing needs. This is because personal change lies at the root of all organizational change.

In this project internal and external evaluators perform different but complementary roles and work at three different levels:

- local evaluation focuses on the groups of staff and students;
- project evaluation focuses on the project team and its management of the initiative; and
- institutional evaluation focuses on senior managers, deans, heads of department and their understanding of change processes at an institutional level.

Comments on the project from around the University include the following.

It made me think about the level at which I teach.

Peer observation has given me valuable insights into how other lecturers teach, and into students' level of knowledge, skills and expectations.

We have been able to incorporate the benefits into course development from day-to-day teaching, to course and module planning.

We discussed issues on which we are not usually able to find time to have a structured debate.

Sharing good practice is a good thing. Newcomers and part-time staff can learn from experienced members of staff and vice versa.

Peer observation has had a major impact on team building.

Reward

There is a need to reward excellence in teaching and learning, since the economic benefits of good teaching, in terms of attracting and retaining students, cannot be underestimated.

Conclusion

The two examples of institutional action to develop capability at the levels of the institution and the individual member of staff are complementary. Success on these fronts is likely to be of benefit to the development of capability in students.

References

Hawkins, P and Winter, J (1997) *Mastering Change: Learning the Lessons of Enterprise in Higher Education*, Sheffield: Department for Education and Employment.

Senge, P (1992) *The Fifth Discipline: The Art and Practice of the Learning Organization*, London: Century Books.

Chapter 14

Training and Enterprise Councils and Capability

Christine Doubleday and Karen Roberts

Editors' introduction

Promoting capability in higher education can be an expensive business and hard-pressed academic staff need to be well-informed about trends in the outside world. They also need good links with employers (and other groups) who share their interest and whose expertise they might find useful. Training and Enterprise Councils (TECs) are among the most helpful of outside agencies in both respects.

In this chapter, two experienced TEC education managers, Doubleday and Roberts, set out the terms under which TECs operate, the policy priorities for which they can provide funding and the kind of help they can give. The TECs' brief substantially overlaps the capability agenda and they are able to help with funding for development projects, provision of information, contacts with employers and the brokering of partnerships. A brief selection of examples of direct assistance given to the development of capability initiatives shows the range of help TECs can give.

Background

There are currently 81 TECs in England and Wales. Scotland has Local Enterprise Companies (LECs) of which there are 22. More recently some TECs have merged with their local Chamber of Commerce to form Chambers of Commerce Training and Enterprise (CCTEs).

TECs were established in 1990 and 1991 with the remit of delivering local training and enterprise strategies. They were a result of the December 1988 white paper 'Employment for the 1990s' and the TEC prospectus which followed (1989). TECs were charged with the task of placing 'education, training and enterprise in the broader context of economic development' and in developing local responses to local issues through local people and communities.

The TECs were set up as independent private companies, generally limited by guarantee with a board of directors selected from local private sector, public sector and community representatives. The directors (up to 15 in number) are unpaid and the structure and composition of the board is specified by the Department for Education and Employment (DfEE) and government.

All TECs are required to obtain and retain licensed status from the government to entitle them to contract with government to act as the private sector, local agent for local economic development. Generally the actual delivery is subcontracted to external providers which are closely monitored and quality assured by TEC staff. As non-profit making organizations any surplus funds remaining after subcontracting or other 'profits' made by the TECs are used for innovative developments or projects which further the TEC aims and priorities and benefit the local economy. Although the majority of funding for TECs originally came through former Employment Department contracts, TECs are increasingly bidding successfully for other funding sources such as European funds, Single Regeneration Budget and employer contributions.

The main aim of every TEC is 'to foster economic growth and contribute to the regeneration of the community it serves. Its special focus is on strengthening the skill base and assisting local enterprises to expand and increase their local competitiveness' (TEC National Council leaflet: TECs – What they are and what they do, June 1995). All TECs are independent, employer-led organizations and will work towards achieving this aim in a variety of ways, depending on the local situation. However, some programmes are common across all TECs, despite being operated differently to meet local needs. These can generally be classified under two main headings:

1. *Business and enterprise:* TECs work in conjunction with local Business Links to support local economic development through business support. The main thrust of business and enterprise work centres around the Investors in People standard which TECs promote as a tool/standard to improve company performance through the development of people. TECs can support companies working towards National Vocational Qualifications (NVQs), support business start-ups and support enterprise initiatives.

2. *Education and training:* TECs are responsible for contracting with government for the delivery of the former youth and adult training programmes. In recent years these programmes have been thoroughly reviewed and improved to ensure the quality of the programmes. Current training initiatives are output-related, clearly focused on achievement of qualifications and the participants obtaining jobs, and include Modern Apprenticeship, Youth Credits and Training For Work programmes.

In terms of education activity TECs will mainly focus on influencing the education sector to be responsive to the needs of employers and individuals. Many TECs are responsible for, or key partners in, Education Business Partnerships and Compacts which aim to strengthen links between education and industry. TECs are also actively involved in promoting the Teacher Placement Service through which placements are arranged for teachers into industry and reciprocal placements are arranged for industrialists into schools. This scheme has been very successful in improving mutual understanding of current educational and industrial practices.

TECs have also worked closely with the further education (FE) and higher education (HE) sectors to help them meet local employers and individual needs. Funds such as FE Development and FE Competitiveness Funds are managed by all TECs and TECs have, since 1994 held a specific role in approving FE college strategic plans as being in relation to the local labour market intelligence.

Role of the TEC in education

In line with overall TEC aims, strategies and priorities, the focus of TEC work in education will be around the competitiveness agenda. TECs will work with all levels of the education sector, often from pre-school through to higher education in order to contribute to local economic development, and improved local competitiveness. As well as the increased focus on lifelong learning strategies and individual commitment to learning, TECs are charged with monitoring and promoting progress towards the National Targets for Education and Training (NTETs). Thus much of the activity of education teams within TECs will be linked particularly to foundation and lifetime targets General National Vocational Qualifications (GNVQs) and attainment levels.

TECs are becoming increasingly aware that in order to meet the national competitiveness agenda and the NTETs they need to influence and collaborate with the HE sector. From our strategic planning mapping exercises, the key areas for interaction can be focused under five main themes:

1. Access and equality of opportunity
   - *HE should be accessible to all individuals and businesses who can benefit from its provision.*
   - TECs can work with higher education institutions (HEIs) to identify ways of increasing the flexibility of provision, eg work-based learning, modularization, credit accumulation, flexible modes of accreditation, customization and innovative uses of technology without dilution or loss of standards.
2. Relevance and quality
   - *HE should be high quality, relevant provision which equips all students to successfully participate in a competitive environment of rapid social and economic change.*
   - TECs can work with HEIs to enhance the employability/capability skills and to promote graduate employment within the small- and medium-sized enterprise (SME) sector. There is also much scope for joint working in the area of work related/enterprise aspect of HE and initiatives to ensure the quality and applicability of teaching and research.
3. Continuity and progression
   - *HE should support all students, actual and prospective, to recognize and realize their full potential.*
   - TECs can facilitate school/FE/training/HE/employer links to ensure continuity and progression and to increase mutual awareness and understanding of the different sectors, particularly within industry–education links. TECs will also have an interest in increasing understanding of the labour market both among staff and students, ensuring appropriate careers advice and guidance and promoting the lifelong learning philosophy.
4. Wider partnerships
   - *HEIs should be creating/embedding mutually beneficial partnerships with a wide range of organizations to enhance the learning experience and contribute to local economic development.*
   - TECs will be working with local partners to identify the needs of the local economy and the contribution that HEIs can make. TECs can facilitate the links, eg within the Single Regeneration Budget (now called the Challenge Fund), utilizing the varying strengths of the different partners and they can also promote fruitful research and enterprise interactions between HEIs and industry.
5. Regional, national, international developments
   - *Most HEIs as autonomous incorporated bodies, promote themselves as regional, national or even international institutions as well as retaining a local perspective.*

- TECs should support this wider activity of their local institutions as contributing to increased local economic competitiveness. They should also capitalize on joint external bidding opportunities in order to attract inward investment to the area.

TECS and the development of capability in HE institutions

TECs work with HE to influence the development of capability within the five themes outlined above at any of three levels of partnership; strategic, developmental and operational. The operational work is most likely to fall under three main areas, employability, access, and guidance and learner autonomy.

1. Employability skills

In order to impact on local competitiveness and to improve the local economy, it is essential to have well-trained, capable, qualified, flexible, motivated and continuously learning/developing individuals. TECs want to influence all levels of education to ensure that those students leaving compulsory education have the skills, knowledge and experience to form the basis of effective lifelong learning and development.

TECs acknowledge the need for subject specific skills and knowledge in specific employment sectors but also hear the constant demand from employers for individuals with key/core skills, motivation and an element of 'common sense'. Individuals who are equipped with the basic key skills – literacy, numeracy and IT and the core skills such as team working, communication, etc, will be better equipped to respond to the changing needs of industry and the constant vagaries of the employment market. TECs recognize that the skills of flexibility and adaptability will be paramount in enabling an individual to remain both employed and employable. For TECs the challenge is to ensure a ready supply of such individuals in order to ensure that the local employment market is satisfied and prepared for the future.

Examples of TEC help with student employability skills

Leeds TEC supported a project at the University of Leeds which aimed to improve the communication skills of medical undergraduates. The different communication situations were identified and written in competence terms and the programme was then incorporated in the second year of the medical course.

Oxford Brookes University has involved employers in the design of a motorsports component to an Automotive Engineering degree and they sponsor students with offers of work-placements. There is no guarantee of jobs following the degree programme but Tom Walkinshaw Racing Ltd, Williams and Reynard have already indicated that the level of knowledge which they now have of the curriculum and the students means that they are reluctant to see the talent they have helped create go elsewhere.

In addition to job specific skills, employers in Oxfordshire identified a need for generic business skills within the high tech sector. The University of Oxford invited employers from high-tech SMEs to help design 'Business Know-How' modules. Five short courses were delivered in March 1997, attracting 22 local delegates. The course is now offered as part of the mainstream Continuing Professional Development programme of the University.

2. Access

TECs will want to ensure that all individuals in their locality have access to education and training which will enable them to achieve their full potential. Barriers to individual progression such as entry qualification will need to be addressed so TECs will be keen to encourage HEIs to consider potential students who, for whatever reason, do not have the typical 2–3 A levels as entry qualifications. This would include those with vocational qualifications (G/NVQ), overseas qualifications or maybe no qualifications but a wealth of experiences. Aspiration may be an access issue in that individuals who lack role models who have experienced HE may not consider HE as an option for them. Thus TECs and HEIs may want to consider mentoring and progression programmes in order to raise aspirations of those under-represented groups who could benefit from higher level learning.

Examples of TEC help with access

All over the country TECs and Education Business Partnerships are working with local schools, FE colleges, universities, community groups and employers to develop intervention strategies which will address the issue of access.

One of the exciting TEC activities in Leeds has been the introduction of a model which enables academic credit to be given for learning achieved through problem-solving at work. This model recognizes that learning in the work-place is equally valid to learning in the university and is currently available from Certificate to Master's level in both University of Leeds and Leeds Metropolitan University.

Heart of England TEC is helping Oxford Brookes University to develop an 'Open Awards' scheme which will allow students to gain credit for modules of learning achieved outside as well as inside the university within a common framework.

3. Guidance and learner autonomy

Just as TECs want to see people achieving their potential, so they are interested to ensure that individuals in their geographical areas are progressing to the most appropriate next step for them and that the already scarce resources in the fields of education and training are not misused or wasted. Thus TECs will be keen to see individuals being guided to the right institution to do the right course, at the right time for them, not being guided by prejudice or lack of accurate information. For some individuals this may mean accepting that the expected route is not always the best route. The choice also has to be the best for the individuals and not the institutions, for example guiding a student towards a Modern Apprenticeship programme after graduation rather than a master's degree because the student concerned may need to develop vocational skills and core skills rather than more academic subject-specific knowledge.

TECs will be keen to see learner autonomy developed in order to instil in individuals the concept of control over their own destiny. If the local economy is to flourish, it needs individuals who will demand to be kept at the forefront of their field and to maintain their employability skills. Those who have developed learner autonomy will be discerning purchasers and participants in lifelong learning, they will want to ensure that any courses they undertake are relevant to their future work plans, and that they receive a high quality product for their investment (both time and money).

Examples of TEC help with guidance and learner autonomy

The Careers for Capability in the Curriculum project, jointly funded by Leeds TEC and Leeds Metropolitan University, aimed to ensure that graduates were adequately equipped to meet the challenges and demands of the world of work. Having identified the needs of employers and the current levels of provision within the University, the second phase of the project then developed curriculum materials and worked with programme teams to ensure that any gaps were plugged and that all students were given the opportunity to develop and demonstrate the skills demanded by the employers.

Finally, TECs want to encourage individuals to maintain lifelong records of achievement. This complements the work in the area of Investors in People from the organizational perspective and encourages individuals to reflect continually on their learning, recognize development in a wide range of environments and identify gaps in their portfolio which can be addressed.

Part 3: Autonomy and Quality

Introduction

The development of student capability has major implications for key processes in higher education, including the assessment of student performance, the way teachers and students relate to one another and the procedures through which student programmes are designed and approved. In Part 2 we presented evidence from individual organizations of how higher education is changing to meet these challenges. In this section experienced practitioners explore some of the more general educational themes which relate to the development of student capability.

Three of the chapters deal directly with students' experiences of greater learner autonomy. Stephenson (Chapter 15) presents a review of some of the pressures placed on students (and to some extent teachers) through the transfer or responsibility from tutor to learner, and suggests that if properly handled, such transfer can be empowering for students and rewarding for their teachers. Evatt and Boyle (Chapter 16) explore ways in which students are being involved in various forms of peer tutoring and support, with consequential benefits for both the helper and the helped. Butcher (Chapter 17) looks at ways in which careers and other forms of guidance are beginning to appear more prominently in the higher education curriculum and envisages the prospect of students placing their own career development at the centre of their educational planning.

The remaining themes relate to course control and quality assurance. If students are negotiating what is learnt and how it is assessed, what safeguards are there that the work they produce is both relevant and up to standard? Anderson, Boud and Sampson (Chapter 18) report on the use of learning contracts as devices for reconciling student initiative with the interests of other stakeholders and present advice to colleagues based on their extensive experience at the University of Technology, Sydney. In the final chapter in Part 3, Yorke (Chapter 19) presents a review of current assessment practice and the very real issues related to level, standards and comparability which have to be addressed when assessment systems are put in place which both support the development of student capability and provide reassurance to the community that degrees and other awards are awarded justly and with appropriate rigour.

Though not a comprehensive coverage of all the themes related to the development of capability in higher education – a major compendium would be necessary for that task – the evidence from the selection in Part 3 should reassure readers that the curriculum model for the development of capability which we present in Part 4 is well-founded in current practice and thought.

Chapter 15

Supporting Student Autonomy in Learning

John Stephenson

Editors' introduction

All students have some responsibility for managing their own learning and are traditionally responsible for the work they put into completion of assignments and revision for exams. This chapter is concerned with helping students who have responsibility for the formulation, management and delivery of the overall strategy of their educational development, and is only incidentally concerned with helping students get on with teacher-determined tasks or working through course materials on predetermined courses, important though these issues are for teachers trying to cope with greater numbers and restricted time. The focus of this chapter is on situations in which students have direct responsibility for aspects of their education which are either not often directly addressed within an institutional setting (such as student motivation and personal development), or for aspects which are the traditional preserve of teachers and accrediting bodies (such as the direction, content, pace, location and assessment of the student's studies).

Responsibility for what?

A full capability approach involves students, preferably in association with other students and in applied contexts, in:

- formulating the strategy of their overall learning based on an awareness of their own development needs (their strengths, weaknesses and aspirations);
- devising a programme relevant to that strategy;
- negotiating approvals for their proposed programmes and access to resources;
- determining the pace, location and character of specific learning activities;
- monitoring actual against planned progress and reviewing the continuing relevance of the programme they planned for themselves;
- demonstrating their achievements, if necessary against external benchmarks;
- critically reviewing the effectiveness of their overall learning experience and the relevance of their original formulation; and
- planning the next stage of their development.

Transfer of responsibility on the scale implied by the above has major implications for the support structures (course design, tutoring, resource management) provided by teachers and institutions. Where students are given responsibility within environments designed for more traditional approaches (invariably the case in the initial stages of curriculum change), tensions can arise for all concerned, particularly the students. This chapter deals specifically with helping students cope with such daunting responsibilities and suggests ways in which teachers and institutions can provide effective support.

Student anxieties and the taking of risk

A number of reports on autonomous learning within formal institutions suggests that most students experience some measure of *disorientation* at some stage of their programmes (Biloruski and Butler, 1975; Ferrier *et al.*, 1981; Taylor, 1986; Stephenson, 1993). Reports further suggest that this disorientation may be an inevitable part of the being responsible, can be addressed and, when overcome, can lead to substantial benefit for the students concerned.

A number of factors can contribute to students' feelings of anxiety: exposure of deeper personal motivations, risk of failure, unfamiliarity of the experience, and locus of control.

Exposure of deeper motivations

Taking responsibility for negotiating the overall strategy of their education forces students to ask fundamental questions about themselves and to share the answers (or lack of them) with others. They need to be clear *and explicit* about why they are in higher education, what is important in their lives, what their longer term future might be. They have to decide how best to use the next two to three years of their lives. They have to commit themselves to a personal direction, or if they are not ready to do so to be clear about any implications of their decision to keep their options open. Evidence from a recent study of non-completion rates shows that younger students are more likely than older students to withdraw prematurely because they have made the wrong choice of field of study (Yorke *et al.*, 1997).

A study of independent study students at North East London Polytechnic (NELP, now University of East London) identified five basic 'primary needs' or life-change motivators which were:

- builders of commitment,
- searchers of identity,
- earners of others' respect,
- provers of personal worth, and
- seekers of total transformation. (Stephenson 1993)

Giving students the opportunity to plan programmes of study which met the needs of their own personal development revealed levels of motivation which went much deeper than the more conventional reasons for joining higher education such gaining a qualification, pursuing an interest, having a good time, responding to family pressure, following their peer group or, in some cases, inertia. Getting to grips with deeper personal motivations relevant to their future can for many students be a difficult, unfamiliar and threatening experience.

As one NELP student reported on her experience of independent study: 'It reaches the parts other programmes cannot reach. It is about yourself and there is no way of getting away from it.'

Autonomous learners feel at risk

Student exposure to risk comes from having to take responsibility for the design as well as the completion of their studies. A number of concerns exacerbate what might otherwise be normal levels of anxiety associated with entering higher education for the first time. Will their ideas be relevant or considered good enough? Who are they to have a say about how they should be taught – it is 'going above their station' (NELP student). What happens if they are not taken seriously? Because deeper motivations are at stake the consequences of failing to get it right, to make the most of the opportunity, are more difficult to contemplate. And for some it may be some time into their course before the direction of their studies finally takes shape, causing anxieties over apparent lack of progress, particularly in contrast with colleagues on other programmes who are rapidly acquiring thick folders of lecture notes. Finally, students have to face the challenge of judging whether work produced by themselves, with little opportunity for comparison with others, is good enough for the award of their degree and for their eventual success in their chosen career.

Even experienced university students embarking on an independent study masters degree programme at Sussex University confirmed feeling at risk. The highest risks were felt by students who placed a high value on successful completion and who felt low levels of confidence that they could do it themselves (Stephenson, 1990).

The overall potential for anxiety amongst institutional autonomous learners is therefore very high. Bilorusky and Butler (1975) report a 'transition crisis of adjusting to the reality of self-directed study' (p.164). Medical students at McMaster University, report Ferrier *et al.* (1981), usually responded to their freedom by 'suffering a period we called the doldrums' (p.130). Marilyn Taylor's work (1986), based on the experiences of a small group of in-service teachers on a self-directed learning programme, discovered that all the students experienced a period of disorientation at some stage of their programmes: 'Disorientation results when the learner's experience diverges from his/her existing assumptions . . . identified by . . . confusion, anxiety, tension, a crisis of confidence, and a withdrawal from others with whom the learner associates the source of confusion' (p.60).

The experience of disorientation 'was common' to all students, says Taylor, though 'it was provoked by different experiences at varying times' (p.67).

Outside their experience and expectations

Most students entering higher education, whether direct from school or as mature students, are unlikely to have had any experience of institutionalized autonomous learning. Mature students will have learned from the 'university of life' but this is often not considered by them as 'real education' or made explicit until its value is explored as part of the programme itself. Teachers from six universities with experience of managing autonomous learning programmes (Higher Education for Capability (HEC) workshop on Autonomous Learning, Nene College, 1997) identified a pervasive feeling among students entering university for the first time that education is something 'which is done to you', and that it is 'the teachers' role to ensure that students will pass provided that students do what is asked of them'.

Locus of control

Another common observation, confirmed by Boud *et al.* (Chapter 18) and Osborne *et al.* (Chapter 10) in this book is the varying readiness of students to take more responsibility for their learning. To some extent what is described as 'lack of readiness' may be staff reaction to initial student displays of resistance or anxiety rather than an actual lack of readiness of students to respond positively to opportunities which they have not previously experienced. But there is a deeper factor involved with student readiness which needs to be taken into account, and that is the extent to which students have a propensity to believe they have the capacity to influence their own lives and surroundings through their own actions, ie whether they have an internal or external locus of control.

Stephenson (1990) characterizes *externally referenced students* as students who feel comfortable with instruction, predetermined syllabuses, judgement by assignment grades and peer comparison and who regard programme planning as a matter for others who know better. The main risk they feel is the possibility of external rejection if they fail to get a qualification – they may be seen by others as 'not being up to it'. *Internally referenced students* prefer learning to instruction, judge relevance according to their own perceptions of their longer-term needs, and need to feel ownership of what they are doing. The main risk internally referenced students feel is that they do not secure the impact they had planned or that deeply cherished aspirations may not be achieved.

In Chapter 1, a crucial distinction is drawn between dependent capability (position Y) and independent capability (position Z), the latter being promoted as the more desirable of the two states. The direct challenge for teachers aiming to help students to become more independently capable is not just to work with students who have an internal locus of control but to help the others to discover that they too have the capacity to become internally referenced. To achieve this, teachers need to understand some of the reasons for resistance and to be aware of strategies which can help students make the transition.

Strategies for developing independent capability

A number of strategies are available to teachers and institutions to help students address the issue of control and to overcome possible resistance or anxieties.

Belief in the value of 'taking it on'

The process of learner managed learning is itself a major strategy for developing independent capability. Even reluctant autonomous learners make progress towards independence when they successfully take on the challenge of their own development within a complex learning environment, see themselves making progress in terms of their deeper motivations and discover that they actually can have an impact on their own lives. As Bandura (1982) has shown, where persons can attribute significant triumph legitimately and directly to their own efforts, confidence in their self-efficacy is considerably enhanced.

Stephenson (1993), reporting on an in-depth study of independent study students, identified 'a cycle of legitimation' through which students pass when transferring from dependence to independence. This cycle of legitimation takes students through three recurring stages: acceptance of themselves as persons (I AM), acceptance of their right to take direct actions concerning their own future (I CAN), and confirmation that their own actions (or studies) have led to achievements in the field to which they aspire and which are recognized by established practitioners (I HAVE). Each time students re-enter the cycle, they have greater *justified* confidence in their ability to manage their own learning and professional development.

Taylor, in the study referred to earlier, identified a similar sequence of development. The in-service teachers moved from a state of 'disorientation' to one of 'exploration' by 'naming the problem' (ie understanding the basis of their disorientation and gearing up to doing something about it), followed by some 'affirming contact or exchange, however brief, with others who are significant to the learner' (p.69). Taylor refers to a sequence of 'reorientation', 'equilibrium' and 'affirmation'. Taylor's sequence, like Stephenson's cycle of legitimation, responds to 'students' need for 'legitimizing emotional states not typically acknowledged as associated with learning' (p.69).

The implications of the above for the development of learner autonomy are clear. Some element of personal risk for the student is not only inevitable but also potentially beneficial. Helping students to recognize and overcome these risks through their own actions can be a crucial part of the process of transition from dependence to independence. To achieve this effect, teachers need to provide structures and procedures which give personal support and reassurance at times of greatest exposure to risk, and provide a critical environment within which students can test the value, relevance and effectiveness of what they produce or do.

Supportive and enabling course structures

Both categories of autonomous learners, the reluctant and the enthusiastic, need the reassurance (for the reluctant) and enabling procedures (for the enthusiast) of a clear course structure with specific tasks, staged outcomes, public criteria for judging progress, procedures for securing help, and advice and ease of access to materials. Uncertainty about the student's own programme should not be exacerbated by any lack of clarity of the 'rules of the game'. For student reassurance, in terms of procedures and criteria, staff need to be seen to know what they are doing.

Few students can enter higher education for the first time with ready-made proposals for the programme they wish to pursue. Time must be provided to help students explore their interests and needs. A life-planning 'syllabus', described as the 'Statement', with specified staged tasks was developed in 1974 at NELP and presented to students as their first major assignment. In today's terms, this assignment would be the equivalent of three modules. Completing the Statement took the student through a logical sequence of five tasks (or, for the reluctant autonomous learner, teacher imposed assignments) which, if completed satisfactorily, would give students a basis for control of their programmes and give others a basis for judging the relevance of what the students proposed. The five tasks were to provide fully argued responses to the following questions.

- Where have you been? (prior experience)
- Where are you now ? (strengths, weaknesses, interests)
- Where do you wish to be? (aspirations)
- What do you need to get there? (what do you need to study, acquire etc?)
- How will you know when you have arrived? (what are you going to produce to show what you have done?)

As shown by Stephenson (1993) and Taylor (1986), the provision of opportunity for affirmation of the student and the student's propositions is of crucial importance to the development of capability. At NELP this was provided by an external validation board consisting of 'the great and the good'. At Manchester Metropolitan University, validation of plans from serving professionals was necessary before students could proceed. These validations not only protected the interests of the establishment in ensuring that student programmes were both serious and relevant, they also provided reassurance to the student that they were capable of putting together appropriate and manageable programmes.

Variations of the above life-planning structure and validation procedures form the basis of many learning contract systems (in this book, Boud, *et al.*, Chapter 18; Osborne *et al.*, Chapter 10; Foster, Chapter 7; Taylor, Chapter 11). A life-planning approach to programme design is also key to integrating careers education into mainstream higher education (Butcher, Chapter 17). Laycock (1996) uses the model for staff development and Manchester Metropolitan University uses it for students entering the final year of the social studies undergraduate programme (Wilson, 1996).

Tutor support for learner responsibility

Supporting autonomous learning requires tutors to go beyond their traditional roles as providers of information and assessing performance. As a consequence, like students, many teachers have anxieties about moving to new ways of working. From their analysis of 256 examples, Stephenson and Weil (1992) identified common concerns such as wariness of unfamiliar techniques, possible loss of status as a subject specialist with less opportunity for promotion, feeling unease at losing their traditional role as 'the authority' and feelings of guilt that they may be abdicating their 'real' duties. There were concerns that students may not learn what they need to learn and the logistics of managing different student programmes might be too difficult or demanding to handle. Many reported feeling exposed, insecure and at risk.

Many more teachers who have made the transition, however, reported finding the change to be both rewarding and intellectually challenging:

To engage students in critical dialogue about fundamental concepts, to be open about their own struggles with particular content areas, to share the pain and excitement of what it means to be a scholar, to help students to find their way through the growing mass of references and information sources, to test assumptions against practice, to help students 'talk it through', and to explore the provisional nature of what we currently accept as knowledge are more challenging and intellectually satisfying activities than the sterile communication of 'certain' knowledge and information. A capability approach, far from de-skilling specialist academics, can give new status to their scholarship. (pp.167–8)

The roles of the 'teacher' of the autonomous learner are more varied and, as the above evidence suggests, more rewarding and demanding than those required of the traditional didactic teacher. Their most important function is to provide an appropriate mixture of personal support and critical feedback. The following roles have been suggested as being crucial by staff attending HEC seminars on autonomous learning.

(a) *Fellow learner*

Tutors need to show an ability to share and celebrate learning, to understand learning blockages and frustrations, and to communicate the excitement of discovery.

(b) *Educational counsellor*

In addition to the obvious role of giving advice on learning needs, this role primarily includes being sensitive to the student's basic personal motivation to study and an ability to guide the student to a more internal focus for judging relevance and achievement.

(c) *Constructive critic*

In the absence of normative feedback, students need personalized feedback on performance which relates to the student's longer-term intentions. The aims of criticism are to provide rigour and encourage self-criticism. Ideally, tutor criticism should focus on student self-criticism.

(d) *Process consultant*

Tutors need to be able to advise students on programme construction, converting aspirations into aims and objectives, monitoring progress, preparing to demonstrate their achievements and gaining access to professional advice.

(e) *Specialist expertise*

The tutor's specialist expertise is often the most valuable source of affirmation of the student's own developing expertise when the tutor is perceived to be taking the learner's own emerging expertise seriously. The tutor also needs to know the difference between 'on the one hand' being available to the student as an expert resource and opening channels to other expertise and resources and 'on the other' being a controlling provider of expertise for the learner – and crucially, to know when it is helpful to switch from one expert role to another.

(f) *Positive attitude to failures*

Autonomous learners make significant progress when they address learning difficulties and learn from failure. Tutors need to be fully supportive of students who make mistakes, encouraging them to see failure as an opportunity for learning. Good tutors of autonomous learners are comfortable with their own failures and are able to talk openly about how they have learnt from their own mistakes.

Support from students

Evatt and Boyle (see Chapter 16) have shown how students can help each other with their learning through formally established peer tutoring schemes on otherwise traditional programmes. On a capability programme, well-managed support groups are particularly important, providing a general culture of interpersonal support where specialist tutorial help is not readily available. In contrast with taught students, autonomous learners have to deal directly with general educational as well as specialist issues. Mixed interest groups can play a positive role in helping students share concerns, explore ideas, exchange experiences and take risks. A home-base can counter the possible loneliness of an individualized programme and provide opportunity for collaborative ventures.

In his study of independent study students, Stephenson (1990) found that cohesive student groups, in which there is understanding and respect for individual differences and needs, are a powerful medium for the experience of acceptance and the taking of risks. Once mutual confidence has been established, such groups can sustain an atmosphere of challenge and rigour, providing a useful and safe context for the testing of ideas and proposals, and the exchange of constructive criticism.

Guskowska and Kent (1994) found that groups with a focus on personal development gave students more confidence in making decisions about their future, including changing direction. Cuthbert (1994) also found personal development groups efficacious in raising students' self-confidence. Evans (1997) gives a graphic account of the workings of learning support sets within the hard-nosed commercial environment of a national supermarket chain:

We decided to use a self-managed learning approach. In this way, people would have to take responsibility for what they learnt and how they learnt it. It began with an assessment of competencies ranging from 'How well do I influence others?', 'Can I do labour forecasting?' and 'Do I understand the legislative framework I operate in?' After an introductory workshop, individuals worked in 'sets' or groups of around six people. From the assessment, they developed a learning contract. It covered their learning objectives for the next six months. This was agreed with their colleagues in the set and with their boss. Each 'set' had a facilitator, a personnel manager who was at the same time a member of their own set. This was modelled from the top of the organization. My colleague who is the Retail Personnel Director and I had our own little set of two with an external facilitator; and we each had our own set which we were an advisor to. I commend self-managed learning as an approach. We have found this extremely valuable in developing the capacity for individuals to take personal responsibility for their own learning ... self-managed learning has helped people develop a commitment to their own lifelong learning.

A focus on learning

One of the most difficult things for autonomous learners is to judge how well they are doing. On traditional courses, comparisons with fellow students are relatively easy to make. Where students are pursuing distinctive programmes of study no such opportunities for easy comparisons exist. It is therefore crucial to the successful introduction of autonomous learning to provide students with the means and tools to monitor their own learning activities and to review the progress they are making.

One widely used approach to this problem is to encourage students to use records of achievement. Records of achievement are particularly helpful when they take the student beyond the mere recording of learning outcomes to reflection on the learning process itself. The better schemes often have titles which convey this purpose, such as learning logs, portfolios of learning and personal review of learning. If being able to manage their own learning is the desired outcome, students need to become conscious of how they learn, to develop the habit of seeking learning opportunities from their experiences and evidence that they can improve performance and understanding through application of lessons learnt from previous experience.

Donald Schon, author of *The Reflective Practitioner* and *Educating the Reflective Practitioner*, gave a live demonstration of reflection in practice when he addressed a HEC conference on Professional Capability in London in January 1996 (Schön, 1996). He was sent a transcript of his answers to questions raised from the floor for proof-reading. Instead, he asked himself two questions. First, 'Why did I answer in that way' and second, 'What have I learnt from the fact that I answered that question in that way?' Each question took him further from the record to an internal debate about his own learning, leading to greater understanding of himself and awareness of the significance of what he already knew.

Programmes need to provide autonomous learners with timetabled space, tutorial support and academic credit for serious reflection on their learning. The student's programme also needs to be responsive to changes the student needs to make as a consequence of that reflection. As students develop an awareness of what they are learning, and how they are learning, their confidence in their ability to manage their learning inevitably grows, as their feelings of anxiety about being at risk subside by the same process. We have seen earlier how dialogue within groups can be a particular help in this regard.

Many contributors to HEC conferences have testified to the efficacy of serious reflection on learning. Here is a very small selection of testimonies given to the 1994 conference on Recording Achievement – Implications for the Learning Experience (reported in *Capability*, 1(1) 1994, 80–5).

Judith George of the Open University in Scotland: 'Reflection gave me knowledge of where I was which in turn gave me justified confidence in my ability; helped me to define my next realistic steps and helped me to make my own judgements.'

Syd Donald, University of Leeds: Statements by language students after using a learning log to describe their year abroad: 'It helped me realize that there is so much I can do for myself, that I can make things happen, that I could be much more in control.' And 'The biggest benefit is in the quality of student–staff exchanges (about my learning) and the consequential feelings of being valued.'

Conclusion

Learner autonomy is only one aspect of capability. It is, however, a significant distinguishing feature of independent capability so its development warrants special attention. What deters many from its wider implementation is concern about possible resistance from students and the adoption of unfamiliar roles for staff. As this brief review of student experiences of autonomous learning shows, it is possible not only to devise mechanisms which cope with these concerns but also to raise the quality of the students' learning experience through the application of these mechanisms. Many examples of these mechanisms exist, but often in isolation. In the next chapter we suggest ways in which the system as a whole might be organized to ensure that more students leave higher education much more capable than when they went in.

References

Bandura, A (1982) 'Self-efficacy: towards a unifying theory of behavioral change', in M Rosenberg and HB Kaplan (eds) *Social Psychology of the Self-Concept*, Arlington Heights: Harlan Davidson.

Bilorusky, J and Butler, H (1975) 'Beyond contract learning to improvisational learning, in N R Berts (ed) *Individualizing Education Through Contract Learning*, Alabama: University of Alabama.

Cuthbert, K (1994) 'Facilitating understanding of group dynamics', in L Thorley and R Gregory *Using Group-based Learning in Higher Education*, London: Kogan Page.

Evans, J, (1997) 'Key skills for tomorrow's world', *Capability*, 3(2), 11–14.

Ferrier, B *et al.*, (1981) 'Student autonomy in learning medicine', in D Boud (ed), *Developing Student Autonomy in Learning*, London: Kogan Page.

Guskowska, M and Kent, I (1994) in L Thorley and R Gregory *Using Group-based Learning in Higher Education*, (pp.49–53), London: Kogan Page.

HEC (1997) Workshop on Autonomous Learning, Nene College (unpublished notes).

Laycock, M (1996) 'QILT – capable institutions?, in *Capability*, 2(2), 42–8.

Schön, D (1996) 'Learning through reflections on conversations', *Capability*, 2(2), 12–16.

Stephenson, J (1990) 'The student experience of independent study', doctoral thesis, University of Sussex.

Stephenson, J (1993) 'The student experience of independent study: reaching the parts other programmes appear to miss', in N Graves (ed) *Learner Managed Learning: Practice, Theory and Policy*, Leeds: World Education Fellowship and HEC.

Stephenson, J and Weil, S (1992) *Quality in Learning: A Capability Approach in Higher Education*, London: Kogan Page.

Taylor, M (1986) 'Learning for self-direction in the classroom, *Studies in Higher Education*, 11(1), 55–72.

Wilson, E (1996) 'Employer links in an honours degree course by independent study', *Capability*, **2**(1), 39–43.

Yorke, M, with Bell, R, Dove, A, Haslam, L, Hughes Jones, H, Longden, B, O'Connell, C, Typuszak, R and Ward J (1997) 'Undergraduate non-completion in England.' Report No 1 in *Undergraduate non-completion in higher education in England*, Bristol: HEFCE.

Chapter 16

Students Supporting Students – An Overview

Jean Evatt and Maggie Boyle

Editors' introduction

Evatt and Boyle report on a selection of initiatives in the UK which are being used explicitly to develop aspects of capability while simultaneously helping their institutions deal with their resource problems. The greatest benefits accrue to the helpers rather than the helped (though their benefit is significant), particularly where they receive training or peer support for improving their understanding of the skills involved and appreciating the extent to which they themselves are developing those skills through the experience. Rewards are discussed including academic credit for peer tutors. Giving groups of students mutual responsibility for managing their learning, it seems, gives students opportunities to develop aspects of capability not normally available through conventional staff-delivered programmes.

Introduction

The practice of students in higher education providing support for each other is far from new and is firmly rooted in the concept of collegiality to which the origins of higher education can be traced. The development of formal mechanisms of student peer support may be seen as a creative response to a rapidly changing environment which has the potential to bring practical benefits to all parties involved: the supporters, the supported, and those with a formal responsibility to ensure that learning occurs.

This chapter seeks to explore the nature of the advantages which can accrue from student peer support schemes to a variety of stakeholders in the higher education system and to give a flavour of the range of student peer support schemes in operation. It goes on to discuss the importance of providing training for students who are supporting others, with some examples of how this is being organized in practice, and touches upon some of the key practical and philosophical issues surrounding how student peer supporters are rewarded.

The content of the chapter derives mainly from a conference, 'Students Supporting Students: Principles and Practice', held in February 1996 under the auspices of the DfEE-sponsored Guidance and Learner Autonomy Project (DfEE, 1996) and from a series of network meetings organized by Higher Education for Capability (HEC) held in the spring and summer terms 1996.

Advantages of student peer support schemes

It is suggested that such schemes present win–win situations for all participants.

For a *participating student group as a whole* the advantages can be summarized as:

- formalizing support relationships between peers – to ensure that they are not left to chance;
- encouraging students to take responsibility for their own learning;
- providing experiential learning gain for all participants;
- creating opportunities for students to provide feedback to the institution about all aspects of the student experience; and
- mirroring mentor–mentee relationships which are increasingly to be found in the world of work.

For *students who are supported* within such schemes potential benefits include:

- access to support which is provided in an environment which is less threatening than a formal teaching situation;
- access to support from a person unconnected with the institution's formal assessment procedures – providing the opportunity to ask questions which might be construed as naive or indicative of a lack of understanding of that which ought to be obvious;
- providing a source of readily accessible support, this is especially relevant to support schemes which are focused on induction to the institution;

- providing new students with a wider social circle than they might otherwise have; and
- providing new students with additional 'listeners' who are more experienced than those at the same stage in their student career but do not represent 'authority'.

Student peer supporters may well be the group with the most to gain from the schemes under discussion. Their potential gains are more fully discussed below with reference to training and rewards but can be summarized as including:

- developing their own understanding and ownership of the curriculum, course, or community, whichever is the basis of the scheme;
- the possibility that the work they do can be accredited either as a formal part of their degree programme or separately as a part of a personal development/record of achievement portfolio;
- the opportunity to develop 'capability' skills; and
- (in some schemes) the possibility of augmenting their income.

Curriculum and pastoral care staff can benefit from:

- a reduction of pressure on their time without the fear that (new) students are being left in a vacuum; and
- the possibility of developing more positive relationships between supporting students, supported students and staff through open discussion and the breaking down of 'them and us' barriers – essentially schemes can create a different social dynamic which enables learning.

For *managers of institutions* schemes have the potential to:

- provide an effective teaching/learning mechanism;
- provide feedback from students engaged in the schemes which can lead to curriculum or service changes which enhance the quality of the student experience; and
- promote the institution as a learning organization which can have a positive effect on its ethos.

In addition such schemes can undoubtedly be viewed as a practical response to the deterioration in the staff:student ratio. It is however important to emphasize that student peer support schemes, if they are to bring about the benefits outlined above, require careful planning and the application of resources. Time and energy must be invested by the institution if gains are to be made.

A range of schemes

Schemes identified at the Northampton conference and by participants in the HEC network meetings included:

- a wide range of activities involving support for new students by existing students;
- student warden schemes which support new students living in halls of residence;
- work carried out by student unions both in training union officers and providing welfare information and personal support services to the student body; and
- mutual self help groups for particular groups such as international students, mature students, part-time students.

In terms of formally supporting the development of capability skills, especially amongst the student 'supporters', course or programme-based activity involving peer tutoring is especially important.

Course-based peer tutoring is a key feature of the induction process at Middlesex University Business School (see below) where a group of returning students work during induction week with new students who are about to undertake the same programme (Frame, 1996). A variant of this scheme, adapted from the United States, where it is widely practised, is one which seeks to put individual students who are about to embark on a particular programme in touch with an individual who has successfully negotiated the first year of the same programme. The possibilities and pitfalls of such 'buddying' schemes have been described in relation to a pilot project undertaken in the Art Department at Nene University College Northampton (Fajkus, 1996).

In other schemes induction is viewed as a process lasting for at least the first term or semester. Oxford Brooks University (Barton and Coloa, 1996) and the University of Wales, Bangor (Linford, 1996) have both developed mechanisms which formally link new and returning students throughout this longer period. These schemes bring together students who have an interest in the same academic discipline and provide the opportunity to discuss study as well as practical issues but are not directly linked to course content.

Peer tutoring systems create difficulties for some academic staff who feel threatened by systems which they perceive as an attempt to replace their expertise by the use of cheap, unskilled labour. It is this resistance which has largely resulted in the failure of the United States system of Supplemental Instruction to make any significant headway in the UK. Such peer tutoring systems as flourish in British higher education institutions tend to operate within clear parameters which clearly delineate the roles of academic staff and student peer supporters.

Keith Topping, Director of the Centre for Paired Learning in the Department of Psychology at Dundee University, has written extensively on the topic of peer tutoring. His contribution to the Students Supporting Students conference report (Topping, 1996) represents a useful starting point for anyone wishing to explore this topic in detail. Also important is the development work carried out by the Peer Tutoring Project at Ulster University (Jordanstown) which has resulted in the publication of a resource pack (Griffiths *et al.*, 1996).

Styles of peer tutoring include cross-year working, by far the most frequent style of working, cascading of information, structured working in pairs in which students might alternate the tutor and tutee roles and some types of group working.

Training student peer supporters

The importance of providing training and support for students who are acting as supporters cannot be over-estimated. Most schemes around the UK have some sort of introductory sessions for intending student peer supporters. Aspects covered include information about how a scheme operates, what support is available and the obligations and commitments the student peer supporter is undertaking.

What skills do peer tutors need?

The most obvious skills relate to the specific role of peer support and are likely to include the ability to *facilitate/model decision-making, problem-solving, study skills* and as well as some subject specific skills. Modelling as well as facilitating skills are needed because the student peer supporter, when faced with problems within the group to which the solution is not immediately obvious, will need to make decisions and problem-solve too. While some supporters may already be confident in these skills most are likely to benefit from the chance to explore them in a 'safe' way – before they are exposed to their group.

Beyond these obvious skills student peer supporters will not be effective if they are not good listeners, knowing how to elicit other students' problems or fears. Skills of *questioning and probing* are required. In other words they need good basic *communication skills*, which are not always well-developed among students. Student peer support systems should be seeking to encourage in all learners reflective skills which will enable them to direct their own learning, a key element in moving towards learner autonomy.

Last but not least, the skills of *negotiation* and *boundary-setting* are vital to student peer supporters who need to be able to structure their interactions within groups. Confidence in this area is about knowing what commitment is required, what it is expected the student peer supporter will deal with and what he or she is expected to pass on. There are important implications here, not only for the training phase but also related to the need for continued support for student supporters throughout the scheme.

The training scheme which helps student peer supporters identify the skills gains they will make (or have made) through their participation ensures that the rewards of participation actually accrue to the students. Those interviewing students often remark how unable students are to capitalize on their higher education experience because they cannot articulate what their development has been. Student peer support training, with an emphasis on reflection and self-awareness should enable them to articulate their experiences and what they have learned.

Some examples of training and support activities

Training across a variety of schemes has included the following elements:

- a frequently-asked question list to help with the information overload in training sessions for student peer supporters;
- a peer support group for student peer supporters;
- active learning sessions to help develop the skills that student peer supporters will need.

Returning students at Middlesex University Business School act as facilitators, guides and mentors in an active induction programme. The training of the returning students for the Middlesex scheme includes short inputs, discussions in small groups and presentations to the whole group. The two most important aspects of the content are, first, encouraging student peer supporters to identify how they will benefit from performing the facilitator role, and second, ensuring they reflect on their own experience of Induction Week, as the basis for establishing rapport with the newcomers. At the same time the involvement of returning students in a peer support role at an early stage introduces the practice of such support to new students.

At the University of Leeds Office of Part-time Education a mentoring scheme is offered to first-year students who have requested a mentor within their discipline. Senior student volunteers make telephone contact around induction time, and follow this up a few weeks later. In the initial contact the mentor will deal with any queries or questions not addressed by the administration process. Often the mentor will arrange to meet the student on campus to talk and show him or her around.

There are three forms of support given to mentors:

1. A *mentoring coordinator* who is readily available if issues arise that the mentor feels ill-equipped to deal with.
2. A *handbook/log book* – offering guidance on such issues as boundary setting, stating explicit skills gained from the experience, providing a place to record the nature of the contact being made.
3. A *support network* – this is a student mentors' group who meet three times during the academic year to review the scheme.

Also at the University of Leeds, in the Department of Philosophy, first year students, as part of their course, are 'proctored' by second-year students. The Department runs a Proctors' Training Course which is a peer support group for peer supporters. All sessions (except the first, which is 50 per cent information transmission) are student-led, some involving active learning. They include opportunities for the student proctors to consider and respond to a set of case studies of real proctoring situations and to discuss problems arising in their proctoring sessions.

Rewards

As indicated above both in the analysis of the advantages of student peer support systems and in discussing the training of supporters, all students participating in such schemes can earn intrinsic rewards. However, in order to recruit supporters it can be important to spell out both the intrinsic, and perhaps more importantly, the extrinsic rewards or benefits to be gained. Not least among these is likely to be the training which is provided for supporters as a prerequisite of the majority of schemes referred to.

Supporters can expect to benefit from increased self-esteem, the opportunity to enhance their personal and interpersonal skills and in the case of curriculum based schemes to improve significantly their own understanding of their subject.

Many schemes also provide opportunities for students to make a small financial gain. Such gains may simply off-set expenses; as for example in 'Welcome' schemes where training and/or the fact that new students may make an earlier start to the first term may involve supporters in extra living costs; or be gains 'in kind'; for example if student wardens are offered reduced rents. Payments to those involved in peer tutoring schemes can cause more problems. Any large scale peer tutoring schemes involving payment of peer tutors might involve unacceptably high total costs or create objections among teaching and support staff.

Increasingly student peer support schemes are seeking to accredit those who take part in the schemes as supporters in some formal way. In the proctoring scheme in the Department of Philosophy at Leeds described above, for example, proctors can gain a course credit for their work. Elsewhere there is a growing practice of formally recording the skills developed by student supporters via personal development portfolio or record of achievement entries which are endorsed by staff.

Conclusion

Formal schemes which promote peer support among students in higher education are apparently being developed at a rapid rate. Their main virtues should be seen in their potential for improving the quality of the higher education experience for a large number of its participants. In addition they can provide an effective means by which rapidly growing and potentially impersonal institutions can present a more human face and provide opportunities for students to develop key interpersonal and transferable skills central to personal capability.

References

Barton, H and Coloa, N (1996) 'Induction and peer support', in *Students Supporting Students: Principles and Practice*, Conference Papers, Northampton, Nene College.

Department for Education and Employment (DfEE) (1996) *Students Supporting Students: Principles and Practice*, Conference Papers, Northampton, Nene College.

Fajkus, J (1996) 'First words: the student mentor's initial contact', in *Students Supporting Students: Principles and Practice*, Conference Papers, Northampton, Nene College.

Frame, P (1996) 'Preparing students to support students at induction', in *Students Supporting Students: Principles and Practice*, Conference Papers, Northampton, Nene College.

Griffiths, S, Houston, K and Lazenbatt, A (1996) *Peer Tutoring* (resource pack) University of Ulster.

Linford, J (1996) 'Peer guide scheme', in *Students Supporting Students: Principles and Practice*, Conference Papers, Northampton, Nene College.

Topping, K (1996) 'The effectiveness of peer tutoring in higher and further education', in *Students Supporting Students: Principles and Practice*, Conference Papers, Northampton, Nene College.

For further details of particular schemes, contact: Philip Frame, The School of Management, Middlesex University Business School; Pat Smith, Office of Part-time Education, University of Leeds; Jim Parry, Department of Philosophy, University of Leeds.

Chapter 17

Supporting Learner-managed Progression

Val Butcher

Editors' introduction

In this chapter Butcher makes the case for learner-managed progression through learning and work, pointing out that, until comparatively recently, autonomy in this aspect of the student's experience had been given little attention. She makes the key point that, from a capability perspective, 'guidance' should be a learner-managed process and not something that is passively received. The Law and Watts model relating to career orientation, she argues, provides a framework which students can use to help them make choices throughout their lives, and is not – as some have claimed – a relatively static model for matching student to career.

The development of career management 'meta-competencies' is being addressed by a number of institutions through their curricula (see examples elsewhere in Part 3): Butcher describes here the way in which a 'Career Learning Log', based on the Law and Watts model, is being used at the University of Leeds. The developments she describes do not diminish the need for expert guidance but, if autonomy is to be encouraged to flourish, then a key attribute of the expert in guidance is the 'handing over' of his or her professional skills to the learner.

The case for self-managed progression

While the concepts of student-managed learning are gaining broad acceptance and currency, driven either by pedagogic values or expediency in the face of growing student numbers, a learner's ability to make effective decisions and transitions through an increasingly diverse series of opportunities in learning and work is too often seen as an *automatic* consequence of enabling learners to negotiate and manage their experiences within programmes of study, particularly if these programmes of study have a work-based component.

More insidiously, with the developments of guidance systems both within and outside higher education, there are often artificial distinctions made between the skills and knowledge learners need to progress through learning and those required to progress through 'work' – employment, unemployment, self-employment.

Recommendations on, and quality standards for, guidance provision in higher education have up to now largely focused on the enhanced provision of information and advice. The National Committee of Inquiry into Higher Education (NCIHE) rightly affirmed that,

... guidance in higher education should be learner-centred, confidential, impartial, equitable and accessible. Given the width of choice afforded by modularization, it is important that students should not be left to find a pathway through the matrix of opportunities open to them without adequate guidance.

The need for enhanced provision for lifelong guidance is also identified:

We support the notion of a lifelong guidance service, based on a partnership between the services inside higher education and those outside. In particular, it is important that students in higher education have access to an external, impartial, and independent source of advice. (NCIHE, 1997, paragraphs 8.42 and 8.50)

While such a focus is undoubtedly necessary and timely, it begs the issue of what autonomous learners can do *themselves* to manage their *own* progression effectively; making use of, but not being dependent on, the quality of guidance provision, whether good, bad or indifferent.

Vivienne Rivis, reflecting on the use of Higher Education Quality Council's (HEQC) (1995) *Guidelines* writes

The *Guidelines* were widely regarded at the time of piloting and publication as being notably student-centred, with their emphasis on learner entitlements. However ... it became apparent that the *Guidelines* had paid less attention to the notion of *student development*, and the role that activities led and determined by students themselves play in their own development, guidance and support. Accordingly, the student development and support section of the *Guidelines on Quality Assurance 1996* (HEQC, 1996) places considerable emphasis on helping students to become autonomous learners, both within and outside their formal studies. (HEQC, 1997, paragraph 2.3, emphasis added)

There is, therefore, a section 'Guidance for progression and career development' which includes within its 'Policy considerations':

Effective policies for supporting guidance for progression and career development are likely to be achieved when institutions . . . have strategies to equip students with relevant skills; particularly the ability to manage their progression, making the best use of the support services available, and to deal with educational and career decisions throughout life. (HEQC, 1997, paragraph 5.1)

The section continues

Institutions can encourage students to develop skills for self-managed guidance and career progression, by:

- facilitating access to impartial, accurate, comprehensive information on learning and career planning, and providing help in interpreting this information in order to choose the most appropriate option;
- helping students to clarify and understand their own experience and to obtain, by formal or informal means, a structured understanding of their personal, educational and vocational development, on which to base informed decisions;
- providing planned learning experiences to enable students to acquire knowledge, skills and competences which can be drawn upon in making personal, educational and career decisions and transitions, including supporting students in their dealings with those who provide or influence learning/employment opportunities;
- negotiating directly with other parts of the institution or external agencies on behalf of specific students for whom there may be additional barriers to progression. (HEQC, 1997, paragraph 5.2)

Although Law (1981) considered the concept of autonomy in relation to careers education and guidance, two recent initiatives have also addressed this subsequently largely unexplored aspect of learner autonomy: the DfEE funded a range of projects and a thematic network 'Guidance and learner autonomy' between 1994 and 1996, and Higher Education for Capability (HEC) has developed a network of member institutions which are 'Supporting student-managed progression'. In the leaflet introducing this new Capability Network, John Stephenson outlined the links between capability and self-managed progression:

An important aspect of capability is being able to manage your own personal, educational, vocational and professional development. This has major implications for the curriculum and its associated support systems. Access support, study skills and careers services are traditionally provided separately from mainstream teaching, but as the 'portfolio society' becomes a reality, we need to find ways of helping students develop the skills to manage their academic and career progression in the context of their previous experience and long-term intentions.

The challenge is to find ways of integrating life planning with mainstream learning so that each can be used for the benefit of the other. Learner-managed learning, a strategy recommended by HEC, has major implications for tutors and university support services. Greater variety of access routes and the switch in emphasis from jobs for life to employability in a world of change are already forcing the pace.

In order for this to be embedded in the philosophy and practice of quality in learning, a number of definitions of commonly used terms need to be re-examined. McNair (1996, p.12) reminds us:

Despite popular prejudice to the contrary, guidance specialists also see the development of individual autonomy as one of their principal objectives: it is no more the business of a guidance specialist to tell individuals how to manage their lives, than it is the business of the teacher of literature to tell students what to think about Hamlet. All would recognize that the ultimate goal is an individual who can act independently and with others, seeking help where appropriate, but with a well-founded sense of her or his own power to control and manage knowledge, skill and events.

'Guidance' therefore, is not a process which is 'done to' a learner, but a learner-managed process using, but not depending upon, the skills of the 'guidance partner'. This must rest upon some degree of congruence in the learner and the guidance worker's assumptions about what attributes and activities secure progression in both benign and adverse circumstances.

Similarly, the term 'career' needs to be reinterpreted in the light of the changing world of work and learning:

'Career' means the sequence of paid and unpaid work and learning throughout an individual's lifetime. It is assumed that a career will be more satisfying to the individual, and more valuable to the community if it builds progressively on developing skills, knowledge and experiences, and is not merely a random collection of experiences. This implies some degree of planning, while recognizing that all plans will need continuous revision in the light of the changing labour market and economy. (Employment Department, 1995, p.8)

The concept of capability is fundamental to this reorientation:

Capability . . . is an integration of confidence in one's knowledge, skills, self-esteem and values . . . Capability is not just about skills and knowledge. Taking effective and appropriate action within unfamiliar and changing circumstances involves judgements, values, self-confidence to take risks and a commitment to learn from the experience. (Stephenson and Weil, 1992, pp.1–2)

Ball and Butcher (1993, p.68) discovered that

The relevance of personal skills development to the process of career planning is not always made explicit by academic staff, who are more likely to limit its relevance to students' academic performance and immediate personal development. There is therefore a need for a clearly articulated model of the career planning process which can be shared by careers advisers, students and tutors alike. Making satisfactory links between the skills required by the academic context and those required in the process of career development remains a continual challenge.

Attributes for successful self-managed progression

What, then, must autonomous learners be able to do in order to extend this self-management to their progression through learning and work?

There has been much debate recently about whether the well-established and well-respected framework developed by Law and Watts (1977) of self-awareness, opportunity awareness, decision learning and transition learning still has currency as a model for careers education in the new 'portfolio' labour market, in which rapidly-changing technology, a global economy and increasingly multinational influences on the nature of opportunities both within and across national boundaries often appear to influence or limit individual opportunity.

Some misunderstand the potential of this model. It does not offer a mere 'matching' process, which links an individual's interests, skills and values to a 'wish list' of appropriate employment, but instead offers a toolkit which, if properly understood and applied, will offer a framework for the individual to progress through learning and work throughout life, making the most effective decisions possible in a series of changing circumstances. Originally written as a developmental model, generations of trainee careers advisers have been encouraged in the past to use this as a differential or 'matching' model and, with the shift into more conscious recognition of learner autonomy, there is now an opportunity to apply this model in its originally-intended developmental manner.

A self-managed approach to 'career progression' (see definition above) requires that autonomous learners, whether making decisions about course programmes or employment opportunities, must be able to do the following.

- Reflect in a structured way on the personal skills, interests and values they have developed so far and those which they wish to develop further in the 'next step' in study or employment. In a 'portfolio' society it is important to take regular 'snapshots' of what has been achieved in learning or work since the last change, and to be able to articulate and substantiate such insights.

- Understand how to research opportunities in learning and work, whether these are the module options available next year, an unfamiliar employment action, setting up a business or the possibility of extending experience by voluntary activity. An ability to challenge long-cherished stereotypes and to extend horizons is also especially important where opportunities are constrained by age, geography, mobility or economic downturn.
- Demonstrate to themselves insight into how they, as individuals, make decisions. They also need an awareness that previous decision-making patterns can be reviewed and changed, or that 'damage limitation' strategies can be identified on the basis of previous bad experiences.
- Take action to implement decisions. Effective action, in small as well as large steps, depends on individuals drawing on the information they have gained about themselves plus the information they have gained about the opportunity (course, research, job, self-employment, voluntary work) and their ability to have insight into their normal decision-making style. Effective action requires orientation (answering questions such as 'Where am I now? Where do I want to be? How do I get there?'); the ability to implement an action plan (including the identification of steps necessary to reach the goal(s); networking, the preparation of contingency plans; and the ability to cope with uncertainty); and the skills to cope constructively with disappointment. However well-prepared, some action plans will prove unviable, and it is important to learn how to review why things might not have worked out as planned, and build this understanding into the next action plan.

These are not sequential processes. The learner/worker can start the process at any point, prompted by the need to make course choices at a particular time, to cope with unexpected redundancy, or to decide to respond spontaneously to an advertisement for a job or course which appeals: the processes then develop in an interactive and cumulative way, so that skills developed at one decision point are used at, and developed further at, successive decision points.

Where learners entering higher education, at whatever point in their lives, have not had the opportunity consciously to develop and own such skills and awareness, these 'meta-competencies' of self-managed progression can be developed within the higher education process and, arguably, the provision of this should be required (and be a focus for quality assurance) in modular and work-based learning programmes where decision points are frequent and the implications of these decisions often significant. As Ball and Butcher (1993) put it:

Too many students may still assume a dependent attitude when broaching the question of their future career. Many may encounter difficulties in carrying out career and life decisions at both an affective and cognitive level. (p.68)

How can the development of these meta-competencies of self-managed progression be encouraged and supported? The processes and documentation of recording achievement offer a valuable delivery mechanism. In his presentation to the second meeting of the HEC Capability Network 'Supporting Student-Managed Progression' Rob Ward, manager of the Recording Achievement in Higher Education Project (Wigan) said:

The development and use of the skills and processes central to recording achievement: 'reflection and review' (of current circumstances, strengths, successes, possible points for development) and 'action planning' (the establishment of personal, educational and/or vocational goals and the planning of strategies by which these might be achieved) facilitate self- and career-management and the development of lifelong learning ... providing a key pivotal mechanism for supporting deeper and more effective learning and a basis for effective career progression.

Research already undertaken with respect to such developments in schools and further education indicated, he said, that

students reporting high levels of involvement in these processes ... were more confident when it came to identifying their own skills, achievements and experiences; presenting evidence in support of these and deciding on short-term goals and targets for themselves and carried these competences into higher education.

Laying the foundations of self-managed progression

An increasing number of higher education institutions are now more seriously addressing the issues of embedding 'career planning' skills in the curriculum through the networks and projects mentioned earlier, although in the earliest stages of development, this presents such a cultural change that, even in institutions with high levels of learner autonomy, this aspect of the curriculum still in many cases equates 'career' with 'employability' or, even more narrowly with self-presentation through curricula vitae. Some build in the development of key skills; understanding of the changing world of employment; the opportunity for work experience and the chance to work with small- and medium-sized enterprises. While all this is both admirable and essential, there is more that can be done to encourage autonomous learners to understand what they are gaining through the management of these experiences in order to support their decisions and transitions during the rest of their lives.

At the University of Leeds, for example, a Career Learning Log has been developed to underpin the masters degree of Research in the Built Environment. It attracts ten credits, but its primary focus is to equip the learners to acquire, own and apply the skills of self-managed progression. Three two-hour contact sessions support this, but the majority of the reflection is undertaken through the Career Learning Log (Table 17.1).

Table 17.1 *The Career Learning Log*

The Career Learning Log has been constructed to support you in:

- Recording key aspects of your experience from:
  - these Careers Development Sessions;
  - other aspects of the course;
  - other parts of your life (where you feel this is appropriate).
- Synthesizing and connecting this experience together, so you can:
  - develop a broader picture of yourself and your achievement;
  - identify your 'next-step' development needs;
  - construct longer-term plans for your future.
- Making use of this synthesis to:
  - plan;
  - prepare for, and implement the next stage of your career progression (whether this is to be further study, to research or development posts in industry, or something entirely different).

The Career Learning Log is constructed around four sections, based on the Law and Watts model (structured self-reflection; making decisions; researching opportunities and taking action) which – as was noted earlier – provides a framework for structured self-progression.

Another illustration of the 'self-managed progression' emphasis of this Learning Log may be found in the section 'introduction to researching opportunities', which demonstrates clearly how learning skills already developed can be directly applied to acquiring and evaluating data about career opportunities – an exercise which, quite shockingly, rarely seems to happen with more highly qualified learners.

Applying the experience in acquiring and analysing information you have gained from your first degree and your MRes is an essential career planning skill. Many students undertake less informed research about their future careers than they would use to write, say, a geography essay.

Once acquired, you will be able to apply these information skills not only to getting information which will help you to choose the next step, but future jobs and courses throughout life. This is a key skill which you are likely to need more and more as the 'normal' graduate employment pattern is more likely to mean that you will move through a series of organizations or occupations, through retraining, further study, possibly self-employment. Even those who remain for many years within the same company or organization are likely, now, to have to take more responsibility for their own career progression.

The Career Learning Log and supporting contact sessions invite learners to apply a high level of academic skill to their personal choices and transitions.

Career and course information can be accessed through three main sources:

- static: printed material/computer database/video;
- people;
- media.

It is important to be aware of the whole range of sources of information, and to get the best use out of them. This requires the same systematic application of processes which you will be familiar with in your academic work.

The assessment guidelines also reinforce this, for example 'researching opportunities' requires learners to

. . . review your recent practice in acquiring information from:

- static sources: printed material/computer database/video;
- people: primary contact/secondary contact;
- media: television, radio, hoardings, advertised vacancies.

Remember the criteria for assessment, which are focused on the extent to which you:

- demonstrate you have used a range of different, but appropriate sources of information;
- review and assess how comprehensive and reliable the information is for your needs;
- demonstrate an awareness of the skills you have had to use to ensure that the information is appropriate and reliable (including what you have learnt from negative and frustrating experiences);
- show how you might use the information to develop and implement your career goals.

The assessment of the log reinforces the key learning issues – that the ability to make effective plans for the 'next step' is not a one-off process and that the relevant competencies do not rest on the outcomes, but on *the extent to which learners can demonstrate that they understand and own the process.*

The Career Learning Log demonstrates one way in which the guidance specialist provides a structure for learning: learners achieve not only short-term understanding about how to find out about a job or course but 'own the process' in ways such that they can apply it in the future. This approach also makes no distinction between the process required to make effective decisions about learning and decisions about work.

Other instances in which student-managed progression is built into the core of a programme can be found elsewhere in this volume (see Osborne *et al.*, Chapter 10 and Gilbert and Reynolds, Chapter 3), and also in HEQC (1997), in which the Council has followed up examples of how a variety of institutions have built upon the *Guidelines* (HEQC, 1996) in developing strategies for student support and development.

The role of 'expert' guidance in self-managed progression

A significant proportion of staff in higher education invest occupational identity in a range of guidance roles. These staff include personal tutors, careers advisers, 'access' officers and student union staff. What, then, of the 'expert' guidance worker?

Della Fazey asserts

To develop autonomy in students the support of well-qualified guidance providers (both specialist and generalist), at all stages of their higher education experience, is essential ... The expertise of the guidance provider relates not only to specific areas in which the provider is working but also in their particular guidance skills which include such competencies as negotiation, listening, problem-solving and referral ... Sensitivity to the very different requirements of individuals – who will vary widely in their autonomy-related abilities and desires – and a willingness to hand over control to the learner, are necessary for the facilitation of autonomy. (Fazey, 1996, p.37)

The key issue, however, for 'expert' guidance providers engaged in developing learner-managed progression is the need to 'hand over' their professional skills in order to equip learners with the ability to tease out key personal attributes and goals and to understand how to research opportunities effectively for themselves. Some cautions about the need to prepare the autonomous learner apply equally to autonomous career progression: Susanna Gladwin (1996) maintains

It is not simply about the knowledgeable tutor transferring what they know wholesale to the student. It is about a process of assimilation and transformation (your knowledge is no good to me, unless I know how to make use of it).

Another member of staff at Middlesex University, Sarah Porter (1996), says,

... we cannot (though we sometimes do) just tell the students they are now 'self-managed learners' and let them get on with it – they must first learn how.

This invariably creates tensions for guidance providers, often overburdened with supporting large numbers of learners who have not yet developed the skills of student-managed progression. It is crucial, therefore, to seek to embed the processes of developing self-managed progression through whole-institutional cultural shifts, and to remember that this process can be developed by a range of methods and by a diversity of university staff and graduate employers. Stephenson and Yorke articulate this through the 'capability envelope' which places a diverse range of student activity into a coherent model to support autonomy in learning and progression (see Part 4).

Stephen McNair describes these processes graphically in 'Putting learners at the centre':

The various activities which we group under the generic name of 'guidance' include 'tutoring', 'advising', 'counselling', 'mentoring', 'careers education', and together enable individuals to find the best options for their particular needs, giving them the skills to reflect on their personal, academic and vocational objectives, to set goals, adopt appropriate learning strategies, cope with crises, review and manage their progress in and beyond formal education. Together, they have a central role to play in enabling individuals to take control of their lives as learners, workers and citizens, in an increasingly uncertain world. (McNair, 1996, p.8)

References

Ball, B and Butcher, V (1993) *Developing Students' Career Planning Skills: The Impact of the Enterprise in Higher Education Initiative*, London: Employment Department.

Butcher, V and Ward, R (1996) 'Career learning log' (unpublished).

Employment Department (1995) 'Prospectus for "Career management in the academic curriculum" project', Sheffield: Employment Department.

Fazey, D (1996) 'Support for student autonomy', in S McNair (ed) *Putting Learners at the Centre*, Sheffield: Department for Education and Employment.

Gladwin, S (1996) 'Support for student autonomy', paper prepared for HEC network, Middlesex University (unpublished mimeo).

HEQC (1995) *A Quality Assurance Framework for Guidance and Learner Support in Higher Education: The Guidelines*, London: Higher Education Quality Council.

HEQC (1996) *Guidelines on Quality Assurance 1996*, London: Higher Education Quality Council.

HEQC (1997) *Monitoring Guidance in Higher Education*, London: Higher Education Quality Council.

Law, B (1981) 'Careers theory: a third dimension?', in AG Watts, D Super and J Kidd, *Career Development in Britain* (pp.300–37), Cambridge: Hobsons.

Law, B and Watts, AG (1977) *School, Careers and Community*, London: Church Information Office.

McNair, S (ed) (1996) *Putting Learners at the Centre*, Sheffield: Department for Education and Employment.

NCIHE (1997) *Higher education in the learning society*, report of the National Committee of Inquiry into Higher Education, London: HMSO.

Porter, S (1996) 'Supporting student-managed progression and students supporting students', paper prepared for HEC Network, Middlesex University (unpublished mimeo).

Stephenson, J and Weil, S (1992) *Quality in Learning: A Capability Approach in Higher Education*, London: Kogan Page.

Chapter 18

Qualities of Learning Contracts

Geoff Anderson, David Boud and Jane Sampson

Editors' introduction

A capability curriculum in which students are encouraged to take responsibility not only for the delivery but also the design of their higher education programme poses particular problems within an institutional context. Learning contracts in their various guises are rapidly emerging as appropriate curriculum devices which appear to offer solutions to those problems by (a) accommodating the different interests of the various stakeholders involved (teachers, employers, institutions and students); (b) providing a manageable common framework for diversity; (c) imposing a discipline for rigour through accountability; (d) stimulating deep approaches to learning; and (e) encouraging students to develop a range of useful skills.

Boud, Anderson and Sampson at the University of Technology in Sydney (UTS) have been using learning contracts for a number of years. In this chapter they report an emerging consensus of support for the effectiveness of learning contracts from a variety of contexts world-wide, despite some voices of caution. The writers draw on the experience of their colleagues at UTS and present the reader with a useful guide to their successful introduction elsewhere. They report on difficulties on good practice and on what is non-negotiable. Finally, they offer some advice to academic staff.

Introduction

Learning contracts provide a way of structuring learning and assessment which allows students significantly to direct their own learning within the overall goals of a course. While they are becoming an increasingly common feature of higher education courses which promote capability, there has been little investigation of the expectations academic supervisors have of either the initial proposal or the completed work.

This chapter outlines the practice of using learning contracts and discusses common concerns which are raised. It draws on the experience of teaching staff who have used this approach over many years to outline the qualities such staff look for in learning contracts, to identify what is non-negotiable in this form of negotiated learning and to suggest ways in which learning contracts can be effectively used in practice.

Using learning contracts and negotiated learning

A typical learning contract as used in higher education is a formal written agreement between a learner and a supervisor which details what is to be learnt, the resources and strategies available to assist in learning it, what will be produced as evidence of the learning having occurred and how that product will be assessed (Knowles, 1975). It also specifies a commencement and completion date for the activity. The contract provides a focus for learning activities which are largely directed by the learner but which earn credit towards an academic award.

Although the most common term used is 'learning contract', in some institutions they are referred to as learning agreements in order to avoid the legal implications of the word 'contract'.

In using learning contracts individual learners are involved with staff supervisors in determining their own learning needs within a particular area. The method provides an opportunity for learners to work on topics of direct relevance and interest to themselves. It also assists learners to develop a better understanding of their own approach to learning and to identify sources of assistance available to them.

Although students are encouraged to propose objectives and assessment criteria the supervisor is expected to:

- participate in negotiating them;
- ensure that the objectives are appropriate for the subject or course;
- work with the learner to consider other relevant issues; and
- generally develop students' thinking about the topic.

The supervisor also has a responsibility to modify the proposed objectives if they appear unrealistic or inappropriate, too ambitious or too simplistic.

A number of claims have been made for the learning contract method with regard to the development of learners, their relationship to learning and the strengthening of their academic skills. The method fosters independence and develops problem-solving skills (Tompkins and McGraw, 1988) as well as being flexible in meeting different learning needs, styles and paces of learning (Galbraith and Zelemark, 1991). It also develops in users some of the competencies required to undertake fully self-directed learning (Caffarella and Caffarella, 1986).

Lane (1988) emphasizes the focus that a contract brings to a learner's activities. It engenders a sense of ownership of the learning process and, by specifying objectives in advance, both parties have an agreed understanding of the expected outcomes. In addition, the method aids the development of such necessary work-related skills as objective setting, negotiation, review and evaluation of one's work and acceptance of responsibility for outcomes.

Brookfield (1986, p.81) has described learning contracts as, 'the chief mechanism used as an enhancement of self-direction (in learning)', although he cautions that, 'the ability to write contracts is a learned skill, and facilitators must spend considerable time helping students to focus on realistic and manageable activities'. He also warns against assuming that the skill required to plan and write a learning contract is some sort of innate ability all learners possess. Malcolm Knowles has long been one of the strongest proponents for the use of learning contracts and considers the contract method to be the educational approach most congruent with the assumptions he makes about adult learners (Knowles, 1986). Stephenson and Laycock (1993) have identified the growing use of learning contracts in the UK and their application in both academic and work-place-related learning. In our own work (Anderson, Boud and Sampson 1996) we have brought together current best practice in the use of learning contracts in order to guide students and teachers.

While there has been considerable discussion of learning contracts as a particular strategy, they are one example of a broader class of teaching and learning approaches which are commonly referred to as negotiated learning. The characteristic of negotiated learning is that programmes of study are jointly determined by staff and students. Negotiation may occur on an individual or group basis and may range in extent from a single assignment to an entire degree programme. Proponents of negotiated learning argue that it is only through processes which explicitly take into account the diverse and specific needs of students within the context of non-negotiable requirements of courses that programmes of study can be created which are flexible enough to address new student populations.

Some concerns about learning contracts

The ways in which the learners and the supervisors are introduced to learning contracts is a recurrent concern in much of the literature on contract learning (Lane, 1988; Tompkins and McGraw, 1988; O'Donnell and Caffarella, 1990; Hammond and Collins, 1991). Careful attention to orienting the users and to developing their skills in using contracts is seen as important, or else the use of contracts may produce anxiety or frustration within the learner. Buzzell and Roman (1981, p.142) cite a case study where simply drafting the 'perfect' contract became a central concern and was seen as a major assignment in its own right. Not surprisingly, feelings of hostility and anxiety were aroused until finally the students came to the realization that the contract was merely a tool, a means to an end and not an end in itself.

Other problems associated with the use of contracts are fairly well documented. Knowles (1986) concedes contracts may not be suitable when the subject matter is new to the learner because decisions about what needs to be learnt can be difficult to make and the resources and strategies available may not be readily identified. O'Donnell and Caffarella (1990) also mention the discomfort teachers and learners may feel with a new and unknown way of doing things, the concern educators may feel about the academic quality of the resultant learning, and the time pressures the method imposes on teachers and learners. Hammond and Collins (1991) see inadequate orientation as the major problem but also mention the possibility that the method may make learners too individualistic and could lessen their ability to compromise and to accommodate others in subsequent situations.

Despite such concerns there is a widely expressed view in the literature that learning contracts represent a useful and often powerful way not only of promoting independent learning and the skills which this develops, but also of tailoring courses to the needs of specific students. That the approach can be used in a variety of situations and with a diversity of learners further enhances its appeal.

What constitutes a good learning contract?

Having used learning contracts as the main vehicle for learning and student assessment in undergraduate and postgraduate courses in adult education at the UTS for many years, we undertook an investigation into the actual practice. The views of 26 staff who had an average of five years' experience in negotiating learning contracts were sought. They were asked to identify what they believed constituted a good proposal for a contract and what they looked for in completed contracts.

Not surprisingly, the single most frequently mentioned characteristic of a contract proposal which staff expected was that it fulfilled the technical requirements of contract formalism, particularly in regard to clear objectives and criteria for assessment. This was followed by equal emphasis on the relevance of the contract to the individual needs of the student and attention to the learning process as indicated by the strategies and resources identified. Direct relevance to the course aims and content, relevance to the student's field of practice and the development of intellectual and learning skills were mentioned by fewer respondents.

While some staff stressed the collaborative nature of the contract proposal, only one required that regular consultation over the life of the contract be explicitly agreed at the outset – others may have taken this as a given or not seen it as important unless specifically requested by the student. It was an expectation of the majority of respondents that the contract would involve either new learning or an attempt to integrate theory and practice through reflection and research. The emphasis in any given contract often depends upon the stage or level of the course in which the contract is undertaken or upon the student's experience in the method. It was clear that staff regard the learning contract method as involving a process of learning and development and that this process is considered just as important as the final product, if not more so (at least at the negotiation stage). The emphasis at the initial stage is very much on the nature of the task to be undertaken by the student and how it will help them grow in his or her role (in our case) as an adult educator.

The qualities looked for in completed contracts indicated the assessment criteria staff use to evaluate contracts and hence the factors which will determine whether or not a student passes the course. However, the system in use in our own courses allows students wherever possible to resubmit unsatisfactory work by rating it 'incomplete' rather than 'fail'. This recognizes the individual nature of learning and that success or failure can only be viewed as relative to the original objectives and the negotiated contract agreement.

Indeed it was the achievement of the contract objectives which the majority of respondents regarded as the main assessment criteria. Through careful negotiation at the outset and subsequent collaborative revision as required during the project, the assessment criteria should be clear to both student and assessor long before the work specified in the contract proposal is completed. Hence most of the responses to this question repeated the qualities determined at the negotiation stage, such as evidence of further reading and research, critical reflection, original thought, and the linking of theory to practice. In addition there was a clear expectation by almost all staff that some attention would be paid to presentation and that this was an important consideration when assessing the completed contract. This aspect involved factors such as completeness, structure and organization, layout, clarity of expression and correct referencing procedures. Other desirable qualities included evidence of learning, a logical argument, a demonstrated awareness of the key issues and the usefulness of the project to the learner. One respondent mentioned the fact that the learner must feel pleased with the completed contract, which links with the findings of Caffarella and O'Donnell (1991) that the notion of a quality outcome in a learning project of this kind has a large affective component based upon the learner's satisfaction with the results achieved. The views of staff in our study are summarized in Table 18.1.

What is not negotiable?

Learning contracts provide considerable freedom for learners to select and design learning experiences relevant to their own particular needs and interests. Yet their use as a vehicle for accreditation in an academic programme naturally imposes certain limitations upon this freedom. For negotiation to be open and productive, any such non-negotiable features must be explicit and transparent from the outset. What are these non-negotiable components of a learning contract?

Assessment criteria

Assessment essentially serves two main purposes: it provides feedback to students regarding their learning and it indicates their level of achievement or competence to others. In a system based upon learning contracts the former purpose takes on an additional significance. Since they are not competing for grades, nor even undertaking similar assignments, learners rely very much on written or oral feedback from staff in the development of their academic competencies during their course. It is therefore important that staff are clear on what is appropriate to expect of students at various stages of their course. While this may or may not be published as a formal policy it is nonetheless helpful if some discussion of this occurs. Naturally the interpretation of assessment criteria will vary according to:

- the level of the course;
- the specific subject in which a student is enrolled;
- the size or scope of the contract; and
- the components which make up the completed work (eg oral, written presentation).

Institutional and staff expectations

In the context of a learning contract, the following were considered to be non-negotiable by staff experienced in the use of contracts as not negotiable:

- the learning plan, in the form of a written contract, must be formally approved by staff prior to the completion of the learning activities;

Table 18.1 *Qualities of learning contracts identified by staff at UTS*

Main qualities of a learning contract proposal	Main qualities of a completed contract
1. Includes clearly expressed, detailed and linked objectives, strategies, resources and assessment criteria.	Clear presentation, complete, well-argued and consistent (eg expression, organization, referencing, etc).
2. Based upon learner's identified personal and professional needs as well as specific course or subject requirements (eg course objectives, competencies, assessment standards, etc).	Meets general standards for the level of the course and specific course criteria.
3. Involves a range of learning activities (including, at least, reading and other investigations).	Evidence of wider reading and investigation (not limited to a few sources)
4. Requires theoretical ideas and concepts to be considered and related to the learner's own practice and experience.	Evidence of critical evaluation of theory and practice.
5. Develops learning-how-to-learn skills of learners.	Indicates use of learning strategies beyond those exhibited in earlier work.
6. Extends learners beyond their existing practice and knowledge.	Evidence of learning beyond normal work (employment) assignments.
7. Involves learners in monitoring both their learning process and the outcomes.	Agreed objectives achieved.
8. Includes realistic tasks and goals achievable within the proposed timescale and availability of resources.	Agreed objectives achieved.
9. Requires learners to engage in a 'deep' approach to their learning.	Evidence of work extending or applying ideas of others.
10. Proposal is actively negotiated having identified the requirements of the parties involved.	(Part of process, not product)

Note: the emphasis on each factor may vary according to the level of the course, the stage of development of the learner and their experience in using a contract approach.

- the contract proposal must fall within the bounds of the subject and be consistent with the objectives or competencies of the subject in which the student is enrolled. In the case of individualized projects which cross subjects the proposal must be consistent with the overall goals of the course;
- for students currently employed, the work presented cannot be solely that produced for a work assignment in their organization. However, such work may form a major part of a contract if agreed by an adviser so long as there is documented evidence of additional subject/course-related learning;
- the completed work must be presented using inclusive language;
- the level of achievement to be demonstrated (in, for example, writing, analysis and skill of performance) must be consistent with the level of course and the stage of the course reached by the student; and
- final work must be submitted each semester by the announced/agreed deadlines.

Factors related to level

The following are also normally non-negotiable features and the interpretation of them can be expected to vary according to the level of the course. However, in the case of a sequence of contracts in an access course, it would not be necessary that each contract met the requirement although the sequence of contracts taken together should do so. The level of a contract can be judged by the extent to which:

- work which is descriptive also attempts to reflect upon personal experience;
- there is appropriate reference to the literature;
- argument is supported by evidence;
- multiple sources are used;
- there is evidence of analysis and critical thinking.

Advice to staff on the effective use of learning contracts

There are three main points of focus in the use of learning contracts: the document which forms the original agreement, the product finally submitted for assessment, and the learning process itself. In the last case continuous renegotiation, collaborative decision-making and student self-determination in relation to outcomes are of prime concern (Tompkins and McGraw, 1988). Hence the supervisor's role is central to the successful implementation of the contract method and may require redefinition at different stages of the project. While the role shift from teacher to facilitator of learning is not new in education contexts, the shift back to assessor upon completion of the project may create difficulties.

The following points summarize our experience and that of our colleagues on using learning contracts effectively.

Roles

- Staff and students must be fully aware that the choice of topic is largely determined by the student but the supervisor is involved in negotiating issues around the topic. The supervisor may also request clarification of objectives; strategies and resources will be discussed mutually; the product will be agreed to in advance but the supervisor will be the judge of whether it meets the course standards. The supervisor will assist and discuss the project but ultimately the student must accept responsibility for its implementation.

Student readiness

- Expect initial confusion and anxiety. This is normal in any situation in which students are asked to take greater responsibility than they are used to. Be flexible and perhaps allow new students to undertake a smaller contract before embarking on a full-scale project.
- When negotiating a possible topic area, start with a problem or an interest. Encourage the learner to consider what difficulties he or she is experiencing within the course or at work, or perhaps what triggers interest in the literature or which competencies need to be developed. These will establish the focus for the learning contract.

Review and renegotiation

- Set aside time to review and, if necessary, renegotiate the contract. This process should continue until the contract is finally submitted.

Tutorial and other support

- The contract method provides the opportunity to make learning relevant and interesting but it does not guarantee that this will happen. Equally, while it provides an opportunity to develop research and study skills, students may still need to be supported in developing such skills. It should not be assumed that all students are naturally self-directed learners. Identify the student's concerns, expectations, strengths and weaknesses early in the advising process and use these to develop appropriate learning strategies.

- Ensure the student has identified as many resources as possible. Resources include people journals and newspapers, radio and television programmes, films and videos recordings, training materials, computer programmes, libraries, government departments, other organizations, etc. Many students fail to look beyond a few books.
- Maintain enthusiasm and a belief in the opportunities the method provides.

Relate to students' longer-term needs and progression

- Monitor the student's learning career and aim for a balance across topic areas when negotiating new contracts. Consider a progression of learning/reflective skills which contracts should display. For example, an initial contract may be about a simple descriptive or narrative account of an event while later contracts would bring in reading and reflection, then critical analysis and finally original theories. An alternative schema would involve restrictive contracts to cover core competencies at first, followed by increasing the options until the student is able to draft complete proposals based on particular interests.

Assessment and feedback

- Establish assessment criteria at an early stage. The student should be in no doubt as to the supervisor's expectations or the institution's academic requirements.
- Provide evaluative feedback as soon as possible. Preferably this should be done in person. Whether or not grades are recorded, it is important for students to feel that their work is valued by being told directly. Similarly, areas of deficiency need to be identified and explained so that amendments can be made.

(Note: a more detailed discussion of all of these issues can be found in Anderson, Boud and Sampson (1996)).

Some staffing issues

By the end of their studies some of our students will have negotiated a very large number of learning contracts. Negotiation of the first few are time consuming for staff but there is a very rapid decrease in the amount of time required as students become confident about organizing their own learning. Staff are used efficiently, they find reading contract work far more interesting than standard assignments, and students express great satisfaction with being able to create a programme which meets their own needs and aspirations. However, the use of contracts implies a shift of staffing from later year courses to first year and new ways of counting staff work-load. While there may be an increase in staff load if there is only a very small amount of negotiated contracts in a course, they have been used *within* the constraints of normal staff resource levels in many professional schools.

Conclusion

This chapter has, for the sake of simplicity, focused on the use of contracts negotiated between individual students and supervisors. Today there is increasing use of other forms of negotiated learning, including negotiations between classes of students and staff and three-way learning contracts for work-based learning negotiated between students, academic advisers and work-place supervisors. It is a rapidly-developing area and offers many opportunities to make courses more flexible while fostering the develop-ment of capability.

Acknowledgement

This chapter draws on a paper by the same authors 'Expectations of quality in the use of learning contracts' originally published in *Capability: The International Journal of Higher Education for Capability*. 1(1) 22–31, 1994.

References

Anderson, G, Boud, D and Sampson, J (1996) *Learning Contracts: A Practical Guide*, London: Kogan Page.

Brookfield, S (1986) *Understanding and Facilitating Adult Learning*. San Francisco: Jossey-Bass.

Buzzell, N and Roman, O (1981) 'Preparing for contract learning', in D Boud (ed) *Developing Student Autonomy in Learning*, (pp.135–44), London: Kogan Page.

Caffarella, RS and Caffarella, EP (1986) 'Self-directedness and learning contracts in adult education', *Adult Education Quarterly*, 36(4), 226–34.

Caffarella, RS and O'Donnell, J M (1991) 'Judging the quality of work-related, self-directed learning', *Adult Education Quarterly*, 42(1), 17–29.

Galbraith, MW and Zelemark, BS (1991) 'Adult learning methods and techniques', in MW Galbraith (ed), *Facilitating Adult Learning*, Malabar, Fla.: Krieger Publishing.

Hammond, M and Collins, R (1991) *Self-Directed Learning: Critical Practice*, London: Kogan Page.

Knowles, M (1975) *Self-Directed Learning: A Guide for Learners and Teachers*, Chicago: Follett.

Knowles, M (1986). *Using Learning Contracts*, San Francisco: Jossey-Bass.

Lane, D (1988) 'Using learning contracts: pitfalls and benefits for adult learners', *Training and Development in Australia*, **15**(1), 7–9.

O'Donnell, JM and Caffarella, RS (1990) 'Learning contracts', in MW Galbraith (ed), *Adult Learning Methods*, (pp.133–60), Malabar, Fla.: Krieger Publishing.

Smith, RM (1982). *Learning How to Learn*. Chicago: Follett.

Stephenson, J and Laycock, M (eds) (1993) *Using Learning Contracts in Higher Education*, London: Kogan Page.

Tompkins, C and McGraw, M-J (1988) 'The negotiated learning contract', in D Boud (ed), *Developing Student Autonomy in Learning*, (pp.172–191), (2nd edn), London: Kogan Page.

Chapter 19

Assessing Capability

Mantz Yorke

Editors' introduction

Capability is a holistic concept which, in a climate in which curricula are progressively being unitized, presents particular challenges to those concerned with assessment. Yorke outlines a number of difficulties with the assessment of capability and points to some developments which have the potential to contribute to the assessment of capability in its fullest sense. Assessment, he argues, is too important to be left to a relatively unconsidered end of the validation/approval process: instead, it probably needs to be given more time than most curricula currently allow, with implications for the distribution of staff time. Further, there is a need, in higher education, for the general level of expertise in assessment to be raised, implying considerable future staff development activity in this direction.

There is probably more bad practice and ignorance of significant issues in the area of assessment than in any other aspect of higher education. This would not be so bad if it were not for the fact that the effects of bad practice are far more potent than they are for any aspect of teaching. Students can, with difficulty, escape from the effects of poor teaching, they cannot (by definition, if they want to graduate) escape the effects of poor assessment. (Boud, 1995a, p.35.)

The assessment of capability has to be considered in the national and institutional contexts. Recently articulated in the report of the National Commission of Inquiry into Higher Education (NCIHE, 1997), there has nevertheless long been a call for higher education to have a vocational relevance: it is often forgotten that this was stated in the first of the four principles for higher education that were expressed in the Robbins report (Robbins, 1963), though in the intervening years it has been given slightly different shades of colouring. The questions have been not whether higher education should serve vocational expectations, but the extent to which, and how, these expectations should be served. The progressive globalization of national economies and developments in communications technology mean that solutions that were appropriate a couple of decades ago are no longer appropriate for a rapidly-changing world of employment. From different positions on the political spectrum, Hague (1991), Reich (1991) and Hutton (1996) all point to a work-force that will be differentiated according to broad, generic skills instead of the traditional segmentation of occupations. Reich, for instance, indicates that the work-force will be subdivided between innovators, generalists, service providers and the providers of more menial services. Higher education serves primarily the first three categories.

As higher education in the UK has expanded over the last two decades (raising the proportion of the 18+ intake from about one in eight to nearly one in three, and markedly increasing the numbers entering at ages greater than 21), so the variety of programmes on offer has expanded. Programme validation and approval has increasingly involved representatives from the world of employment, and there is now less 'supply-side determinism' by institutions regarding programme content. The introduction, in the late 1980s, of the Enterprise in Higher Education (EHE) Initiative by the then Manpower Services Commission (later the Employment Department) provided selected institutions with extra funding to implement the development in students of skills related to employment. The term 'transferable skills' will be used here for convenience, though transferability is a more problematic concept than some of the rhetoric on the subject tends to allow. Transferable skills can be seen, for convenience, as being complementary to 'academic skills', though the two are considerably interwoven – often inextricably.

There are many expressions of the transferable skills desired by employers, as the NCIHE (1997) points out. Lists of desired skills tend to include most of the following:

- communication
- numeracy
- use of information technology
- critical analysis
- problem-solving
- capacity to manage one's workload
- ability to relate to others
- teamworking
- ability to learn throughout life.[1]

The risk of listing transferable skills in this way is that they may become segregated in curricula and miss the integration that is necessary for the demonstration of the capability to handle the 'messiness' of problems in the real world.[2] There is plenty of evidence from a variety of fields that problems often do not present themselves in a form for which a standard solution can satisfactorily be applied: acknowledgement of this point is provided, for example, by Meehl (1957), who entitled an article 'When shall we use our heads instead of the formula?' (recognizing that people do not present as standard psychological textbook cases), and by Morgan and Murgatroyd (1994), who talk of total quality in the service sector in terms of the ability of the service provider to make the correct *differentiated* response to the client (ie they acknowledge the uniqueness of the client-problem combination). As Stephenson has made clear in Part 1, it is this 'non-standardness' of problems, coupled with the pace of development in the world, that make capability so much more than the ability to display expertise in learned routines. This has profound implications for curricula and, within curricula, for assessment. Before we get into assessment, however, we need to spend a little time on curricula.

Curricula in higher education have changed markedly in structure in recent years, in response to demands for greater flexibility for students and for more economical use of resources. It is debatable which driver has been the stronger, not that this matters for the present purpose, where the implications of the outcomes for capability and its assessment form the crux of interest. Flexibility has been captured through the unitization of curricula, now almost always within a semesterized academic year. Curricular units are increasingly being expressed in terms of learning outcomes, though the link between expectations and the assessment of achievement is quite frequently not as strong as it might be. Part of the difficulty stems from the problem of reconciling programme aims (which are of necessity broad and general) with the more specific expected learning outcomes of the component units.[3] The integrative nature of capability brings this issue to the fore.

Unitized curricula will address most, if not all, of the skills listed above: for example, Chance (1994) describes how transferable skills are embedded in a compulsory core of modules in geography at Oxford Brookes University. The difficulty however, from a capability perspective, is that different skills may be emphasized in different units, with the result that integration may be left to some kind of project unit (or suchlike) or perhaps to the student's (unassessed) capacity to make connections between the various components of his or her learning.[4] The situation can be symbolized in Figure 19.1, in which the blocks represent curricular units, and the shaded blocks indicate where skills such as those listed above are emphasized: the point of the symbolization is to demonstrate the risk of disconnection between the skills.

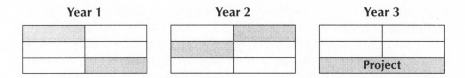

Figure 19.1 *Symbolization of a unitized curriculum in which transferable skills are emphasized in a proportion of units.*

An option that has been piloted in the School of Media, Critical and Creative Arts at Liverpool John Moores University (JMU) is the award of a National Vocational Qualification (NVQ) at Level 1 for the transferable skills component of their studies, as a complement to the degree. For this, the student has to produce evidence that he or she has acquired the skills specified in the schedule for the award. This goes some way to ameliorate the fragmentation of transferable skills in a unitized curriculum.

Sandwich and some professional programmes (eg Social Work, Teacher Education) use one or more periods in employment to develop students' awareness of, and skills related to, the world of work. For some of these programmes the period of placement is assessed, and the assessment provides the certification that the student is a fit person to practise in the profession. For others, the assessment may be relatively token, or it may – as it does at JMU and a small number of other institutions – lead to a senior award of City and Guilds of London Institute in addition to the degree (see Jackson *et al.*, Chapter 9).

Assessment is a vital part of curriculum design, but is often given less detailed attention in the validation and approval process than it merits. There are three main purposes of assessment: diagnostic, formative and summative. The diagnostic purpose, as far as student ability is concerned, is relatively little used in higher education but, as greater emphasis is placed on the student's learning from learning packages, the diagnosis of strengths and weaknesses prior to engaging with the materials becomes of particular importance. Formative assessment provides feedback to students regarding their progress, with the aim of assisting learning: it is one of the weaknesses of the unitization of curricula that the duration of many units makes the setting and grading of assignments for formative purposes much more difficult to achieve than in 'traditional' year-long segments of courses. Summative assessment is undertaken in order to provide judgement about the student's achievements: where this is in the form of question papers in an examination hall, the likelihood is that little feedback will be given to the student other than the mark or grade. Even so, there is some formative component to summative assessment (either explicit or implicit). There is a second angle to the diagnostic purpose of assessment, which relates not to student attainment but to the quality control procedures operated by an institution. The three purposes of assessment can be presented in an elaborated configuration such as that of Table 19.1, though the distinction between the three purposes is, for some items, not as clear-cut as presented here – for example, the level of achievement at the end of a unit can comprise a summative judgement regarding the award of academic credit.

Table 19.1 *Purposes of assessment* (From Yorke (1995), with acknowledgement to Atkins *et al.* (1993))

Learning	To motivate students
	To diagnose strengths and weaknesses
	To provide feedback
	To consolidate work done to date
	To establish the level of achievement at the end of a unit
Certification	To establish the level of achievement at the end of a programme
	To underwrite a 'licence to practise'
	To demonstrate conformity with relevant external regulations
	To select for employment, further training, etc
	To predict future performance
Quality control	To assess the extent to which a programme has achieved its aims
	To judge the effectiveness of the learning environment
	To provide feedback to staff regarding their individual effectiveness
	To monitor standards of achievement over time

Summative assessment is of obvious importance to higher education's external stakeholders, even if it is not without controversy. There seems now to be an annual debate over whether the standards of degrees are declining with the massification of the system (particularly in the former polytechnics), running in parallel with that relating to whether the increasing pass rate at A level betokens an easing of that examination. In this rather fevered environment, it is not surprising that the former Higher Education Quality Council (HEQC) was pressed by government to conduct various investigations into standards in higher education[5], and, to those who have studied the matter, that it is difficult to reach unequivocal conclusions about the relationship between standards and time.

Assessment is particularly important to students, in the sense that assessment specifications send signals to them about what is valued, and hence about those aspects of their studies on which they might concentrate with advantage. If transferable skills are not given a measure of prominence in assessment schemes, then students will not be particularly encouraged to work on them. The Final Report of the Graduate Standards Programme (HEQC 1997c, paragraph 5.2.13) draws attention to the problem: '. . . it is not always clear how far the development of generic skills is made explicit in the curriculum, nor what relative value is placed on them in the process of assessment.'

Capability draws attention to the same point, but is, through being integrative, more difficult to signal to students.[6] Some institutions have sought to deal with this problem: the University of North London is in the throes of implementing a 'capability curriculum' (page 39, Chapter 4), and the University of Wolverhampton (see Gilbert and Reynolds, Chapter 3), Oxford Brookes University and De Montfort University are among institutions working along broadly similar lines, even if their terminology is somewhat different. One of the problems here could be that, as Shaw (1996) found, departments were stronger on the promotion of capability than on its assessment. Institutional mission, on Shaw's evidence, is a necessary but insufficient condition for the full development of capability.

Assessment methods tend to fall into one of two categories, norm-referenced and criterion-referenced, though the boundary between the two is more blurred than is typically appreciated. Norm-referenced assessments are those in which the student's performance is compared with those of his or her peers. Performances are assumed to be consistent with the normal, bell-curve, distribution, and success or failure is determined by where the student stands in relation to peers. Assessments in the United States, where grade-point averages (GPAs) are used as scores, have thrown up some extreme examples of norm-referenced assessment, where students getting high GPAs are nevertheless deemed to have failed because the mean GPA was itself even higher.[7] Norm-referencing can equally work to the benefit of students (as one editor of this volume is personally aware) where an apparently inadequate performance turns out to have been comparatively good with reference to the performances of peers.

The potential inequity of norm-referencing has contributed to the interest in criterion-referencing, but the latter has probably been more prompted by questions from outside the education service which have asked what students can actually *do* as a result of their period of study. The behavioural objectives movement of the late 1950s and 1960s, stimulated by Bloom's (1956) *Taxonomy of Educational Objectives*, led to an emphasis on mastery learning and specific competences. When education was conceived in these terms, there was no necessity to believe that performances should be normally (in the statistical sense) distributed: theoretically every student could obtain full marks, though for practical purposes the concept of mastery was slightly diluted to a '90/90' criterion of teaching success such that 90 per cent of the class attained a score of 90 per cent.[8] The problem with the criterion-referenced approach was that attempts were made to identify everything that the student could learn during a programme, resulting in very lengthy lists of objectives that turned out to be unmanageable in practice. The behavioural objectives approach lives on, however, in the assessment regime associated with NVQs in the UK, in which students have to attain a set of learning outcomes across a range of relevant circumstances.[9]

In practice, however, norm-referenced assessments contain tasks on which students have to demonstrate a satisfactory level of performance (ie there is a measure of criterion-referencing, often not very clearly specified and with inadequacy in respect of one component able to be compensated by an above-par performance elsewhere). Criterion-referenced assessments are based on expectations that are normative in underlying character.

From the point of view of higher education, and especially from a capability perspective, both norm-referenced and criterion-referenced assessment present problems. For the reasons noted above, the former may not give appropriate recognition to a student's performance (whether it be good or poor), whereas the latter may require a level of specification of expectations for learning that is too precise for the complexity that aspiring diplomates and graduates need to be able to address. At the lower levels of competence-based programmes, where the exercise of relatively limited skills is involved, there may be little difficulty: to take an example that is trivial in one sense (but not in another), the wiring of an electric plug simply has to be done correctly in order not to electrocute someone. As one moves higher in a competence framework, the competences that have to be displayed become more complex, subsuming lower competences and requiring the *selection* of competences appropriate to the problem at hand. As an example, one needs only to look at the framework for NVQs (National Council for Vocational Qualifications (NCVQ), 1991; 1995) to see how, as one progresses from level 3 to level 5 (ie through those levels that bear a relationship to higher education), the expectation is that the certificate-holder is able to handle, with increasing autonomy, more complex situations and the management of others. From the perspective of assessment, both with reference to this example and more generally, people will vary in the extent to which they are successful in various components of achievement. One person might be particularly creative at problem-solving (ie scoring high on complexity and autonomy) but only moderately skilled as a manager, whereas another might be a good manager (demonstrating a high degree of autonomy and the capacity to handle a different kind of complexity) without being particularly creative.

At these higher levels of performance it may well be better to lay out expected performance in general terms and to expect individuals to demonstrate the ways in which they have fulfilled such relatively broad expectations.[10] It is perhaps worth stressing that, where the *detail* of performance is concerned, the emphasis is switched from prior expectation of outcomes to *post hoc* recognition that what has been achieved is consistent with the general expectations for the award. The generic assessment question is thereby switched from something like 'Can you do this?' to 'How have you satisfied, through your work, the aims stated for your particular programme of study?'

Holmes (1996) captures the distinction in a different way, by suggesting that there are two ways of looking at capability. The first is to treat it as an attribute. This can be described, criteria can be established, performances can be set up against these criteria, and judgements about performances can then be made: this corresponds to 'Can you do this?' This view he disfavours. The alternative perspective, which is consistent with the second generic assessment question above, sees capability as indivisible into sub-units, and requires that it be assessed in a holistic manner analogous to Eisner's (1979) 'connoisseurship' with respect to criticism in art. For Holmes, capability provides a discursive warrant for judgement about individuals' capacity to function in the future, rather than a tightly-specified grid of expectations. Under this discursive warrant, the expectation of capability (Part 1) is that the student should:

- show that he or she has taken appropriate and effective action;
- explain why he or she took that action; and
- articulate what he or she has learned from the experience.

This might imply a credit-bearing integrative overlay to the curricular components that have been undertaken, as is suggested in Wolf and Silver (1995).

In their review of capability practice, Stephenson and Weil (1992) noted that most examples of capability assessments did not contribute towards students' degrees.[11] Since then, and for a variety of reasons, transferable skills have risen up 'the assessment agenda', but it is debatable whether in many institutions these have been integrated in a manner consistent with expectations of capability. Stephenson and Weil did include a number of examples of innovation in assessment which reflected *aspects* of capability – the use of portfolios of performance (in the field of public relations), submission of consultancy reports (civil engineering), the use of records of progress and achievement (teacher education), and peer assessment (business studies) but in which the more wide-ranging notion of capability was at best implicit.

A few contributions did, however, address the assessment of capability more fully. In the field of fine art, students were recorded as being expected to show:

- that personal research and critical reflection had been directed towards arguing a coherent case in their final project;
- breadth and depth; and
- awareness of modes of thought, practices and disciplines other than those of the main study (Stephenson and Bromly, 1992, p.40.)

and, in cultural studies modules linked with the EHE Initiative, final assessment was noted as being negotiated and based on portfolios containing the student's curriculum vitae, a personal development statement, a critical account of the work-shadowing that had been undertaken, and a dossier containing their preparation for interview (Weil and Melling, 1992, p.122.)

The general picture regarding the assessment of capability is little different now. If anything has changed it is probably in the assessment of work-based learning, where in a number of instances students are being encouraged to reflect critically and constructively on what they have achieved. Examples include the following.

- Taylor (Chapter 11) reports that students are expected to provide a narrative to accompany evidence of work-based activity, which links it to relevant theory.
- Osborne *et al.* (Chapter 10) describe how reflective analysis can be used, for instance, to show how a setback was translated into positive learning, or to justify the exclusion of a particular line of inquiry that might otherwise have been construed as a significant 'gap' in learning.
- Winter and Maisch (1996, p.99ff) give, as part of a broader discussion of validity and authenticity, examples of students' reports on their own practice, and the way in which triangulation has been used to authenticate what they have claimed.

We shall return later to the nature of the assessment process regarding capability (and some of its implications), limiting ourselves for the present to observing that the outcomes of this process have to be assessed 'in the round'.

A number of consequences follow from adopting Holmes's 'discursive warrant' approach to assessment.

- Performances have to be judged, rather than be measured. Failure in a curricular component may be able to be redeemed by the student's demonstration that he or she has learned from the failure. One of the problems of modular schemes (and it is more evident in some than in others) is that of compensation for failed modules: the critical question to be asked is whether it is essential to the student's award (for example, in respect of a licence to practise) that he or she passes particular modules.

- If precise measurement is inappropriate, then fine scales of grading (such as percentages) are also inappropriate. What, in the context of the assessment of capability, would a mark of 64 per cent signify, for example?[12]
- Validity, *against expectations relating to capability*, is quite likely to be respectable. As with any assessment, it is of critical importance. Limitations on validity inhere in the ability to state with reasonable meaningfulness what is expected; the ability of staff to judge in the holistic sense described by Holmes; and the extent to which the work is truly that of the student.
- Reliability, in the sense of replicability of performance, is problematic, for the simple reason that the task is very unlikely to reappear in precisely the same form a second time. As far as capability is concerned, it is probably more useful to look at reliability in terms of consensus among assessors. Fine discriminations are unlikely to be consensual regarding what will almost certainly be a complex set of evidence, but the chances are better that consensus can be achieved with respect to broad categories of judgement.[13] A difficulty with the assessment of capability is that of ensuring that performances deemed to fall into a particular category would do so in a different institution: the only solution (though it is difficult to achieve satisfactorily with the complex evidence likely to be provided under a capability expectation) is, as Brown and Knight (1994) suggest, that of inter-institutional moderation.
- Equity demands an approach not dissimilar to the judgement of ice-skating, in which the skaters embed certain movements, such as a double-axel or a toe-loop, within a flowing programme of their own choosing. In ice-skating, however, marks are awarded for both technical merit and artistic impression, whereas the assessment of a performance in higher education will relate to students' self-chosen activities and is likely to take place with reference to a single scale. The onus is on the educational assessor to justify why he or she regards two (different) performances as being of equivalent standing, or why one is superior to another. Equity has to be approached in terms of ordered categories[14], rather than in terms of measures such as percentages.

The assessment of capability also has implications for institutional economy. To assess properly a complex piece of work or a portfolio of evidence takes time, and this is doubled if a reliability cross-check is implemented. If such assessments take time, then the necessary time has to be built into curricula and not left as an afterthought whose implications only become clear some way downstream of the validation and approval process. The implications of the proper assessment of capability (in both formative and summative senses) are perhaps more radical than they might appear at first sight, since they are likely to require some considerable redistribution of time within the curricular framework.

The discussion above has almost slipped into considering assessment from a summative perspective, but a consideration of the development of capability in students necessarily contains a strong formative dimension. Indeed, the formative and summative can be brought more closely together under a capability expectation than is typical of assessment in general – but this requires a rethink of the role that assessment plays in the curriculum.

Capability requires, among other things, self-awareness. This implies the ability of a student to assess his or her performances and development: examples were noted earlier in this chapter of reflection in respect of work-based learning[15], and other examples appear in Cuthbert (1993, especially pp.102–103)[16] Boud (1995b) makes a strong case for the contribution of self-assessment to learning, but despite the influence of the EHE Initiative and other encouragements to develop employment-related skills in higher education, formal self-assessment is encompassed in a small minority of curricula. Two aspects of capability in particular point to the importance of self-assessment: the need to be able to articulate the 'what' and 'how' of achievement (intended or completed), and the ability to learn from experience. The capability-oriented curriculum, therefore, brings together the formative and summative: Boud (1995a, p.42), though not writing with capability particularly in mind, remarks that 'Good assessment now is that which both closely reflects desired learning outcomes and in which the process of assessment has a directly beneficial influence on the learning process', and Heywood (1994, p.136) comments in similar vein that '[t]he role of the curriculum designer in enterprise learning is to reconcile the function of assessment in learning with the function of assessment in certification . . .'

If Boud's and Heywood's point applies to capability (as we believe it does), then the assessment regime needs to allow for dialogue between teacher and learner[17] about intentions, methods, achievements, and consequent learning. To be able to give a valid assessment of what the learner has gained from the educational experience implies a thoroughness of understanding on the teacher-assessor's part: this requires both time and a measure of expertise in assessment, neither of which are currently in abundance in UK higher education. How might the implied challenge be met?

The extension of the time which can be devoted to each individual's work cannot satisfactorily be solved by incremental changes to curricula, since –

to strike one particular (and accentuated) comparison – it takes far longer per person to discuss achievements and progress than to give marks to an examination script. The 'capability curriculum' needs not only to transcend the subdivision of programmes (particularly those that are unitized) but also to make space for assessment *as part of the learning activity*.[18] This would imply for many programmes a reduction in teacher/learner contact in activities such as formal presentations and a greater reliance on various forms of self-directed learning, some (if not all) of which will be cooperative in character. The basic curricular issue is the rebalancing of the relationship between the quantity and quality of teacher/learner contact, as the Dearing Report (NCIHE, 1997, paragraph 8.13) argued. Within that rebalancing the role of assessment as a medium for learning needs to be emphasized.

The second issue, expertise in assessment, is just as substantial. It means not only that many staff will need to reconstrue the purposes of assessment, but also that they would need to engage in activities aimed at developing their methodological repertoires. A useful aid in this respect, as well as standard texts on assessment, is the Assessment Strategies in Scottish Higher Education (ASSHE) inventory of assessment practice in Scotland (Hounsell *et al.*, 1996), not least because exemplars are more useful in conveying understanding than relatively abstract statements, as Wolf (1995) shows. Gonczi *et al.* (1993) and Heywood (1994) make clear that, in order to assess holistically, it is necessary to possess an extensive repertoire of assessment methods and to know when any particular method might or might not be validly used. To assess *capability* in an integrative way, therefore, requires more than swapping one assessment method for another, since it demands the following abilities:

- to see the student's performance in the subject discipline in relation to the performance in a broader setting;
- to identify the extent to which the student can justify his or her course(s) of action;
- to determine the degree of success of the student in working with others, where this is applicable;
- to come to a view about the student's learning from experience (even if the actual achievements on an assignment were not particularly meritorious[19]); and
- the capacity to argue convincingly to an external examiner or other interested party that the final judgement reached was fair.

In their description of the development of the Accreditation for Social Services Experience and Training (ASSET) Programme, Winter and Maisch (1996) exhibit a substantial move in this direction. The advantage they had was that the ASSET Programme was tied to a specific occupational area[20] in respect of which a set of general educational expectations could be elaborated. The ASSET Programme therefore lessens a difficulty noted by HEQC (1997a, paragraph 6.18), that students often feel a need to concentrate on the subject-specific aspects of their programmes rather than on transferable skills or general cognitive attributes which are less easy to pin down. Where a programme of study is connected less firmly to a profession than is the ASSET Programme the broader educational expectations will tend to be more general, leaving open the extent to which the skills developed in the higher education context can be transferred 'outside'.

The assessment of capability demands considerable expertise in assessment, yet this is in relatively short supply across higher education: this is a matter to which the HEQC's Graduate Standards Programme might have given more emphasis.[21] To develop expertise in assessment – and this is needed across higher education whether or not a capability-oriented curriculum is being used[22] – will require a considerable investment in staff development, involving not only institutions themselves but trans-institutional bodies such as subject associations.

This chapter cannot be brought to a close without making one second-order point – that what has been said about assessment applies also to external examiners, since – in general – they come from academic institutions and many will not have made a study of assessment methodology. It is widely acknowledged that the external examiner system is under strain (Yorke, 1994; Silver *et al.*, 1995). The Dearing Report recommends, *inter alia*, that the external examiners of the future should be approved by the new Quality Assurance Agency and that they should undergo familiarization, training and preparation for their role (NCIHE, 1997, paragraphs 10.93–94). Though the report was not explicit on the point, the case for the development of external examiners' conceptual and technical expertise in assessment is compelling.

Conclusion

The assessment of capability is, if it is done properly, a complex and time-consuming task which probably requires more 'curriculum space' than is typically allowed, with obvious implications for curriculum design. Unitized programmes present particular challenges, since often the assessments that are undertaken are dis-integrated and allow no overall view (other than, at best, a highly inferential one) of the extent to which a student has developed capability. Some of the issues are taken up in Part 4 in a discussion of the 'capability envelope'.

Among the examples of practice that have been cited there are some pointers towards ways in which the assessment of capability might be developed, but the reader will appreciate that 'quick fixes' are very unlikely to be successful. There is, in any case, a need for greater expertise in assessment across higher education (whether or not capability is being assessed): given that relatively few staff have a developed understanding of assessment theory and practice (and as the Final Report of the HEQC's Graduate Standards Programme recommended), educational development activity in this direction is a necessity.

References

AGR (1995) *Skills for Graduates in the 21st Century*, Cambridge: Association of Graduate Recruiters.

Allen, MG (1993) *Improving the Personal Skills of Graduates: A Conceptual Model of Transferable Personal Skills*, Sheffield: Employment Department.

Assiter, A and Shaw, E (eds) (1993) *Using Records of Achievement in Higher Education*. London: Kogan Page.

Atkins, M, Beattie, J and Dockrell, WB (1993) *Assessment Issues in Higher Education*, Sheffield: Employment Department.

Bloom, BS (1956) *Taxonomy of Educational Objectives: Handbook (Cognitive domain)*, London: Longmans Green.

Boud D (1995a) 'Assessment and learning: contradictory or complementary?', in P Knight (ed), *Assessment for Learning in Higher Education*, (pp.35–48), London: Kogan Page.

Boud, D (1995b) *Enhancing Learning Through Self-assessment*, London: Kogan Page.

Brown, S and Knight, P (1994) *Assessing Learners in Higher Education*. London: Kogan Page.

Chance, J (1994) 'Integrating transferable skills into geography through a compulsory core', in A Jenkins and L Walker (eds), *Developing Student Capability Through Modular Courses*. (pp.63–9), London: Kogan Page.

CIHE (1996) *A Learning Nation*, evidence to the National Committee of Inquiry into Higher Education, London: Council for Industry and Higher Education.

Cuthbert, K (1993) 'Records of achievement in relation to personal learning', in A Assiter and E Shaw (eds), *Using Records of Achievement in Higher Education* (pp.97–105), London: Kogan Page.

Eisner, EW (1979) *The Educational Imagination: On the Design and Evaluation of School Programs*, New York: Macmillan.

Elton, L (1998) 'Are UK degree standards going up, down or sideways?', *Studies in Higher Education*, **23**(1).

Entwistle, N (1994) *Teaching and the Quality of Learning*, London: Committee of Vice-Chancellors and Principals.

Gonczi, A, Hager, P and Athanasou, J (1993) *The Development of Competency-based Assessment Strategies for the Professions*, Canberra: Australian Government Publishing Service.

Graves, N (1993) 'Assessing learner-managed learning: problems of process and product', a case study of the University of East London, in Graves, N (ed) *Learner Managed Learning: Practice, Theory and Policy*, (pp.89–95), Leeds: Higher Education for Capability and the World Education Fellowship.

Hague, D (1991) *Beyond Universities: A New Republic of the Intellect*, London: Institute of Economic Affairs.

Harvey, L, Moon, S and Geall, V (1997) *Graduates' Work: Organisational Change and Students' Attributes*, Birmingham: Centre for Research into Quality, University of Central England.

HEQC (1996b) *Inter-institutional Variability of Degree Results: An Analysis in Selected Subjects*, London: Higher Education Quality Council.

HEQC (1996c) *Threshold and Other Standards: The Views of Four Subject Groups*, London: Higher Education Quality Council.

HEQC (1997a) *Assessment in Higher Education and the Role of 'Graduateness'*, London: Higher Education Quality Council.

HEQC (1997b) *Graduate Standards Programme: Final Report Volume 1*, London: Higher Education Quality Council.

HEQC (1997c) *Graduate Standards Programme: Final Report Volume 2 (Supplementary Material)*, London: Higher Education Quality Council.

Heywood, J (1994) 'Enterprise learning and its assessment in higher education', (report no 20). Sheffield: Learning Methods Branch, Employment Department.

Holmes, L (1996) 'Reframing the ability-based curriculum in higher education', unpublished paper, University of North London.

Hounsell D, McCulloch, M and Scott, M (1996) *The ASSHE Inventory: Changing Assessment Practices in Scottish Higher Education*, Edinburgh: Centre for Teaching, Learning and Assessment, University of Edinburgh and Napier University, in association with the Universities and Colleges Staff Development Agency.

Hutton, W (1996) *The State We're In* (revised edition), London: Vintage.

Labour Party (nd) *Lifelong Learning: A Consultation Document*, London: The Labour Party.

Meehl, P (1957) 'When shall we use our heads instead of the formula?', *Journal of Counselling Psychology*, **4**, 268–73.

Morgan, C and Murgatroyd, S (1994) *Total Quality Management in the Public Sector*, Buckingham: Open University Press.

NCIHE (1997) *Higher Education in the Learning Society*, report of the National Committee of Inquiry into Higher Education, London: HMSO.

NCVQ (1991) *Guide to National Vocational Qualifications*, London: National Council for Vocational Qualifications.

NCVQ (1995) *NVQ Criteria and Guidance*, London: National Council for Vocational Qualifications.

Reich, RB (1991) *The Work of Nations*, London: Simon and Schuster.

Robbins, L, Chairman (1963) *Higher Education* (report of the Committee appointed by the Prime Mininster under the chairmanship of Lord Robbins, 1961–63, (The Robbins Report)), London: HMSO.

Shaw, M (1996) '. . . from rhetoric to reality', paper prepared for the Higher Education for Capability Assessment Network meeting, Institute of Education, University of London, 11 July (mimeo).

Silver, H, Stennett, A and Williams, R (1995) *The External Examiner System: Possible Futures*, London: Quality Support Centre, The Open University.

Stephenson, J and Bromly, T (1992) 'Capability through art and design', in J Stephenson and S Weil (eds), *Quality in Learning: A Capability Approach to Higher Education*, (pp.21–44), London: Kogan Page.

Stephenson, J and Weil, S (1992) *Quality in Learning: A Capability Approach to Higher Education*. London: Kogan Page.

Weil, S and Melling, D (1992) 'Capability through Humanities and Social Sciences', in J Stephenson and S Weil (eds), *op cit*, (pp.104–26).

Winter, R and Maisch, M (1996) *Professional Competence and Higher Education: The ASSET Programme*, London, Falmer.

Wolf, A (1995) *Competence-based Assessment*, Buckingham: Open University Press.

Wolf, A (1996) 'Vocational assessment', in H Goldstein and T Lewis (eds), *Assessment: Problems, Developments and Statistical Issues*, (pp.209–30), Chichester: Wiley.

Wolf, A and Silver, R (1995) 'Measuring "broad skills": the prediction of skill retention and transfer over time', (research report no 61), Sheffield: Department for Education and Employment.

Yorke, M (1994) 'The external examiner system – in crisis?' in M Yorke (ed), *External Examining for Capability*, (pp.2–4), London: Higher Education Quality Council.

Yorke, M (1995) 'The assessment of higher order transferable skills: a challenge to higher education', in M Yorke (ed), *Assessing Capability in Degree and Diploma Programmes*, (pp.5–12), proceedings of a conference held in Liverpool on 8 February 1995, Liverpool: Centre for Higher Education Development: Liverpool John Moores University.

Yorke, M (1997) 'The skills of graduates: a small enterprise perspective', *Capability*, 3(1), 27–32.

Notes

1. Sources include AGR (1995); CIHE (1996); Harvey *et al.* (1997) and Yorke (1997). See also Allen (1993), or, perhaps more accessibly, Entwistle (1994), for a conceptual model which embraces a considerable number of transferable skills, and which many have found helpful.

2. See Hunt and Frier (Chapter 5) for an expression of concern that giving separate attention to 'key skills' might lead to their dis-integration from the curriculum, with negative implications for transferability.

3. Those who remember the programmes instituted in the mid-1970s by the Technician Education Council may recall the broad statements of intent for the programmes as a whole and that very many of the programme units sought no more than to inculcate the skills of application (in the sense used by Bloom, 1956). The puzzle that had to be solved was how a collection of building blocks with relatively limited cognitive ambitions could be brought together into a programme which sought to achieve aims that related to the higher order Bloomian objectives of analysis, synthesis and evaluation.

4. Less likely to be satisfactory is the idea of a separate study unit on vocational skills, which was a proposition put forward by the Labour Party (nd) in the period leading up to the general election of 1997. This would, in itself, fail to provide the integration necessary for capability.

5. See, *inter alia*, HEQC (1996a, b; 1997b).

6. There is, as Graves (1993) observes, a danger of a student pursuing independent study on a front that is too narrow to enable him or her to have sufficient breadth of context in which to locate the work (and presumably any action stemming from it). Graves thus draws attention to the tension between 'process' and 'product', and the need to find an appropriate equilibrium. The same issue arises *a fortiori* in respect of capability which, probably in the majority of cases, is intended to span a wide range of intended outcomes.

7. This is one of the manifestations of grade inflation which has beset higher education in the US over the last couple of decades, and which is feared by some to be affecting higher education in the UK (though hard evidence on the point is difficult to find). Elton (1998) attributes the upward trend in the classification of degree awards in the UK to an increase in the amount of coursework, and argues that this amounts to a general change in courses while the measuring instrument has remained unchanged.

8. Other criteria have also been suggested, such as 80/80.

9. See Wolf (1995, 1996) for critique of competence-based assessment which covers technical, organizational and human aspects.

10. Or, less asymmetrically, to construct learning agreements (see Anderson *et al.*, Chapter 18).

11. Stephenson and Weil (1992, p.176).

12. Those who favour percentage marking tend to have difficulty with questions such as 'What do I have to do to obtain the remaining 36 per cent?' unless the assessment is made up of elements to which the answer is unambiguously right or wrong.

13. See the discussion in Brown and Knight (1994, p.14ff).
14. Statistically speaking, in the hazy overlap between categorical and ordinal (ranked) data.
15. Taylor, this volume; Osborne *et al.*, Chapter 10; and Winter and Maisch (1996, p.99ff).
16. Self-reflection is not without its dangers, as Assiter and Shaw (1993, p.151ff) show in their book on records of achievement. It could, under certain conditions, turn into self-surveillance; it is at risk from social desirability bias; and some aspects of personal experience may not be appropriate for inclusion in assessment methodologies.
17. The distinction is not as clear-cut as, for convenience, it is presented here.
18. It is wasteful of higher education to conduct end of unit or end of programme assessments without taking the opportunity to further students' learning. See also Heywood (1994, pp.146–51) and Boud (1995b) for argument in favour of including self-assessment in higher education.
19. Or, to put it more bluntly and paradoxically, the extent to which failure could be construed as success. Or, put yet another way, how does one value the ability to perform in the future against the relative inability to demonstrate the appropriate level of expertise in respect of a particular assignment? There is a tension here between two of the purposes of assessment noted in Table 19.1 – those of certifying actual achievement and prediction of future performance.
20. The approach was subsequently extended to engineering.
21. To be fair, HEQC (1997b, paragraphs 5.13 and 7.2) does refer to the need to give a higher priority to the training and development of assessors. However, the same paragraph exemplifies the point by referring to the ways in which awards are determined, rather than to the need for clearer conceptualization of what assessments are trying to achieve and for greater expertise in the actual practice of assessment.
22. See NCIHE (1997, paragraph 9.43) on this point.

Part 4: The Way Ahead

Chapter 20

Creating the Conditions for the Development of Capability

John Stephenson and Mantz Yorke

Editors' introduction

Delivering student capability in higher education has major implications for the culture, structures, procedures, practices and management of higher education institutions and their programmes of study. In this chapter we present a capability model of a higher education curriculum which draws heavily on the advice and experience reported in earlier thematic chapters on learning contracts (Boud et al.), peer support (Evatt and Boyle), careers and guidance (Butcher), supporting learner autonomy (Stephenson) and assessing capability (Yorke).

This emerging model, called the Capability Envelope, is an ideal in the sense that it is a collation of different people's experience, and realistic in that its various components have been tried and tested somewhere within most higher education institutions. Later in the chapter we explore the implications of such a model for the culture and organization of higher education institutions. Finally, we present a list of challenges for the various stakeholders whose actions will be needed if progress towards this ideal is to be made.

An ideal capability curriculum?

In Chapter 1 (see Figure 1.1, p 5) two contrasting contexts in which people need to be capable were characterized as position Y (the familiar world) and position Z (the unfamiliar world). Higher education, it was argued, should help students become proficient in both contexts. For most students position Y is represented by the specialist content of their studies. Preparation for position Z, it was further argued, is achieved through *the process* by which students engage with and use that content for their own educational development, and the extent to which they exercise personal responsibility for that process. The challenge for curriculum designers is to give as much opportunity as possible for learners to manage their own development while ensuring that what is regarded within the intended specialist area as *essential learning* is satisfactorily covered.

Many universities, through their faculty interests, library stocks, specialist workshops and, more recently, modular structures are geared to the presentation and delivery of what *they* define as essential learning. Judgement of the relevance of what is delivered is usually the prerogative of academic staff, in some cases with the assistance of outside bodies. In a position Y context it is sufficient to structure the curriculum in ways which are resource-efficient, educationally effective and intellectually coherent. Many teaching staff are comfortable working in this manner and, as reported elsewhere in this book and its predecessor (Stephenson and Weil, 1992), some are wary of moves towards a more student-managed approach.

When academics determine the direction and purpose as well as the content of students' studies they are, in effect, restricting students' opportunities to develop their capacity to be effective in position Z to their engagement in live projects and other open-ended assignments. From the students' perspectives, their future is their unfamiliar context, their position Z. When given the opportunity to imagine and define their potential future and the responsibility to devise a programme of study which will help bring it about, students experience the personal risk and exposure described in Chapter 15. Successfully completing such a programme, particularly within a demanding and rigorous educational environment, builds their belief in their power to perform in new and demanding circumstances.

The Capability Envelope

The Capability Envelope (see Figure 20.1) is a curriculum framework which accommodates the different demands of preparing students to be capable in both position Y and position Z. The Capability Envelope:

- gives students responsibility to formulate and manage their own strategic educational development according to their distinctive circumstances and longer-term aspirations;

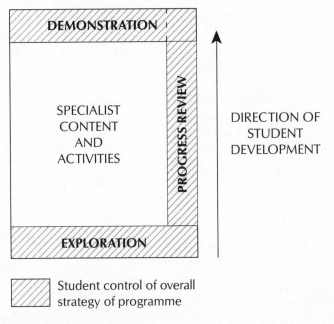

Figure 20.1 *The Capability Envelope*

- ensures that students develop intellectual, specialist and personal skills and qualities relevant to effective performance in life and at work;
- meets the needs of key stakeholders such as professional bodies, custodians of academic standards, future clients (in the case of vocationally-oriented programmes) and the community at large;
- can, where necessary, accommodate current modes of delivery of specialist content;
- accommodates a wide range of resources and learning opportunities in the community and employment and the greater availability of resources through electronic and other media; and
- can be implemented within the specialist and general resource constraints of higher education.

The Capability Envelope is a sequence of stages formally established as part of the total programme and is wrapped around the specialist content. The Envelope begins with an Exploration Stage in which students are helped to plan and negotiate approval for their programmes of study; continues with a Progress Review Stage running through the main study phase, in which students are helped to monitor and review their progress; and ends with a Demonstration Stage in which students show what they have learnt through its application to real situations relevant to their intended career.

Each of these three stages relates to the other two, giving an overall coherent structure to the learners' programme of development which is managed by the learner. The Exploration Stage builds on the students' prior experience and looks ahead beyond the completion of the programme. The Progress Review Stage monitors progress according to the plans which emerge from the Exploration Stage and facilitates changes in response to experience and evolving aspirations. What is demonstrated at the end of the programme is what was planned at the beginning or renegotiated on the way. A final critical review of the whole process provides a basis for the students' plans for the next stage of their development. The Capability Envelope provides both a structure and a process for the autonomous management of lifelong learning, whether on campus, at work, or in life generally. People who adopt the central features of the Envelope as a habit are, we argue, independently capable.

Exploration Stage

Education is essentially a journey. Like explorers, autonomous learners need to construct a map of the terrain, acquire a set of tools by which to navigate, be aware of where they are starting from, have some notion of a possible destination and be willing to adjust both the destination and the route in response to greater understanding of the terrain and themselves acquired as the journey progresses. The purpose of the Exploration Stage is to help students to prepare plans for the rest of their programme and to secure academic registration of those plans as leading to an approved qualification.

In order to prepare plans which meet the demanding requirements of registration, learners need with the support of institutional staff to:

- appraise their experience and become aware of their strengths and weaknesses;
- explore their career or other long term aspirations;
- identify the specialist expertise and personal skills and qualities they will need in order to achieve those aspirations;
- plan an appropriate programme of learning activities;
- give thought to how they will demonstrate the relevance of what they have learnt to their intended career or employment; and
- become aware of the general requirements of the award for which they are working.

The above activities can be conducted in peer groups with tutor supervision supported by a programme of exploratory activities, specialist inputs and contacts with key stakeholders. On professional courses such as medicine and civil engineering, for instance, dialogue with professional practitioners at these early stages is essential. Careers advisers also have a key role to play. Once likely areas of study have been identified, projects, placements or assignments can be used to help students become familiar with key concepts and essential components and to provide some initial exposure to the good practice which they are aiming to attain.

The interests of key stakeholders, such as professional bodies and employer groups, and the general requirements of the HEI for the level of the intended award can be accommodated formally through the general criteria for the approval of student plans and the composition of the groups charged with judging the appropriateness of those plans. Non-negotiable content, such as formal legal requirements for some professional courses, can be part of the criteria for approval, provided students have the right to show where, how and at what stage such requirements will be demonstrated within the programme as a whole.

The amount of time needed for an Exploration Stage will depend upon the scale of the programme being prepared. For whole degree programmes, as in the Leeds Work-based Learning programme, it can last 10 to 12 weeks. For shorter one-year programmes, anything from two to four weeks of intensive activity may suffice.

The Exploration Stage can be a valuable learning experience in its own right, for which credit can and should be given. Much of this learning relates to personal qualities which come from the experience of taking responsibility within an uncertain environment (see Chapter 15) The processes of planning and negotiation promote the development of general and specialist skills and an understanding of the scope, key features and relevance of the area of study (see Boud *et al.*, Chapter 18, Foster, Chapter 7 and Osborne *et al.*, Chapter 10 in this book, and the final chapter of *Using Learning Contracts in Higher Education* by Laycock and Stephenson, 1993). Academic staff wary that students may spend several days or weeks before any 'real content' is given can be reassured that such activity leads to a high level of motivation and commitment which more than compensates for any apparent 'loss' of time.

Progress Review Stage

Once programmes are approved and running, students need time and opportunity to monitor their progress, review their aspirations in the light of experience and judge the continuing relevance of their studies to those aspirations. 'Learning sets' are particularly useful for these purposes, providing students with opportunities for dialogue, intellectual challenge, personal support and exchange of experience with peers.

The formal agenda for these sets can include:

- the preparation of learning logs or personal reviews of learning (see Chapter 15);
- the renegotiation or clarification of plans in response to experience;
- preparing student feedback on the relevance of particular learning activities provided by the institution;
- formulating demands for different provision by the institution;
- negotiating access to remedial assistance;
- addressing conceptual and practical issues related to the final demonstration of learning; and
- raising students' awareness of the emotional, intellectual and practical aspects of taking responsibility for managing their own development.

The Capability Envelope provides time, space and tutorial support for learning sets to meet at regular intervals throughout the students' programme. The frequency of supervised meetings can vary, but on a long programme (eg an undergraduate degree programme) once a month might be sufficient.

The Progress Review Stage is the main means through which students retain ownership of their programmes of study. As with the Exploration Stage, the Progress Review Stage provides opportunities for significant learning through discussion about the relevance of the specialist·content and reflections on their progress towards their planned future. In recognition of this learning, students should receive credit towards their final award, thereby justifying the allocation of scarce resources to this valuable activity.

Demonstration Stage

In this Stage, students are helped and given time and space to prepare a demonstration of *what they can do* as a result of the studies they have completed, allowing assessment to be based on the students' *integration and application* of component specialist skills and knowledge in the context of their intended vocational, personal or professional aspirations. The form of this demonstration of capability will be that which is most appropriate to the nature of the student's programme and can include a range of formats such as performances, exhibitions, project reports and dissertations.

In addition to being asked to demonstrate that they can use their newly acquired specialist skills and knowledge students are also asked to present a *Personal Review of Learning* covering the appropriateness and relevance of their original plans, the learning activities which followed and, crucially in view of the importance of lifelong learning, their plans for the next stages of their continuing development. Assessment of students in the Demonstration Stage judges both the extent to which students can successfully manage their own learning and development and the extent to which they have understood and effectively used the specialist material they have acquired.

Preparation for the final demonstration of capability is a learning experience in its own right, providing students with opportunities to develop a range of communication and presentation skills and to review the relevance of their learning to their future lives and/or employment. Marshalling material for these purposes is a challenging intellectual test. The Capability Envelope gives full recognition to the educational value of student-led assessment by making assessment a part of the learning programme itself, not an event which takes place after the programme is over.

Inevitably, there is a greater variety of material for assessment than on most conventional courses, raising the issue of comparability of student achievement. Comparability is assured by the use of generic criteria related to the general level of the award being sought, similar to those being developed by Leeds Metropolitan University and the University of Leeds and reported in Chapter 6 and Chapter 7. Assessment against those criteria is appropriately the responsibility of the university whose award the student is seeking; it is the responsibility of the students to show how what they have done is worthy of that award. The ability to judge the quality of one's own work is an important feature of being independently capable and is validated (or not) by the external assessment of that work.

The Capability Envelope and specialist content

The Exploration, Progress Review and Demonstration Stages of the Capability Envelope provide a framework of support for the *process* of students' taking responsibility for the overall strategy of their learning. Within this supportive framework, *specialist content* can be provided through a variety of learning modes, including unsupervised student-managed learning environments such as multimedia, the Internet, independent study and work-placements as well as more conventional teacher-student learning environments including taught modules, workshops and large lectures.

One advantage of the Capability Envelope is that not all specialist teachers need to be converted to the capability approach. In the Capability Envelope it is possible to envisage a capability student who has planned and negotiated an overall programme leading to, say, a civil engineering qualification asking for instruction in some aspects of mathematics related to material stress analysis in order to overcome a particular blockage to his or her progress. At that moment in the student's programme, it would appear to a casual observer that the student is in a highly dependent mode when in fact it is the student who is in control of the learning.

Formally delivered content, therefore, can be timetabled in the normal way and made available to those who need it without detracting from the development of the autonomous learner. By (a) giving students control of how it is presented for final assessment, (b) basing assessment on the *subsequent use* rather than the immediate possession of skills and knowledge and (c) expressing key requirements as criteria for judging final performance, specialist tutors can provide *specialist input without detracting from students' control* of their overall educational development. It is also likely, however, that tutors providing such inputs can expect to be pressed by students on the relevance and adequacy of what the tutors present.

By the same token, other students will have the motivation and tools to pursue specialist content without direct supervision. Reading lists, placements and electronic media can support those students pursuing major projects or independent study, perhaps with only occasional support from a supervisor. Over-coverage of the field can be a problem for some students given licence to pursue their enthusiasm.

Implications of information technology (IT) and the Capability Envelope

In *The Learning Revolution*, Gordon Dryden and others have argued that new technology is already leading to accelerated learning outside conventional modes of teaching and schooling (Dryden and Voss, 1997). In recognition of this trend, and the growing importance of IT in employment, the Dearing Report urged higher education institutions (HEIs) to make more provision for the use of IT and proposed that development of IT skills should be a priority for all students. By focusing on student-managed learning, the Capability Envelope is an ideal curriculum model for helping students to make effective use of new technology.[1]

Virtual networks of learners are emerging on a global scale, often extending beyond the campus into community centres, cafes, offices and factory floors. Some observers consider there is real prospect that only a few prestigious institutions (perhaps only 20 world-wide) or individuals will be supplying interactive learning materials in each main subject field to anyone who can get on-line and, for a fee, offering accreditation (Pauling, 1998). While many academic staff will prefer to continue to filter information for students, particularly at the undergraduate level, some movement towards the rationalization of content provision of the kind envisioned by Pauling is highly likely.

We believe that students need professional support for managing their engagement with new technology and that this professional support can best be given within formal institutions through the three stages of the Capability Envelope. The Exploration Stage enables students to judge the relevance of sources to their overall educational development, the Progress Review Stage provides a forum for dialogue, reflection and exchange thereby promoting greater understanding of material encountered, and the Demonstration Stage focuses students' attention on the application of what they have learnt in the context of their intended employment or further development. The use of learning sets reduces the risk of isolation and allows the development of interpersonal skills.

The Capability Envelope and staffing resources

The Dearing Report on higher education concluded that pressure on staff resources inevitably means a switch to greater learner autonomy, particularly in the contexts of raising the quality of learning and promoting lifelong learning:

It is not for us to offer institutions a compendium of learning strategies to enable them to achieve excellence in a world in which it is unrealistic to expect a return to former staff to student ratios. But it seems plain that an effective strategy will involve guiding and enabling students to be effective learners, to understand their own learning styles, and to manage their own learning. We see this as not only directly relevant to enhancing the quality of their learning while in higher education, but also to equipping them to be effective lifelong learners. Staff will increasingly be engaged in the management of students' learning, using a range of appropriate strategies. (NCIHE, paragraph 8.15)

Many colleagues who would otherwise support a capability approach assume that because it relies on individually negotiated programmes of study it must inevitably be more expensive than conventional schemes and hence, under today's resource constraints, be uneconomic to run. We believe the Capability Envelope addresses some of the concerns they raise.

The Capability Envelope makes it possible to cost and resource the main activities associated with learner managed learning. Two factors make this possible: the separation of activities which support student control of the strategic development of the programme from the provision of specialist subject inputs, and the giving of academic credit for learning which accrues from managing that strategy. Because the three Stages can attract credits for student learning each can be funded in the same way as any other credit earning activity.

Each Stage can be organized on the basis of learning sets, similar to those tested and advocated by Judith Evans of Sainsbury (see Chapter 15). Such sets need staff time for setting up and maintenance, augmented by specialist inputs on process issues such as planning and study skills. These learning sets can be self-managed, supervised or a mixture of both. A typical arrangement would involve one tutor with responsibility for several learning sets of five or six students each. The tutor can meet his or her learning sets as one whole group or less frequently as separate sets, and/or receive reports of meetings of self-managed sets.

In the early stages of the Exploration and Demonstration Stages, staff contact is likely to exceed the normal levels of support offered to conventional students, but this is compensated by much lower levels of input at times when students are pursuing their programmes. During the Progress Review Stage, for instance, sets may need to be supervised only once a month. As a consequence, the total staff commitment to the envelope activities is likely to be front-loaded with a smaller peak at the end, but the total number of hours for the year need not be greater than the total currently deployed in more familiar ways of working. During the pilot programme of the University of Leeds Work-based Learning Programme, for instance, it was found that the overall actual (as opposed to the perceived) contact was less than standard university practice though the peak periods were more demanding of staff than the average working week (Foster, 1996, pp.35–6).

Supply side or demand side accounting?

Some colleagues' perceptions of the costs of capability-oriented learning are related to their experience of content delivery models in which staff time is allocated on a standard weekly basis. In a learning model such as the Capability Envelope, in which weekly patterns vary during the year, a more appropriate basis for costing is the number of learning credits earned. It is possible to speculate on how a 'demand side' funding system based on student learning credits, in which funding follows learning, might be used to support the Capability Envelope.

Table 20.1 illustrates an approach to accounting staff time on an Exploration Stage based on learning credits in two contrasting examples. Each example has key figures in common:

- the unit of resource for full-time students as allocated by the Higher Education Funding Council in England (HEFCE);
- 120 credits per year;
- 24 credits earned by the Exploration Stage (as in the University of Leeds–Leeds Metropolitan University work-based learning scheme);
- the use of learning sets of five students per set and clusters of five sets; and
- because of the wide variety of practice, an assumed range of £30 to £50 per hour for staff time based on part-time hourly rates, as used in a number of universities for costing purposes.

Table 20.1 *Possible staff allocations to students during Exploration Stage*

Key variables	Example A		Example B	
	Classroom-based	Science & Technology	Classroom-based	Science & Technology
a HEI income per FT student (English standard rates 98–99)	£2900	£5200	£2900	£5200
b Total credits per year	120	120	120	120
c Income to HEI per student credit (a ÷ b)	£24	£43	£24	£43
d Credits from Exploration Stage	24	24	24	24
e Total income to HEI per student on Exploration Stage (c * d)	£580	£1040	£580	£1040
f % HEI income spent on academic staff	30%	30%	50%	50%
g Proportion of staff time spent on student contact	0.3	0.3	0.6	0.6
h Funds for individual contact on Exploration Stage (e * f * g)	£52	£94	£174	£312
i PT hourly teaching rate	£50	£50	£30	£30
j No of hours staff contact available for individual student (h ÷ i)	1.04	1.87	5.80	10.40
k Students per set	5	5	5	5
l Funds available for Learning Set – staff contact (h * k)	£261	£468	£870	£1560
m No of hours staff contact available for learning set (l ÷ i)	5.2	9.4	29	52
n Number of sets per cluster	5	5	5	5
o No of hrs staff contact available for cluster (m * n)	26	47	145	260
p Individual student contribution to central services in Exploration Stage (e–h)	£528	£946	£406	£728

Example B gives a higher priority to teaching than Example A as represented by a higher share of its income being devoted to academic staff salaries (50 per cent compared to 30 per cent) and has a higher proportion of staff time spent on student contact (0.6 compared to 0.3).

In Example A, five clusters of learning sets 'earn' 26 hours of contact time for classroom-based subjects and 47 hours for science and technology. In Example B, with a higher teaching profile, the figures are 145 hours and 260 hours respectively. Table 20.1 also shows (line p) the amount of student-generated income which goes towards overheads and central services.

Table 20.1 is not intended to do other than demonstrate that learner managed learning in the context of the Capability Envelope *can be* costed on the basis of learning credits. It is for readers to judge the extent to which their own HEIs could manage to support the Envelope within their own internal expenditure priorities.

A supply side basis for costing staff

An alternative basis for allocating staffing resources to the Capability Envelope is to use student staff ratios (SSRs) and the tutor's total *annual* contact time with students. For instance, an SSR of 30:1 and an annual student contact load of 550 hours for each academic means that 18.33 hours per annum are available for one-to-one contact. Learning sets of five students therefore have access to 91.66 hours per annum. If the Exploration Stage takes up 20 per cent of the annual programme, then 18.33 hours (91.66 × 20 per cent) are available for each set, or 91.66 hours are available for clusters of five sets.

Other considerations

As reported above, specialist information is becoming more readily available through new technology, so much so that it will become increasingly uneconomic for HEIs to use an expensive resource, staff time, to provide a progressively less expensive commodity, information. On the other hand, assisting students with the process of managing their own learning of material made available by other means is a high value activity leading to high level capability which is not necessarily replicable by multimedia. Converting as much of the routine presentation of specialist content to media other than face-to-face contact will eventually allow more staffing resources to be devoted to supporting student learning thereby raising overall cost effectiveness while raising the quality of higher education, thus achieving the cost-effectiveness desired by Dearing (NCIHE, 1997, paragraph 8.15).

Moreover, if students are pursuing their specialist studies through the medium of a major project, it is likely that their productive learning will be based as much on library search and external placements as on direct input from tutors. *In extremis*, it is possible to envisage a situation in which, for some highly motivated and self-actualizing students, the Capability Envelope is the only regular contact they have with university staff.

The Capability Envelope and modular structures

Many British universities have restructured their undergraduate programmes by breaking down their subject content into modules in order to enable students to select routeways according to their needs and interests.

Modular structures are essentially supply-side solutions to the problem of providing student choice. The mode of teaching does not, as a consequence of modularization, necessarily change from being teacher-led to being learner-led. Classroom and teacher availability are major constraints on what students can learn, particularly where modules are defined in terms of minimum student numbers and hours of classroom contact. Rules of engagement often restrict student choice to a fixed number of modules each year and, in many cases, to pathways determined explicitly or implicitly by preconditions.

In the interests of fairness (ie uniformity of treatment), all students taking the same module are assessed in the same way, irrespective of their reasons for taking the module, their prior experience and the place of that module in their longer-term programme. Assessment therefore tends to focus on the possession of the learning outcomes specified by the module, not on the effective use of that learning – integrated with other specialisms obtained elsewhere on the students' programmes – in the context of the students' intended areas of post-programme activity. Indeed, over-assessment of the student with consequential examination fatigue for both students and staff is a common criticism (one large faculty in a major British university told HEC that it conducted 50,000 assessments each year on its undergraduate programmes – 2,000 students taking 12 modules per annum each double-marked with a proportion further marked by external examiners). Overall assessment in these circumstances is often confined to the addition of marks gained in each contributory module assessment.

Modular programmes are also criticized for an apparent lack of concern for the overall coherence and relevance of each student's programme of study. Despite these and other criticisms and limitations (HEQC, 1997), a modular structure of one kind or another is likely to remain a fact of life in most institutions. Modules provide a convenient basis for flexibility of provision, the distribution of resources and the monitoring of outcomes.

In Part 2 of this book, we presented evidence of how the process of module definition is being used by some institutions to promote greater student capability through (a) the formulation of learning outcomes based on key skills and capabilities and (b) by the use of generic criteria to allow a greater variety of forms of assessment and student initiative. The Capability Envelope takes these trends further and allows a modular structure to be used to develop independent capability (see also Laycock, 1994; and Zahran Halim and Zaidah Razak, 1994). Three features need to be established to accommodate a modular structure within a Capability Envelope:

1. The Capability Envelope is defined as being equivalent to a number of modules (see Figure 20.2). For instance, the Exploration Stage could be deemed to be equal to, say, six parallel and integrated half modules at the start of the session. This would allow the Exploration Stage to be resourced and the students to be given credit for its successful completion (by the presentation of a detailed plan and justification of the remainder of the programme).

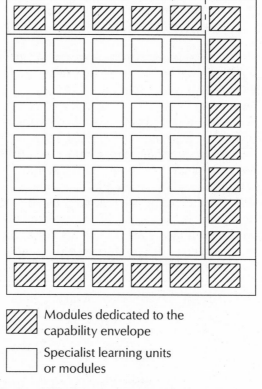

Modules dedicated to the capability envelope

Specialist learning units or modules

Figure 20.2 *The Capability Envelope in a modular course*

2. The definition of specialist modules is relaxed (a) to accommodate activities not dependent upon teacher availability in classrooms (eg 'paper modules' such as reading lists leading to assignments, independent study modules, a variety of placements including the workplace, use of IT sources) and (b) to allow a greater variety of size and duration of learning units leading to appropriate numbers of learning credits.
3. Formal contributory assessment switches from the end of each module to the use of generic and specific criteria which have to be met through a synoptic assessment in a Demonstration Stage at the end of year or programme. Module assessment would be confined to the presentation of feedback on progress, perhaps channelled through Progress Review Stage modules.

Such an approach in modular based institutions would:

- foreground the coherence of student programmes of study;
- reduce the burden of assessments, and make assessments meaningful in terms of the overall relevance of the programme;
- ensure that students provide an explicit rationale for the choice of modules;
- give students a basis for monitoring the continuing relevance of their programmes of study; and
- enable the institution to provide and recognize a much greater variety of learning opportunities than the formal timetable and physical resources would normally allow.

Partial Capability Envelope on a modular scheme

Where a programme has a high proportion of 'essential content', as in some vocational courses, or where academic staff wish to proceed to a capability model in stages, the first two years of a three-year programme can be organized on a traditional basis with the whole of the final year left open to negotiation and leading to a final demonstration of the student's learning from the programme as a whole. In a modular scheme, it is possible to use one or two full modules in the second year as an Exploration Stage, leading to the Registration of a *negotiated* programme for the final year. Assessment of those year two modules devoted to the Exploration Stage would be contributory to the students' final awards. A staged progression to a full Capability Envelope would also appeal to those students who, at the outset, prefer to adopt a relatively dependent stance towards their programmes, as would the opportunity to mix taught modules and more open-ended activities according to the students' readiness to take full responsibility.

The Capability Envelope and vocational qualifications

Many countries, including the UK, New Zealand and Australia are building national frameworks of qualifications for skills required for, or developed in, the work-place. Many of these qualifications, or components of these qualifications, have relevance to higher education students preparing for particular employment. The Capability Envelope allows students to justify the taking of such qualifications during periods of work placements and to show in their Demonstration Stage the relevance of their learning from that experience when they are being finally assessed for their degree. There would be no need for institutions to attempt to reconcile the different traditions of academic campus learning and work-based training since the relevance of each is judged by what the student can do at the end of the programme as a whole.

The Capability Envelope and work-based learning

The Capability Envelope is particularly suitable for work-based learning schemes which lead to university qualifications. Examples from the University of Leeds, Middlesex University and Southern Cross University presented in Part 2 of this book embody many of its features, such as student negotiated programmes, learning contracts, learning sets and a final demonstration of capability.

The openness and flexibility of the Envelope allow full cooperation between the university and the employer over the nature of the students' programmes and the criteria for their registration and final assessment. Students can pursue programmes which consist entirely of work-based projects or which comprise a mixture of projects and campus-based modules. Learning sets can be set up at work or on campus with tutors from either location.

The Capability Envelope and the development of skills

Capability as defined in this book is an integration of skills, knowledge and personal qualities used appropriately and effectively in changing circumstances. To be consistent with this definition, skills development and assessment should not be isolated or 'bolt-on' but should be essential part of the educational process.

By directly and actively involving students in planning, negotiating, implementing and demonstrating their learning – and reflecting on their progress – the Capability Envelope enables students to develop a wide range of important and high level skills in the context of their mainstream studies. Laycock and Stephenson, in their book *Using Learning Contracts in Higher Education*, summarized those skills in Table 20.2.

Table 20.2 *Opportunities for skills development through learning contracts*

Activity	Skills, understanding and personal qualities
Planning	Self-appraisal, context awareness, target-setting, scheduling, creativity, decision-making, problem formulation.
Negotiating	Communication (oral and written), awareness of others' needs, justification of relevance to self and external context, clarity of purpose, resource awareness, competence in formal procedures.
Implementing	Self-organization, monitoring skills, adaptation to experience, application of knowledge, working for a purpose, working with others
Demonstrating	Presentation, communication (oral and written), evaluation of performance, dialogue with experts (clients, assessors), self- and peer-assessment.
Reflection	Conceptual development, understanding (knowledge, self, external context), problem reformulation, awareness of personal needs (knowledge and skills) for further development.

Adapted from Laycock and Stephenson (1993, p.173)

The Capability Envelope gives students the opportunity to develop and demonstrate all of the skills and qualities in Table 20.2, and to do so within an overall capacity to manage their own continuing learning and development.

A Capability Continuum

The Capability Envelope represents what we consider to be an ideal, and as such may never be fully representative of what happens in any one institution, given the plurality that exists in aims, needs and structures.

Nevertheless, we argue that the achievement of student capability as we and others have defined it has major implications for the culture, style and structures of programmes and the institutions which support them. Individual programmes, departments or staff may wish to progress towards capability-based curricula (many have already done so), and there are many legitimate stops on the way.

As a guide to teachers, programme developers and institutional managers, we present in Table 20.3 two polarized extremes focused on what, in the

Table 20.3 *The Capability Continuum*

Feature	Institutional control model	Learner development model
General stance	Supply-side determined, with a nod towards student choice.	Learner development within a general framework.
Main curricular focus	Specialist knowledge and intellectual skills, with personal skills and qualities in a subsidiary position, often seen as 'bolt-on'. Integration may or may not happen – rather left to chance. TRANSMISSION OF KNOWLEDGE	Integration of specialist knowledge with personal skills and qualities into effective action; the development of the learner to be an 'effective operator' in the world, whether in employment or society more generally. DEVELOPMENT OF AUTONOMY
Programme control	Specification by teachers, in some cases in conjunction with external agencies. PRE-DEFINED CONTENT	Frameworks of procedures and generic criteria of level within which programmes can be negotiated by learners, bearing in mind the expectations of external agencies as appropriate. FRAMEWORKS FOR LEARNING
Programme boundary	What the teachers (and others, where relevant) know and specify. TEACHER-DETERMINED	Students' strategic personal development, bearing in mind expectations regarding standards and external constraints. LEARNER-DETERMINED
Programme structure	Substantially pre-determined by supply-side considerations. CONSTRICTING	Open to negotiation within an enabling framework, provided that student can successfully argue the case for his/her proposed programme. ENABLING

(continued over)

Feature	Institutional control model	Learner development model
Programme coherence	Coherence determined by sequence and integration of subject content. RELEVANCE TO SUBJECT	Coherence judged by relevance to individual student's personal and professional development. RELEVANCE TO LEARNER
Expected learning outcomes	Specific. Largely prescribed in advance. Greater emphasis given to study unit than to programme as a whole. FRAGMENTED	Generic. Open to revision as the student learns. Programme focus dominates over that of the study unit. INTEGRATED
Status of personal skills and qualities	Though recognized as valuable, many treated as of secondary importance and not featuring in assessment. SUBSIDIARY	Seen as integral to the programme, and treated as such in assessment practice. INSEPARABLE
Admission	Selection according to suitability for prescribed programmes. Based (retrospectively) on qualifications and experience. APL/APEL is seen as a surrogate qualification. STUDENT FITS SPECIFICATION	Admission according to (potential) readiness to use the resources for own development, taking qualifications and experience into account, confirmed at validation of programme. APL/APEL is seen as the start of a continuing development. SPECIFICATION FITS STUDENT
Primary curricular activities	Teaching; setting assignments. Students expected to demonstrate learning through formal examinations, hence revision is a significant activity. DIRECTIVE	Learners supported in the planning, monitoring and self-direction of their work and in reflection on what has been learned. Dialogue with peers and experts; exchange of criticism; and feedback. SUPPORTIVE

(continued over)

Table 20.3 *(Continued)*

Feature	Institutional control model	Learner development model
Focus of assessment	'Do you know/can you do this?' Grading against (assumed) common standards. CLOSED	'What can/will you do as a result of following your programme?' Assessment against generic criteria on a holistic basis plus ability to review own learning. OPEN-ENDED
Role of the teacher	The expert through whom what student learns is filtered. AUTHORITY	Knowledgeable facilitator of student learning, providing personal support and intellectual rigour. CHALLENGING GUIDE
Institutional supply of resources	According to specified curricular units' requirements. Confined to students on defined unit/module. Constrains student learning. PRESCRIPTIVE	Learner-negotiated access where s/he is working outside prescribed curricular units, including off-campus. Follows and supports student learning needs. RESPONSIVE
Primary mode of monitoring	Via attendance, and assignments, examinations set in prescribed curricular units. CONTROL	Via achievement of generic learning outcomes, the perspective being the programme rather than the unit. In addition, students to monitor own learning and to judge own performance. DEVELOPMENT
Academic guidance and support	Often confined to which units the student should select, where choice can be exercised. DISPENSABLE	Central activity. Concentrates on helping students clarify and fulfil their strategy for the programme and the achievement of the generic learning outcomes that they have elected to pursue. INDISPENSABLE

(continued over)

Feature	Institutional control model	Learner development model
Careers and the world outside HE	Incidental, for FT students; consideration often limited to near the end of the programme. PERIPHERAL	Central to the student's strategy, influencing what is studied and the ways in which learning objectives are pursued – programme seen as a stage in a lifelong learning career pattern. CENTRAL
Quality assurance	Validation of prescribed programme/modules. Checks outcomes of components rather than total experience. Focus also on teaching and immediate graduate employment. INSTITUTION-ORIENTED	Validation of individually-negotiated programmes designed by the student. Various checks that outcomes meet generic criteria. Focus also on support systems for learning and continuing employability of graduates. LEARNER-ORIENTED
Research/ scholarship	The preserve of the teacher and research students. EXCLUSIVE	Encouraged and celebrated in students at all levels. INCLUSIVE
Capability outcome	**Dependence**	**Independence**

light of the evidence we have seen, seem to be key features that need to be addressed. We have caricatured the two extremes as an *Institutional Control Model*, and a *Learner Development Model*. The descriptions of each extreme of each feature beg many questions, some of which are answered in our description of the model in the previous section and the challenges which follow in the final section of this chapter. Others will require a longer discussion than space allows in this book. Nevertheless, despite all the caveats, we feel it is a useful exercise for staff to decide where they, their departments and institutions stand in relation to the grid's polar dimensions. To undertake such an exercise is a good way of focusing attention on the issues which we feel need to be addressed.

Finally, as a bit of serious fun, the 'ready reckoner' grid in Table 20.4 is presented as a workshop tool for assessing the extent to which the overall culture and infrastructure of a course, department or HEI are supportive of the development of capability. In any one instance some features may be more supportive than others, revealing where priority action needs to be taken if further progress towards capability is to be made. We envisage many responses will lie within the 2 to 4 range. Some course activities, such as distance learning materials, could be placed towards either end of the continuum depending on how they are controlled and used on the programme.

Some challenges for the stakeholders

The Dearing Report has drawn attention to the pressures for change and the growing importance of self-managed learning as a preparation for lifelong learning. Employers are looking for graduates with the capacity for initiative and adaptability while higher education institutions are having to cope with greater numbers and more varied groups of students within diminishing units of resource. New technology has already revolutionized the way information is stored and accessed and is creating new arenas and networks for learning. Changes in the way higher education is delivered are inevitable.

We have shown in Part 2 how some institutions are already addressing these issues and are making significant progress along the capability continuum. A further 400 examples have been presented at various HEC events. We have presented one conceptual model, grounded in practice, for consideration and have suggested the general directions in which the organization of higher education needs to continue to move.

Creating the conditions for the development of student capability presents major challenges for all involved in higher education. Many of the challenges listed by Stephenson and Weil (1992) are being met, but new challenges have appeared and some old ones have become more urgent.

Table 20.4 *The Capability Continuum ready reckoner*
(See the Capability Continuum (Table 20.3) for elaboration of terms.)

Feature	Institutional control model	Rating	Learner development model
Main curricular focus	TRANSMISSION OF KNOWLEDGE	1 2 3 4 5	DEVELOPMENT OF AUTONOMY
Programme control	PRE-DEFINED CONTENT	1 2 3 4 5	FRAMEWORKS FOR LEARNING
Programme boundary	TEACHER-DETERMINED	1 2 3 4 5	LEARNER-DETERMINED
Programme structure	CONSTRICTING	1 2 3 4 5	ENABLING
Programme coherence	RELEVANCE TO SUBJECT	1 2 3 4 5	RELEVANCE TO LEARNER
Expected learning outcomes	FRAGMENTED	1 2 3 4 5	INTEGRATED
Status of personal skills and qualities	SUBSIDIARY	1 2 3 4 5	INSEPARABLE
Admission	STUDENT FITS SPECIFICATION	1 2 3 4 5	SPECIFICATION FITS STUDENT
Primary curricular activities	DIRECTIVE	1 2 3 4 5	SUPPORTIVE
Focus of assessment	CLOSED	1 2 3 4 5	OPEN-ENDED
Role of the teacher	AUTHORITY	1 2 3 4 5	CHALLENGING GUIDE
Institutional supply of resources	PRESCRIPTIVE	1 2 3 4 5	RESPONSIVE
Primary purpose of monitoring	CONTROL	1 2 3 4 5	DEVELOPMENT
Academic guidance and support	DISPENSABLE.	1 2 3 4 5	INDISPENSABLE
Careers and the world outside HE	PERIPHERAL	1 2 3 4 5	CENTRAL
Quality assurance	INSTITUTION-ORIENTED	1 2 3 4 5	LEARNER-ORIENTED
Research/scholarship	EXCLUSIVE	1 2 3 4 5	INCLUSIVE

Score:
17–30   Heavily institutionally-focused; probably unaware of need to develop capability.
31–44   Institutionally-focused, but with a few features of capability being used.
45–58   Some way down the road leading to the development of capability.
59–72   Distinctly oriented towards learner development and capability.
73–85   Congratulations. You are truly developing independent capability. Tell the world!

We conclude this chapter by listing some of the challenges which key stakeholders can take on as their contribution to the creation of an effective higher education for capability.

Students

The biggest challenge for most students is to overcome their understandable reluctance to take responsibility for their own learning. Previous educational experiences have often reinforced a dependent mode while the feelings of being at risk when taking responsibility within uncertainty are real. Greater awareness of the value of independent capability in a changing world can help overcome this reluctance.

Students are responding to the challenge of capability when they:

- See their studies in terms of a phase in lifelong learning.
- Expect to contribute actively to their own development: dependence on teachers will not be enough. They need to accept that they will be expected to negotiate at least some of the details of the curriculum that they intend to follow.
- Take the 'long view' about their development, and avoid short-termism in fulfilling assignment briefs. A high grade today may not imply that sufficient underpinning knowledge, understanding and skill has been acquired for more advanced work tomorrow.
- Are prepared to take risks with their learning, and not fear failing (though this implies a different response to failure from teachers and course managers, particularly on assessment-driven modular schemes).
- Are prepared not to have easy bases for comparisons with peers, since they are quite likely to be doing different things even when they are in the same academic group.

Teachers

Teachers, of course, have a crucial role to play, not just as the immediate providers of higher education but also through their participation in course design, membership of professional bodies and contributions to the general culture of higher education. Many colleagues are wary of 'giving up control', fearful that students may not cover essential ground if left too much to their own devices. Other colleagues have found it rewarding to establish a new shared learning relationship with students and have been impressed at the work students can cover when encouraged to do so. We have also come across many colleagues who are keen to change but who find the general context in which they work to be more towards the 'wrong end' of the capability continuum.

Teachers are beginning to meet the challenge of capability when they:

- Value each student's reason for participating, starting point and personal aspiration and recognize that these characteristics are important to the student's overall progress and development.
- Are aware of the new demands being placed on graduates in the workplace and are able to convey to students the importance of self-reliance, initiative and personal skills.
- Aim to facilitate student autonomy in learning. This will be a major challenge to many, for whom the basic 'model' is one of passing on knowledge filtered through themselves. The capability approach requires the teacher to be a *facilitator* of the student's learning: a guide to what, for the students, is likely to be unfamiliar terrain and across which they will be expected to make their own ways, rather than a coach driver who takes a group together along a precisely-specified route.
- Support the development of 'transferable skills' through their own subject teaching as well as more specifically academic expertise. For some disciplinary areas, this will require a sea change in teaching approach: others will see this as merely confirming existing practice.
- Make it clear to students that they are trusted to do the necessary work, and that teachers will not expect to control their activity closely.
- Are prepared to negotiate with students regarding the latter's learning assignments.
- Acknowledge, in assessment, when students have demonstrated that they have learned from an assignment even though the assignment itself may have been carried out unsuccessfully. There is a need to accept the possibility of success stemming from apparent failure.
- Get together in order to share experiences of the 'capability' approach in action, in order to identify the causes of successes and failures and to facilitate the sharing of good practice.

Curriculum designers

Curriculum design is particularly important, hence the emphasis we have given in this chapter to the Capability Envelope as a model. We recognize that radical change is difficult to introduce within institutions where most of the administrative, managerial, financial and quality assurance infrastructures are geared to more traditional course designs. As our examples in Part 2 show, one has to begin either slowly, gaining confidence with each small change within existing programmes (as has been the case in the UK with the Enterprise in Higher Education Initiative), or totally, within a controlled discrete area where a new infrastructure can be developed to support a totally new course design, as in the University of Leeds

Work-based Learning Scheme (Chapter 7). The Middlesex example (Chapter 10) showed how a successful scheme can have a knock-on effect in other areas of the university through the involvement of colleagues in servicing the new scheme.

Student resistance to autonomy has been discussed at length in Chapter 15, showing how care is needed to ensure that students are fully briefed about the reasons and benefits of greater autonomy and that colleagues are aware of the importance of student anxiety and risk. In some cases, it will be prudent to develop schemes in which students can experience different levels of autonomy according to their readiness. Indeed, the Capability Envelope, when used with a modular programme which allows combinations of independent study and taught modules, should be ideal for this purpose. Alternatively, schemes can be developed which allow greater student autonomy in stages, with the final year being a complete Capability Envelope.

Course designers are responding to the challenge of capability when they:

- Bear in mind that curricula constitute stages within lifelong learning, and are not closed entities. As a consequence, they need to ensure that for many students institutional careers services contribute appropriately to the learning experience.[2]
- Accept that, while the general aims an institution holds for (say) its degree programmes need to be maintained (not least in respect of considerations relating to standards), the actual expected learning outcomes of/for the student are likely to develop organically as s/he grows in experience, and may change from those that may have been specified/agreed at the outset.
- Have continually to the fore the need to support the development of both academic and 'transferable' skills. This need will be met in different ways in different institutional cultures, and can be expected to contain a measure of negotiation between the student and the institution about the nature of the study programme to be pursued.
- Give serious thought, when planning to design a full Capability Envelope, to the rebalancing of the distribution of teaching and support resources across types of activity and time. The traditional allocation of teaching resources, for example, gives an even spread across time: under the Capability Envelope there is likely to be a need to front-load and end-load staff time-commitment, with the corollary that staff time-commitment will be lower in the middle of the relevant period.
- Recognize the importance to the student of serious reflection on progress and give credit for the learning which comes from that reflection.
- Consider how all the resources which support teaching and learning can best be brought to bear on the student experience.

- Recognize and accommodate the greater range of sources of material and learning environments being provided by new technology.
- Give thought to how assessment may be made more holistic and less fragmented: this is of particular relevance to modular schemes in which performance (typically over the last two years of a first degree course) is seen in terms of aggregation of 'mini-performances' in respect of individual modules.
- Devise methods of recording assessment outcomes (or, at least, ensure that students can present their achievements succinctly) in order to be of practical utility in the labour market, bearing in mind that lengthy records of achievement are unlikely to be considered by employers.
- Acknowledge that the concept of educational 'level' needs to be expressed in terms of transparent generic criteria which allow comparability of performance to be judged across a wide variety of contexts and by a range of modes of assessment.
- See assessment as a learning experience, in which students are encouraged to show what they can do as a result of their learning, to review the relevance of their learning to their continuing development and to explore how it relates to the generic criteria for the award they are seeking.
- Find ways of cross-checking that work submitted for assessment is really that of the student him/herself, and of ensuring that sufficient time is available for this to take place.
- Find ways of ensuring that students do not undesirably repeat experiences in different parts of their total programme of study. This is a particular issue for modular schemes, and some institutions have been able to specify modules in such a way that this problem is minimized.
- Continue to involve employers appropriately in programme design and validation[3] – but also to involve, where appropriate, externals who are not employers but who are able to contribute to the development of capability.

Institutional managers

Institutional managers have responsibility for two major factors relevant to the development of capability programmes: the overall culture of the organization and the allocation of resources. In addition to the challenges ascribed to curriculum designers above, institutional managers can have significant influence on course design and innovation through their staff promotion policies and culture of decision-making. Line management systems can, of course, be used to stimulate and support change from the top, but more often than not they can discourage innovations initiated by staff at operational levels, particularly within environments where league tables of successes against traditional measures are the dominant measures of success and where zero tolerance of error discourages the learning of new techniques by experimentation. Most modern corporations are moving towards a culture which encourages and supports learning by staff at all levels (see Chapter 1 pages 7–9) and have built in appraisal systems which reward and recognize initiatives aimed at enhancing the company's ability to serve the needs of its clients better and to improve readiness for new market conditions. The capability curriculum needs an environment in which learning from experience is rewarded, valued and celebrated at all levels and in all institutions (including staff and programme development). In some HEIs, it is assumed that because the business is one of learning (indicated by the scholarship of staff and research students) the institution is, *ipso facto*, a learning organization.

The importance of the institutional culture is twofold: it encourages people to take the risk of developing new kinds of programmes, and it gives all staff an awareness of the rewards and challenges of learner managed learning.

Institutional managers are responding to the challenge when they:

- Commit themselves to staff development and appraisal systems which focus on staff plans for their own development (Laycock, 1996).
- Use student appraisal systems which focus on the relevance of what is learnt to students' longer term needs and aspirations, the extent to which students are given responsibility, and the development of personal skills, and not (as sometimes happens on conventional practice) on the formal delivery of material.
- Give prominence in their promotions policy for achievements in staff and programme development.
- Base the distribution of resources, including staff time, on the changing learning needs of students rather than distribute students according to allocation of resources.
- Pursue policies of open access to all university resources and in a variety of places, consistent with minimum controls of valuable and dangerous materials, thus enabling students to pursue specialist interests which move outside the normal boundaries of the department or programme in which they are registered.

Professional and statutory bodies

The professions have a lot to gain from a higher education system which is located more towards the independent capability end of the capability continuum. Good professional practice includes the capacity to make independent judgements, monitor one's own effectiveness, and exercise autonomy in continuing professional development as circumstances change.

Professional and statutory bodies have considerable influence over the practice of higher education through the conditions they impose for the recognition of programmes of study. Withdrawal of such recognition could lead to the closure of courses, and hence academics tend to act cautiously when seeking approval for innovative programmes.

Professional and statutory bodies respond to the challenge of capability when they:

- Acknowledge, in a time in which specialist knowledge rapidly becomes obsolete, that capability is of superordinate importance. Encouragement should be given to institutions which seek to develop capability curricula that may look rather different from those with which they are familiar, but that seek to develop equally valid portfolios of skills. The capability curriculum should be construed as 'equal but different'. As a first step, enterprising professional and statutory bodies might wish to support (and even sponsor) pilot developments of this kind.
- Give as much importance, when setting conditions for the accreditation of courses, to the learning process as they do to specialist outcomes, and to the demonstration of capability through the effective use of knowledge and skills in a professional context as to the possession of knowledge and expertise.
- Exercise control of standards of courses through the rigour and appropriateness of the procedures and criteria used for the validation and registration of student-negotiated programmes and the assessment of final demonstration of the student's overall capability.
- Reconsider the relationship of their accreditation to the outcomes of programmes in higher education. It may be preferable, in the context of lifelong learning, that individuals should gain full accreditation at some time after, rather than contemporaneously with, the award of a degree.

Quality and standards

As stated at the beginning of this book, judgements about quality should look beyond the extent to which something is fit for its purpose to the fitness of the purpose itself. We have argued that the development of independent capability within a demanding university context is a high quality purpose since it directly and appropriately prepares people for the challenges they will face in life and at work in a changing world.

The criteria and procedures used for quality assessments of students, courses and institutions inevitably have a direct impact on what is measured or recorded. 'The practice becomes the measurement'. Criteria and procedures for judging quality in higher education, in the context of the Dearing review, should both reward and encourage the development of capability approaches, not subvert them.

Quality and standards procedures encourage capability when:

- Institutions appreciate (as they do in respect of other types of curricula) that there are two foci for internal quality assurance regarding capability – the capacity of programmes to encourage the development of capability (in effect, the aspirational aspect of the programmes) and the actual outcomes of programmes (in effect, the achieved standards).
- Examination boards have mechanisms through which holistic capability achievements can be recognized. The arithmetical cumulation of grades from modules may well not be sufficient for assurance that the capability intentions of curricula have been fulfilled.

The newly-established Quality Assurance Agency (QAA) will assist the development of capability if it:

- Is willing to recognize that standards differ between and within institutions in both level and type, and that the two kinds of difference should not be confused. Regarding the latter, a capability curriculum seeks to develop a different profile of skills from some more traditional curricula. Both types of curricula have their place, but it should not be inferred automatically that the capability programme, because it is different, is in some way inferior to the traditional – it is different but equivalent.
- Continues the practice, currently inbuilt into quality audit and quality assessment, of using criteria of quality which are related to institutions' own aims and objectives, and ensures that scrutiny panels appreciate that some institutions are seeking to achieve capability outcomes instead of more traditional outcomes.
- Leads a review of the utility of the honours degree classification and other traditional features which do not relate particularly well to the notion of capability.

Employers

Employers have a great deal to gain from greater graduate capability and from participation in the capability envelope. The profile we have painted of the independently capable graduate, as someone who is effective in both position Y and position Z, is consistent with most profiles of 'what employers want' published in recent years (particularly by Harvey et al., 1997, and see Chapter 1 for further discussion on this). The openness of the Exploration, Progress Review and Demonstration Stages to participation of groups relevant to the students' longer term needs gives employers real opportunities to participate, where relevant, as partners in the students' education, through representation as members of registration panels;

involvement in the learning contract signed at the end of the Exploration Stage; or by provision of learning opportunities directly relevant to both the employer's and students' needs.

The three work-based learning schemes described in Part 2 show how capability programmes can be attractive to employers including small- and medium-sized enterprises (SMEs). SMEs need recruits who possess at least three characteristics: readiness for immediate operation (to hit the ground running); a range of personal skills and qualities which make them effective in a variety of interpersonal situations; and the capacity to drive change from within and to manage their own continuing development without recourse to expensive release to taught courses. SMEs also have a lot to gain from student placements since such placements will be focused on real projects which are used both for the student's education and employer's benefit.

It is therefore very much in employers' interests to support (or at least not restrain) the development of student capability.

Employers are responding to the challenge when they:

- Continue to collaborate where possible with higher education in order to contribute to curriculum development and to inform themselves about what higher education is aiming to achieve, and is achieving.
- Continue to make available opportunities for work-experience within curricula.
- Look very carefully at what institutions are trying to achieve with their students, and what graduating students are offering to them. The danger is that employers will use institutional reputation as a filter ('Did you get your degree from the University of Tradition, or from De Novo University?'), without appreciating that the latter has been seeking to develop the generic capability that employers actually say that they need (and that labour market analyses indicate are needed) for many types of employment.
- Educate their staff with regard to the benefits of lifelong learning, and where appropriate seek partnerships with higher education institutions in order to maximize the value that the latter can offer in respect of employment-related lifelong learning.

Government and government agencies

Training and Enterprise Councils (TECs), Local Enterprise Companies (LECs) and Government Regional Offices are responding to the challenge of capability when they:

- Continue to seek ways to support the bringing together of higher education and employers, to their mutual benefit. TECs and LECs are in a particularly good position to strengthen the relationship between small- and medium-sized enterprises and higher education.

The Department for Education and Employment is responding to the challenge when:

- In the light of the success of its Enterprise in Higher Education Initiative, it takes the opportunity further to support the development of capability through higher education. Two routes through which this is being achieved are via its developmental prospectus and via developmental projects.

References

Dryden, G and Voss, J (1997) *The Learning Revolution,* Auckland: The Learning Web Ltd.

Foster, L (1996) *Comparable but Different: Work-based Learning for a Learning Society,* Leeds: University of Leeds.

Harvey, L, Moon, S and Geall, V (1997) *Graduates' Work: Organisational Change and Students' Attributes,* Birmingham: Centre for Research into Quality, University of Central England.

HEQC (1997) *Managing Flexible Curricula in Higher Education: the Architecture of Modularity,* London: Higher Education Quality Council.

Laycock, M and Stephenson, J (eds) (1993) *Using Learning Contracts in Higher Education:* London, Kogan Page.

Laycock, M (1994) 'The use of learning contracts in undergraduate modular programmes, in A Jenkins and L Walker (eds), *Developing Student Capability through Modular Courses,* (pp. 125–32), London: Kogan Page.

Laycock, M (1996) QILT – 'capable institutions', *Capability,* **2**(2), 42–8.

NCIHE (1997) *Higher Education in the Learning Society,* report of the National Committee of Inquiry into Higher Education, London: HMSO.

Pauling, B (1998, in press) *The Virtual University,* London: Kogan Page.

Stephenson, J and Weil, S (1992) *Quality in Learning: A Capability Approach in Higher Education,* London: Kogan Page.

Zahran Halim and Zaidah Razak, (1994) 'Learning units: a framework for implementation strategies', *Capability,* **1**(1), 62–70.

Notes

1. By new technology we include the following: electronic storage, dissemination and retrieval of information; on-line exchanges between distant

tutors and students or members of groups; intelligent interaction and engagement with data and texts; virtual learning environments for situations which would otherwise be prohibitively expensive or dangerous; external networking with fellow experts; student access to the best expertise, wherever it is, from anywhere with a computer, a modem, a telephone line and power.

2. There are still broader issues here, in that the overall aim of the institution may encompass the wider concept of citizenship. Also many part-time students will be in employment and will already have a good idea of the directions in which they want their careers to develop.

3. Employers' time is usually given on a goodwill basis, and it is important for institutions to make the most effective use of their contributions: this may not best be achieved by involving employers in validation meetings.

Index